Geo. B. McClellan

The two great facts, which the public is too apt to forget, are these—that General McClellan by unwearied efforts made the army what it is, out of very raw material, and thus prepared it for the brilliant encounters in which it has been so eminently successful—and that the failure, as yet, to accomplish the great purpose in view, namely, the capture of Richmond, is owing to the entire overthrow of his plan, by taking away a part of his command and by withholding McDowell's troops from him. Ever since, he has been endeavoring to prevent fatal disaster to his reduced army, and yet with it accomplished that splendid movement to James River, of which, as the *World* says, "the head of the rebel government, himself a soldier, in open admiration declared, that with the exception of the retreat of Moreau, through the Black Forest, a retreat upon which, more than upon any of his victories, rests his great fame as a general, the operations of McClellan furnished the most magnificent example which modern history presents of the rescue of a great army from apparently irretrievable ruin."

LIFE

AND

CAMPAIGNS

OF

GEORGE B. McCLELLAN

MAJOR-GENERAL U.S. ARMY.

BY

G. S. HILLARD.

PHILADELPHIA:
J. B. LIPPINCOTT & CO.
1864.

TO THE

Army of the Potomac,

WHOSE COURAGE, CONDUCT, AND PATRIOTISM
BEAR RECORD ALIKE TO THEIR OWN GLORY AND TO
THEIR UNSHAKEN DEVOTION TO THE

Noble Commander

WHO WAS PERMITTED, FOR A TIME, WITH CONSUMMATE
WISDOM AND ABILITY,
TO LEAD THEM ONWARD IN THE PATHS ALWAYS
OF HONOR AND OFTEN OF VICTORY.

PREFACE.

The purpose of this work is to exhibit General McClellan's title to the gratitude and admiration of his countrymen by simply telling them what he has done. The treatment he has received has made it, indeed, necessary sometimes to take the attitude of controversy, and to assail others in order to do him justice. But this has been done no more than the interests of truth required.

G. S. H.

Boston, August, 1864.

CONTENTS.

CHAPTER I.

CHAPTER II.

CHAPTER III.

CHAPTER IV.

CHAPTER V.

CHAPTER VI.

CHAPTER VII.

CHAPTER VIII.

CHAPTER IX.

CHAPTER X.

CHAPTER XI.

CHAPTER XII.

CHAPTER XIII.

APPENDIX.

LIFE

OF

MAJOR-GENERAL McCLELLAN.

CHAPTER I.

THE name of McClellan, common in many parts of the United States, is borne by the descendants of a Scotch family, the head of which was Lord Kirkcudbright. The last nobleman of this name died April 19, 1832, when the title became extinct. Three brothers of the name emigrated to America about the middle of the last century. One went to Maine, one to Pennsylvania, and one to Connecticut: from the last of these the subject of this memoir is descended.

GEORGE BRINTON McCLELLAN was born in Philadelphia, December 3, 1826. He was the third child and second son of Dr. George McClellan, a distinguished physician, a graduate of Yale College, and the founder of Jefferson College, who died in May, 1846. His mother, whose maiden name was Elizabeth Brinton, is still living. The eldest son, Dr. J. H. B. McClellan, is a physician in Philadelphia;

and the youngest, Arthur, is a captain in the army, attached to the staff of General Wright.

The first school to which George was sent was kept by Mr. Sears Cook Walker, a graduate of Harvard College in 1825, and a man of distinguished scientific merit, who died in January, 1853. He remained four years under Mr. Walker's charge, and from him was transferred to a German teacher, named Schipper, under whom he began the study of Greek and Latin. He next went to the preparatory school of the University of Pennsylvania, which was kept by Dr. Crawford, and in 1840 entered the University itself, where he remained two years. He was a good scholar, and held a high rank in his class, both at school and in college; but he was not a brilliant or precocious lad. His taste was for solid studies: he made steady but not very rapid progress in every thing he undertook, but he had not the qualities of mind that make the show-boy of a school.

In June, 1842, he entered the Military Academy at West Point, being then fifteen years and six months old. He went there in obedience to his general inclination for a military life. He had no particular fondness for mathematical studies, and was not aware that they formed so large a part of the course of instruction at the Academy. Having a modest estimate of his own powers and attainments, it was a source of surprise as well as pleasure to him to find, at the examination in January, 1843, that he was coming out one of the best scholars in the class.

The Academy was at that time under the charge of Colonel De Russey. Among his classmates were several persons who have served with distinction in the army of the United States, as well as some whose mistaken sense of duty led them at the breaking out of the civil war into the ranks of the Confederates. Among these latter was that remarkable man, Thomas Jonathan Jackson, better known by his far-renowned name of Stonewall Jackson, who in his brief military career seems to have combined all the dash and brilliancy of one of Prince Rupert's Cavaliers, with the religious enthusiasm of one of Cromwell's Ironsides.

Young McClellan was a little under the prescribed age when he entered the Academy; but his manly character and sound moral instincts were a sufficient protection against the dangers incident to all places of education away from the pupil's own home, and from which the vigilant care and absolute power of the Government cannot entirely guard the young men committed to its charge at West Point. He showed at the start a more careful intellectual training than most of the youths admitted to the Academy. His conduct and bearing throughout his whole course were unexceptionable. His deportment then, as always, was singularly free from that self-assertion which is frequently seen, but not always pardoned, in men of superior powers. He showed perseverance, a strong will, and resolute habits of application. His acquisitions were not made without hard work, but, when made, they were securely held. At the close of the course at West Point, he stood second in general rank in the largest class which had ever left the Academy. In Engineering and Geology he was first. The highest scholar in the class was Charles G. Stewart, now a major of engineers. He came out first because he was more uniformly strict in complying with the rules and regulations of the Academy, as well as more attentive to its regular studies.

McClellan was graduated in the summer of 1846, before he had completed his twentieth year. Few young men have ever left West Point better fitted by mental discipline and solid attainments for the profession of arms than he. He had also a precious gift of nature itself, in that sound health and robust constitution which are large elements of success in every department of life, but without which distinction in a military career is almost hopeless. He was of middle height, and his frame was well proportioned, with broad shoulders and deep chest. His muscular strength and activity were very great, and all manly exercises came easy to him. He was patient of heat and cold, capable of severe and long-continued application, and able to sustain fatigues and exposures under which most men would have broken down. Such he was at the age of twenty, and such he is now. Aided by strictly temperate habits, his body has always been the active and docile servant of his mind. In all the toils and exposures of his military life, in sickly climes and at sickly seasons, he has preserved uninterrupted good health. He could to-day discharge with ease the duties of a common soldier in any arm of the service; and in the shock of encountering steel, few men would be more formidable, whether on horseback or on foot.

At the close of his student-life, a new impulse had been given to the military spirit of the country, and of the army especially, by the breaking out, a few weeks previously, of the Mexican War. The brilliant victories of Palo Alto and Resaca de la Palma (May 8 and 9, 1846), gained against immense odds, had shed new lustre upon American arms, and opened to the officers of the army the prospect of a more congenial and animating employment than the dreary monotony of a frontier post or a harbor fort. McClellan went at once into active service as brevet second lieutenant of engineers, and was assigned to duty as junior lieutenant of a company of sappers and miners*

* Sappers and miners form a part of the Corps of Engineers. They are employed in building and repairing permanent fortifications, in raising field redoubts and batteries, in making gabions and fascines, in digging trenches and excavating galleries of mines during sieges, and also in forming bridges of rafts, boats, and pontoons. Their duties require higher qualities, mental and physical, than those of the common soldier. A sapper and miner must have a strong frame, a correct eye, steady nerves, and a certain amount of education. It may be well to add, for the benefit of civilians, that gabions are baskets made of twigs, which are filled with earth and used as screens against an enemy's fire; that fascines are bundles of twigs, fagots, and branches of trees which are used to fill up ditches, form parapets, &c.; and that pontoons are a kind of flat-bot-

then in the course of organization at West Point, under charge of Captain A. J. Swift. The first lieutenant was G. W. Smith, now a general in the service of the Confederate States. Captain Swift had studied the subject in Europe; and he instructed his lieutenants, and the latter drilled and exercised the men. The summer was spent in training the company, and in preparing their equipments and implements. It was a branch of service till that time unknown in our country, as since the peace of 1815 our army had had no practical taste of war, except in an occasional brush with the Indians, where the resources of scientific warfare were not called into play.

The duties in which Lieutenant McClellan now found himself engaged were very congenial to him, and he devoted himself to them with characteristic ardor and perseverance. In a letter written in the course of the summer to his brother, Dr. McClellan, with whom his relations have always been of the most affectionate and confidential nature, he says, "I am kept busy from eight in the morning till dinner-time. After dinner, I have to study sapping and mining until the afternoon drill, after which I go to parade. After tea, we (Captains Swift, Smith, and myself) generally have a consultation. Then I go to tattoo. The amount of it is that we have to organize by the 1st of September the first corps of engineer troops that have

tomed boat carried along with an army for the purpose of making temporary bridges.

ever been in the country. The men are perfectly raw, so that we have to drill them; and we are now (to-day) commencing the practical operations to prepare us for the field. Smith and I have been in the woods nearly all the morning, with the men, cutting wood for fascines, gabions, &c. We have now fifty men, and fine men they are too. I am perfectly delighted with my duties."

Lieutenant McClellan sailed with his company, seventy-one strong, from New York, early in September, 1846, for Brazos Santiago, and arrived there immediately after the battle of Monterey. They then moved to Camargo, where they remained for some time. Thence they were transferred to Matamoras in November, and from this point started on their march to Victoria, under the orders of General Patterson. Before leaving Matamoras, Captain Swift was taken ill, and the company was left under command of Lieutenant Smith.

At Victoria the company joined the forces under General Taylor, and were assigned to the division of regulars under command of General Twiggs, with whom, in January, 1847, they marched to Tampico. The distance from Matamoras to Tampico is about two hundred miles. The intervening country is unfavorable for the march of an army; and every thing necessary for the support of the troops had to be carried with them. The sappers and miners found frequent occasion for the exercise of their skill in making and repairing roads and bridges. They did excellent service, and were assisted by men detailed from other corps, for that purpose, from time to time.

The company arrived at Tampico in the latter part of January, and remained there about a month, and then sailed for Vera Cruz. They landed, March 9, with the first troops which were disembarked, and immediately began to take an active part in all the operations of the siege. The officers and men did a large part of the reconnoitring necessary to determine the plan of the siege, the officers reporting immediately to Colonel Totten, the chief of engineers, and executing in detail the works subsequently prescribed by orders from head-quarters. The corps of engineers, including the company of sappers and miners, encountered great difficulties in drawing the lines of investment and in constructing batteries, arising from the nature of the ground, which was broken into innumerable hills of loose sand, with dense forests of chapparal between. In common with all the troops, they suffered from scarcity of water and the excessive heat of the weather. But nothing could exceed the zeal of the officers or the cheerful obedience of the men. Their valuable services were duly recognized by the able and accomplished chief of the department of the service to which they were attached, as appears by a letter addressed to the commander-in-chief, as follows:—

CAMP WASHINGTON, BEFORE VERA CRUZ,
March 28, 1847.

SIR:—Before leaving camp with the despatches in which you inform the President of the United States of the brilliant success which has attended your attack upon this city and the Castle of San Juan d'Ulloa, I seize a moment to solicit your attention to the merits and services of the officers of engineers who have been engaged in that attack.

If there be any thing in the position, form, and arrangement of the trenches and batteries, or in the manner of their execution, worthy of commendation, it is due to the ability, devotion, and unremitting zeal of these officers. By extraordinary and unsparing efforts, they were enabled, few as they were, to accomplish the work of many; and, so far as the success of your operations before this city depended on labors peculiar to their corps, no words of mine can overrate their services.

The officers thus engaged are Major John L. Smith, Captains R. E. Lee and John Sanders, First Lieutenants J. L. Mason, P. G. T. Beauregard, and I. I. Stevens, Second Lieutenants Z. B. Tower and G. W. Smith, Brevet Second Lieutenants G. B. McClellan and J. G. Foster.

The obligation lies upon me also to speak of the highly meritorious deportment and valuable services of the sappers and miners attached to the expedition. Strenuous as were their exertions, their number proved to be too few, in comparison with our need of such aid. Had their number been fourfold greater, there is no doubt the labors of the army would have been materially lessened and the result expedited.

I have the honor to be, very respectfully, your obedient servant,

JOS. G. TOTTEN,
Colonel and Chief Engineers.

MAJOR-GENERAL W. SCOTT,
Commanding the Army of the United States, Mexico.

The city of Vera Cruz and Castle of San Juan d'Ulloa were surrendered to the American forces on the 29th day of March, 1847, the articles of capitulation having been signed two days before. On the 8th of April, the army, with the exception of a regiment of infantry left behind to serve as a garrison, began its march into the interior, numbering in all about eight thousand five hundred men. They were soon made to feel that their path of progress was not without difficulties and dangers. At Cerro Gordo, sixty miles from Vera Cruz, a Mexican army, thirty-five thousand strong, under the command of General Santa Anna, was found posted in a mountain-pass, a position of great natural strength, fortified and defended by powerful batteries, bristling with cannon. But, in spite of superior numbers and of almost impregnable defences, the enemy's position was assaulted and carried, and his forces utterly routed, on the 18th of April, by the American army, in one of the most brilliant battles on record, in which the skilful plans of the commander-in-chief were carried out and crowned with success by the zeal and energy of all the subordinate officers and the splendid courage of the men. The company of sappers and miners had reached the place on the day before the battle, and shared in the dangers and honors of the field. Lieutenant McClellan, with ten of his men, was with General Pillow's brigade on the left, with directions to clear away the obstacles in front of the assaulting columns. This was a service of no common danger, as the heavy and well-served Mexican batteries in front swept the space before them with a most destructive fire, under which Pillow's command, mostly composed of volunteers, reeled and fell into confusion. General Pillow, in his official report to the commander-in-chief, says, "Lieutenants Tower and McClellan, of the Corps of Engineers, displayed great zeal and activity in the discharge of their duties in connection with my command."

After the battle of Cerro Gordo, Lieutenant McClellan accompanied the advance corps under General Worth on the march to Puebla, passing through Jalapa and Perote, and arriving at Amozoque, a small town twelve miles from Puebla, on the 13th of May. Our officers did not dream of finding any portion of the enemy here, and the usual precautions adopted to guard against surprise were somewhat relaxed. On the morning of the 14th, the soldiers were busily occupied in cleaning their arms and accoutrements, in order that they might enter Puebla in good trim, when a drummer-boy, who had strayed in advance of the pickets, ran in and gave the alarm that the enemy was approaching in force. The staff-officers mounted and galloped to the front, and discovered the advance of a body of Mexican lancers from twenty-five hundred to three thousand in number. The long roll at once called the troops to arms, and the different regiments were quickly paraded. Lieutenant McClellan, who was in a house on the side of the town nearest the enemy, at once sprang upon his horse and rode out to observe them. After riding a few hundred yards, at the turn of a street he came upon a Mexican captain of cavalry riding into the town to reconnoitre. Each was alone, and both were armed with sabres and pistols. The Mexican officer turned; but his opponent, being better mounted, pursued, overtook him, and compelled him to surrender. The two went back together, and, while on their way, the Mexican officer suddenly put spurs to his horse and attempted to draw his pistol; but Lieutenant McClellan caught him again, and gave him to understand that if he renewed the attempt to escape, he should be obliged to put a bullet through him. After this the two rode together quietly, and Lieutenant McClellan surrendered his prisoner to his commanding officer. The Mexican cavalry were checked by the well-served guns of our artillery, and retired without doing us any damage.

At Puebla a pause of several weeks was made in the progress of the army, in order that its numbers might be increased by reinforcements and that due preparations might be made for a march upon the city of Mexico. And here seems a fitting place to introduce that portion of the official annual report of Colonel Totten to the Secretary of War in which he speaks of the services of the company of sappers and miners and their officers, though it was not drawn up until a somewhat later period:—

"The law adding the company of sappers, miners, and pontonniers (otherwise called engineer soldiers) to the Corps of Engineers, was passed on the 15th of May, 1846. On the 11th of October following, this company, seventy-two strong, landed at Brazos

Santiago; having in the interim been enlisted by great exertions on the part of several engineer officers, and been organized and drilled by Captain A. J. Swift and Lieutenants G. W. Smith and McClellan, of the Corps of Engineers. The captain being disabled by sickness at Matamoras, Lieutenant Smith led the company, as part of Major-General Patterson's division, in the march from that place to Tampico,—a march in which the services of the company, constantly in advance and engaged in removing impediments and making the road practicable, were of great value. The company landed with the first line on the beach at Vera Cruz, being then again under the command of Captain Swift; who, in his desire to lead in its dangers and toils, strove nobly, but vainly, against an inexorable disease. A too ardent sun prostrated him at once, depriving the country of his services at a moment when his high and peculiar attainments would have been of the greatest value. During the siege of Vera Cruz, I was a witness to the great exertions and services of this company, animated by, and emulating, the zeal and devotion of its excellent officers, Lieutenants Smith, McClellan, and Foster. Since the surrender of that place, we have no official accounts giving the particular employments or engagements of the company. We know only that it has been on the march with General Scott's army to the city of Mexico. I will venture to say, however, that the opportunities of that service have been profited of, by the sergeants and rank and file, as well as by the commissioned officers, to display the highest qualities as soldiers, demonstrating, at the same time, the great advantage to armies, however engaged in the field, of possessing troops well grounded in the peculiar exercises of engineer soldiers."

On the 7th of August the American army, numbering not quite eleven thousand men, began their march from Puebla, starting upon an enterprise which would have been pronounced extremely rash had it not been crowned with success, but which, having been successful, ranks among the most daring and brilliant in the annals of war. A mere handful of men, volunteers and regulars, undertook to capture a city of nearly two hundred thousand inhabitants, strong in its natural defences, and protected by numerous works, constructed by able engineers, in conformity with the most approved rules of military science. Around it was distributed an army of thirty-five thousand men, composed of regular troops and volunteers, and comprising artillery, cavalry, and infantry. These were by no means despicable soldiers, and they often fought with a courage which extorted the respect of their enemies. Their artillery in particular was well served and effective, as our troops often learned to their cost. The weak points in the Mexican army were the want of courage and want of capacity in its officers, just as the weak point in the civil history of that unhappy country has been the want of rulers who were at once honest and able. Had the Mexican officers been men and soldiers like our own, history might have had a different record to make upon the event of the Mexican War.

Lieutenant McClellan's company of sappers and miners was attached to the second division of regulars, under command of General Twiggs, which formed the advance of the army. Soon after leaving Puebla, they were joined by General Scott, the commander-in-chief. Our troops entered the Valley of Mexico on the 10th, and General Scott fixed his head-quarters for the time at Ayotla, a village on the northeastern edge of the Lake of Chalco, about nine miles east of the fortified position of El Peñon, which was carefully reconnoitred on the 12th and its great strength fully discovered. On the next day, another reconnoissance was pushed upon the route by Mexicalcingo. This was pronounced by General Scott the most daring reconnoissance of the whole war, as the small corps of observation was obliged to pass close by the strong position of El Peñon and to leave it for a considerable space in the rear. In both of these reconnoissances Lieutenant McClellan took part; and in one of them he was saved from probable death or captivity at the hands of about a dozen Mexican lancers by Lieutenant Beauregard and three dragoons.

When, in consequence of the great strength of the defences at El Peñon, the project of advancing upon Mexico by the great road from Puebla, and assaulting it upon the eastern side, was abandoned, and it was determined to march round the southern shore of Lake Chalco and attack the city on the south and west, the company of sappers and miners was transferred to General Worth's division, which now took the lead, and the company moved at its head to San Augustin, occasionally repairing the roads as far as was practicable. As soon as General Santa Anna learned this movement of the American forces, he withdrew the greater portion of his troops, with several pieces of artillery, from El Peñon and Mexicalcingo, where he had been expecting the first shock of battle, and, establishing his head-quarters at the hacienda (hamlet) of San Antonio, began to labor upon the lines of defence in that vicinity.

On the morning of the 18th, General Worth's division was moved forward a couple of miles on the causeway leading from San Augustin to San Antonio, and took up its position in front of the latter place, the men encamping on both sides of the road. Here a careful reconnoissance was made of the defences of San Antonio, in which Lieutenant McClellan took part. His company was then transferred to General Twiggs's division, and moved at its head, across the Pedregal, to Contreras. During the first day of the battle of Contreras (August 19), Lieutenant McClellan, while reconnoitring, ran into a Mexican regiment, and had his horse shot under him by a musket-ball. On the same day, while posting Magruder's battery, he had another horse killed under him by a round shot. Still later, while in temporary command of a section of the same battery whose officer had been mortally wounded, he was knocked down by a grape-shot which struck plump upon the hilt of his sword. "Stonewall" Jackson, who belonged to Magruder's battery, relieved Lieutenant McClellan from command of the section, and the latter then took charge for some time of a battery of mountain-howitzers whose officer had been wounded, and, after a day of severe toil and great exposure, rejoined his company, which was at San Geronimo, a small village on the western edge of the Pedregal,* a little north of Contreras.

At a very early hour the next morning (August 20) the intrenched camp of General Valencia at Padierna was stormed and carried at the point of the bayonet by the left wing of the American army, under the command of General P. F. Smith. This was the battle of Contreras, of which General Scott says, in his official report, "I doubt whether a more brilliant or decisive victory—taking into view ground, artificial defences, batteries, and the extreme disparity of numbers, without cavalry or artillery on our side—is to be found on record." In this battle Lieutenant McClellan's company of sappers and miners led General Smith's brigade of regulars in its attack on the flank of the enemy, and is thus mentioned in the report already quoted from:—"In the mean time,

* The Pedregal is a field of broken lava, about nine miles south of Mexico, nearly circular in form, and about two miles in diameter, entirely impracticable for cavalry or artillery except by a single mule-path, and only practicable for infantry at a few points.

Smith's own brigade, under the temporary command of Major Dimmick, following the movements of Riley and Cadwallader, discovered opposite to and outside of the works a long line of Mexican cavalry, drawn up as a support. Dimmick, having at the head of the brigade the company of sappers and miners under Lieutenant Smith, engineer, who had conducted the march, was ordered by Brigadier-General Smith to form line faced to the enemy, and, in a charge against a flank, routed the cavalry."

In the reports of the officers immediately commanding, honorable mention is made of Lieutenant McClellan and his corps. General Twiggs says, "Lieutenant G. B. McClellan, after Lieutenant Callender was wounded, took charge of and managed the howitzer battery (Lieutenant Reno being detached with the rockets) with judgment and success, until it became so disabled as to require shelter. For Lieutenant McClellan's efficiency and gallantry in this affair, I present his name for the favorable consideration of the general-in-chief." And again, "To Lieutenant G. W. Smith, of the engineers, who commanded the company of sappers and miners, I am under many obligations for his services on this and many other occasions. Whenever his legitimate duties with the pick and spade were performed, he always solicited permission to join in the advance of the storming-party with his muskets, in which position his gallantry, and that of his officers and men, was conspicuously displayed at Contreras as well as Cerro Gordo."

General P. F. Smith, in his report, says, "Lieutenant G. W. Smith, in command of the engineer company, and Lieutenant McClellan, his subaltern, distinguished themselves throughout the whole of the three actions. Nothing seemed to them too bold to be undertaken, or too difficult to be executed; and their services as engineers were as valuable as those they rendered in battle at the head of their gallant men."

General Smith, it will be noticed, speaks of "three actions" in which the officers of the company of sappers and miners distinguished themselves. These include the battle of Churubusco, which was fought on the same day (August 20) with the battle of Contreras, and in which the company took part, both in the preliminary reconnoissances and in the conflict itself.

After the battles of Contreras and Churubusco, hostilities were suspended by an armistice which lasted till September 7. On the 8th the severe and bloody battle of Molino del Rey was fought, at which Lieutenant McClellan was not present. On the 13th the Castle of Chapultepec was taken by assault, in which also he did not take part, but during the night of the 11th, and on the 12th, he built and armed, mostly in open daylight and under a heavy fire, one of the batteries whose well-directed and shattering fire contributed essentially to the success of the day.

Immediately after the fall of Chapultepec, and on the same day, the company of sappers and miners was ordered to the front, and took the lead of General Worth's division in one of the most difficult and dangerous movements of the assault upon the city of Mexico,—the attack of the San Cosme garita, or gate. Of the nature of the important services performed by the company and its officers at this point, and also after the capture of the city, a correct notion may be formed from the statement contained in the report of Major J. L. Smith, of the Engineer Corps:—

"Lieutenant G. W. Smith, commanding the sappers, arrived on the ground some time after this, while our troops were in front of the battery at the garita,—the other batteries on the road up to that point having been carried. Being the senior engineer present, he was ordered to reconnoitre in front and ascertain the state of the enemy's forces, and particularly whether it would be necessary to move our heavy artillery forward. He reported his opinion that the advancing of the heavy pieces should be suspended, and that the sappers should advance under cover of the houses, by openings made in the walls of contiguous houses; and, this being approved, he proceeded, in the manner proposed, until he reached a three-story house about forty yards from the battery, and was enabled from the roof to open a fire upon the battery which drove away the enemy's troops, who in their retreat succeeded in carrying away one of the guns. Part of his force then descended to the road to secure the battery, but was anticipated by a body of our troops, which entered on the right as the sappers were about entering on the left. The sappers were then moved forward until they reached strong positions on both sides of the rear, capable of affording shelter to our troops, although the enemy occupied in force a large convent, one hundred and fifty yards in advance, and had batteries on the next cross-street. These facts being reported, a brigade was sent to occupy the strong positions referred to, and at ten P.M. further operations were suspended for the night.

"At three o'clock next morning, a party of the sappers moved to the large convent in advance, and found it unoccupied. Lieutenant McClellan advanced with a party into the Alameda, and reported at daylight that no enemy was to be seen. The sappers then moved forward, and had reached two squares beyond the Alameda, when they were recalled. The company during the day, until three P.M., were engaged in street-fighting, and particularly in breaking into houses with crowbars and axes. In this service they killed a number, and made prisoners of many suspicious persons.

"Lieutenant McClellan had command of the company for a time in the afternoon, while Lieutenant Smith was searching for powder to be used in blowing up houses from which our troops had been fired upon, contrary to the usages of war. During this time, while advancing the company, he reached a strong position, but found himself opposed to a large force of the enemy. He had a conflict with this force, which lasted some time; but the advantage afforded by his position enabled him at length to drive it off, after having killed more than twenty of its number."

A few words may here be added, to explain a little more in detail the proceedings of the sappers and miners in making their way through the houses to which Major Smith refers. At the gate of the city a powerful and well-served battery swept the street with continued discharges of grape-shot, so that it was impossible to move down directly in front of it. The problem was to take the battery or to drive the Mexicans from their guns. The houses on both sides were built mostly in continuous blocks, with an occasional interval or vacant lot. The walls of the houses were of *adobe*, or light volcanic stone. The operation of breaking through them was thus conducted. A detachment of the sappers and miners, led by an officer, entered a house at the outer end of the street, with the proper tools and implements, and made a breach in the party or division wall large enough for a man to go through to the next house, and so on successively. Lieutenant McClellan led the party on one side of the street. It was a highly dangerous service, as every house had Mexican soldiers in it, and there was continuous fighting until the Americans drove out the occupants. It was Lieutenant McClellan's duty—or at least he considered it to be so—to pass first into the opening. In one instance, where it was necessary to cross a vacant space between two houses which did not join, he nearly lost his life by falling into a ditch of stagnant water. The party at length forced their way through the houses till they reached those which overlooked the battery, and where they could fire upon the Mexicans who manned the guns. These having been shot or driven away, the Americans descended from the houses, took the guns, and turned them on the gate, which was forced, and the city entered.

On the 14th day of September, 1847, General Scott, with six thousand five hundred men, the whole of his effective army remaining in the field, entered and took possession of the city of Mexico. With the exception of a few slight skirmishes, this was the close of the war in that part of the country.

CHAPTER II.

No minute and detailed account has been given of those military operations in Mexico in which Lieutenant McClellan was engaged,—which, indeed, could not have been done without swelling this part of the memoir to a disproportionate bulk. Our aim has been merely to present a continuous and intelligible narrative of what was done by him. The movements of the campaign, its sieges, assaults, and battles, were planned by others; and he can claim no higher merit—though this is not inconsiderable—than that of having faithfully executed the orders received from his superiors in rank. Nor has the moral element involved in the Mexican War —the question how far it was provoked or unprovoked, or how far we were right or wrong—been taken into consideration. Such an inquiry has now become as obsolete as would be a discussion of the moral judgment to be passed upon the conspirators who took the life of Julius Cæsar. But no candid person, whatever he may think of the merits of the contest, can deny that the conduct of the war and its results reflected the highest honor upon the courage of the American army, both regulars and volunteers, as well as upon the skill and accomplishments of our officers. Not that there were not grave errors committed, both at Washington and in the field; not that the volunteers did not sometimes show the infirmities of raw troops; but these shadows in the picture were as nothing to its lights. The whole campaign was especially remarkable for the brilliant, dashing, and reckless courage displayed in it,—for that quality which the French call *élan*, which is so captivating to civilians, and for the want of which so much fault has been found with our officers and soldiers in the present civil war. But the tactics in the Mexican War were founded upon and regulated by an accurate knowledge of the enemy; and the distinguished and veteran soldier who led our armies in that campaign would never have taken the risks he did had the Mexican soldiers been like those in the Southern army, and the Mexican officers men like Lee, Johnston, Jackson, and Beauregard.

The public mind judges of military movements and of battles by the event: the plan that fails is a bad plan, and the successful general is the great general. Without doubt, this is a correct judgment in the long run; but in particular cases the rule could not always be applied without injustice. Hannibal was defeated by Scipio at Zama, and Napoleon was defeated by the Duke of Wellington at Waterloo; but it does not follow that Scipio was a greater general than Hannibal, or the Duke of Wellington than Napoleon. Mexico was taken by a series of rapid and daring movements, and Richmond has not yet been taken; and thus the inference is drawn that, had the latter city been assailed in the same way as the former was, it too would have fallen, as Mexico did. But those who reason thus forget the sharp lesson we learned at Bull Run,—a disastrous battle forced upon the army by a popular sentiment which ignorantly clamored for the dash and rapidity which accomplished such brilliant results in the Valley of Mexico. Nelson won the battle of Aboukir by a very daring and dangerous plan of attack, which had the good fortune to be successful. Cooper, in his preface to the last edition of "The Two Admirals," says that had he attacked an American fleet in the same way he would have had occasion to repent the boldness of the experiment; but then Nelson, who, like all great commanders, was a man of correct observation and sound judgment, would probably not have tried such an experiment with an American fleet.

To Lieutenant McClellan his year of active service in Mexico was of great value in his professional training; for it was a period crowded with rich opportunities for putting into practice the knowledge he had gained at West Point, and which was still fresh in his mind. The corps of engineers attached to the army was so small that much work was of necessity exacted from each officer, and higher responsibilities were devolved upon the younger men than would have been the case in any European army. Lieutenant McClellan had an unusually large experience both of field-work and in the investment of fortified places. And it is no more than just to him to add that he proved himself equal to every trust laid upon him. His knowledge of his profession was shown to be thorough, exact, and ready, and his coolness and self-possession on "the perilous edge of battle" was like that of the bronzed veteran of a hundred fights. The number of men in our country—indeed, in any country—competent to pass a correct judgment upon military measures and military men, is not large; but upon this select body Lieutenant McClellan had made his mark during the Mexican War, and he was recognized by them as a soldier upon whose courage, ability, and devotion his country might confidently repose in her hour of need.

Lieutenant McClellan remained with his company in the city of Mexico, in the discharge of garrison-duty, till May 28, 1848, when they were marched down to Vera Cruz and embarked for home, arriving at West Point on the 22d of June. After his return he was brevetted first lieutenant for conduct at Contreras, and afterwards captain for conduct at Molino del Rey, which latter honor he declined, as he had not been present in the battle.

He was afterwards brevetted captain for conduct in the capture of Mexico, and his commission was dated back to that period.

Upon his return, his company was stationed at West Point, and he remained there with them till June, 1851, much of the time in command. His leisure hours were spent in studies connected with his profession. Among other things, he prepared an elaborate lecture upon the campaign of Napoleon in 1812, which was read before a literary society. Of this discourse he thus speaks in a letter to his sister-in-law:—"Well, it is over at last; and glad I am of it. I read the last part of my Napoleon paper last night. I have been working hard at it ever since my return, and the ink was hardly dry on the last part when it was read. The affair amounted to one hundred and eleven pages in all; and they compliment me by saying that it gave a clear explanation of the campaign: so I am contented. I hardly know, but I have an indefinite idea that we have had fine weather since I returned. I have some indistinct ideas of sunshine, and some of rain; but I have been so intently occupied with the one subject that I have thought of but little else. Now I must go to work with my company. I've enough to do to occupy half a dozen persons for a while; but I rather think I can get through it. I have had no time to read any of Schiller; but now I will go at it. I have some thought of writing a paper on the Thirty Years' War for our club."

His familiar letters breathe a strong desire for a more stirring and active life than that he was now leading, the monotony of which was the more keenly felt from its contrast with the brilliant excitements of the Mexican campaign. In one of his letters he tells his correspondent that his highest pleasure is to fall in with some comrade of the war, and talk over its hardships, perils, and successes and revive their impressions of the glorious scenery of Mexico. And yet he was never idle. Here is a specimen of his habits of work, taken from a letter to his brother, Dr. McClellan, dated January 10, 1849:—"On Christmas day, orders were received here from the Chief Engineer, requiring plans and estimates for several buildings to be furnished him for the Military Committee of the House, by to-day at latest. Among those required was a barrack for our company; and I had to make all the drawings: the barrack had to be planned and drawn in the short time allotted; and from two weeks from to-day until last Saturday night at twelve o'clock, I drew every day, morning, afternoon, and night, working Sundays, New-Year's day, and all. I had to make eight different drawings on the same large sheet, fifty-two inches by thirty-two, all drawn accurately to a scale, all the details, &c. painted: so, you may imagine, I had my hands full."

In the winter of 1849–50, he prepared for the use of the army a Manual of Bayonet Exercise, mostly taken from the French of Gomard. This was submitted by General Scott, the commander-in-chief, to the Secretary of War, in which he strongly recommended its being printed for distribution to the army, and that it should be made, by regulation, a part of the system of instruction. The recommendation was adopted by the War Department, and the manual was officially printed. It forms a small duodecimo volume of about a hundred pages, with a number of plates in outline.

In June, 1851, Captain McClellan was ordered to Fort Delaware, as assistant to Major John Sanders in the construction of the works there. Here he remained till near the close of the ensuing winter.

Early in March, 1852, Captain Randolph B. Marcy, of the Fifth Infantry, was directed by the War Department to make an exploration of the country embraced within the basin of the Upper Red River; and Captain McClellan was assigned to duty with the expedition. The other officers accompanying it were Lieutenant Updegraff and Dr. Shumard. Captain J. H. Strain, of Fort Washita, and Mr. J. R. Suydam, were also with it, but not in any official capacity. The private soldiers were fifty-five in number. There were also five Indians, serving as guides and hunters. Up to this time the region round the head-waters of the Red River had been unexplored by civilized man; and the only information we had as to the sources of one of the largest rivers in the United States was derived from Indians and semi-civilized Indian hunters.

The expedition started from Fort Belknap, upon the Brazos River, on the 2d of May, and marched to Red River at the mouth of the Little Witchita, and up the right bank of the latter stream to the mouth of the Big Witchita, where they crossed Red River. Proceeding westward, between Red River and a branch of Cache Creek, they struck the north fork of Red River at the west end of the Witchita Mountains, and followed that stream to its source in the Llano Estacado, or Staked Plain. Here an excursion was made to the valley of the Canadian River, at Sand Creek, in order to verify the position of the party by the survey which had been made along that stream by Captain Marcy in 1849. They then travelled south to the Kech-ah-que-ho, or main Red River, and, leaving their train at the place where the river comes out from the bluff of the Llano Estacado, ascended it to the spring which forms its source. From this they returned down the left bank of the river to the Witchita Mountains, which were examined, and thence they proceeded to Fort Arbuckle, on the Washita River, in the Indian Territory, arriving there July 28. Here the expedition terminated.

Captain Marcy brought back his command without the loss of a man. In his Report he says, "I feel a sincere regret at parting with the company, as the uniform good conduct of the men during the entire march of about a thousand miles merits my most sincere and heart-felt approbation. I have seldom had occasion even to reprimand one of them. All have performed the arduous duties assigned them with the utmost alacrity and good will; and when (as was sometimes the case) we were obliged to make long marches, and drink the most disgusting water for several days together, instead of murmuring and making complaints, they were cheerful and in good spirits. I owe them, as well as the officers and gentlemen who were with me, my most hearty thanks for their cordial co-operation with me in all the duties assigned to the expedition. It is probably in a great measure owing to this harmonious action on the part of all persons attached to the expedition that it has resulted so fortunately." Of Captain McClellan the introduction to the Report speaks thus:—"The astronomical observations were made by Captain George B. McClellan, of the Engineer Corps, who, in addition to the duties properly pertaining to his department, performed those of quartermaster and commissary to the command. An interesting collection of reptiles and other specimens, in alcohol, was also made under his superintendence, and put into the hands of Professors Baird and Girard, of the Smithsonian Institution, whose reports will be found in the appendix. For these and many other important services, as well as for his prompt and efficient co-operation in whatever was necessary for the successful accomplishment of the design of the expedition, I take this opportunity of tendering my warmest acknowledgments."

The party were received with peculiar warmth of welcome by the garrison at Fort Arbuckle; for they were supposed to have been all massacred by the Comanche Indians. The account was brought by a Keechi Indian, and was so circumstantial and minute in every particular, and showed so perfect a knowledge of the movements of the expedition, as well as of its numbers and equipment, that it was believed to be true. The report was carried to the

United States; and for several weeks the relatives of Captain McClellan mourned him as dead.

Captain Marcy's Report was published by order of Congress, and is one of those books which many receive, but few read. And yet it is well worth reading; for it has that fresh and spontaneous charm of style which we so often observe in the writings of superior men who are not men of letters by training and profession, and who tell us in a plain way of what they have seen and done. Besides a graphic and animated description of the country traversed by the expedition, it contains an excellent account of the Indian tribes that roam over it,—not that impossible creature, "the noble savage" of the poet, the sentimental red man of the novelist, nor yet the degraded outcast that withers in the shadow cast by the white man and grafts upon his own wild stock all the vices of civilization; but the Indian as he really exists,—a mingled web of virtues and vices, and certainly holding no low place upon the scale of savage and nomadic life.

And the remark which has just been made as to Captain Marcy's Report may be further extended; and it may be said that comparatively few persons know any thing of what may be called the civil victories of the American army. How few there are who are aware of how much has been done for science, and especially for geographical science, during the last thirty or forty years, by the able and accomplished officers of the regular army!—what toils and hardships they have endured, what perils they have met, and what laurels, unstained by blood and tears, they have won! One might feel indignant at the injustice which deals out what is called fame with so unequal a hand, were it not for the reflection that men who are competent to add to the intellectual wealth of the world, and enlarge the domain of knowledge, have learned to take popular applause at its true value, and to find in the faithful discharge of honorable duty a satisfaction which is its own reward.

After his duties upon Captain Marcy's expedition had ceased, Captain McClellan was ordered to Texas as chief engineer on the staff of General P. F. Smith. He sailed from New Orleans, accompanying General Smith, August 29, and arrived at Galveston on the 31st. In a letter to his brother, dated September 3, he says, "Galveston is probably the prettiest and most pleasant town in Texas. It is built on a perfectly level island, which forms a portion of the harbor, and near the point. The houses are all of frame, with piazzas, and very pretty and neat: all are surrounded with shrubbery. They have there the most beautiful oleanders I ever saw: they, with many other flowers, the banana, china-tree, orange, lemon, palm, &c. &c., present, you may imagine, a charming relief to the monotony of the level site. There is almost always a fine breeze and an elegant surf. The roads were excellent when we were there, on account of the frequent rains, which pack them down."

From Galveston he accompanied General Smith in a tour of military inspection, visiting Indianola,

St. Joseph's, and Corpus Christi. Of this last place he writes, "Corpus is about two miles from the head of Corpus Christi Bay, which is separated from Nueces Bay by a reef of sand. The shore makes a beautiful curve, near one end of which the town is built. The old camp of General Taylor was on the beach where the town stands, and extended some mile and a half or two miles above it. The positions of the tents are still marked by the banks of sand thrown up to protect them against the Northers. It is a classical spot with the army, there are so many old associations, traditions, and souvenirs of many who are now no more. The country round Corpus is very beautiful. Below, towards the bay (gulf, rather), it is a rather flat country, alternately prairie and chapparal, the prairies interspersed with 'motts'* of live-oak and mesquite,† covered withal by a luxuriant growth of grass. The chapparal is the prettiest growth of that nature I remember to have seen. It is, of course, tropical,—that is, composed of the cactus and the stiff thorn-covered bushes peculiar to the Southern latitudes; but the ground even now is covered with a great variety of beautiful flowers, and the whole makes up a very pretty country."

From Corpus Christi they proceeded to Fort Merrill, thence to San Antonio, and from there to Camp Johnston, on the Concho River, where they arrived October 24.

---

* "Mott," a local word, meaning a grove, or clump, of trees.

† "Mesquite," an indigenous tree of the acacia kind.

Here Captain McClellan found orders relieving him from duty on General Smith's staff, and assigning him the charge of the surveys for the improvement of the harbors on the coast of Texas from Indianola to Rio Grande, embracing Brazos Santiago, Corpus Christi, Lavacca, and the San Antonio River. This change of employment, transferring him from the land to the sea, was not exactly to his wish; but he set about his new duties with his usual promptness and energy. We find him at Corpus Christi in January, 1853, diligently at work upon estimates and reports; and on the 13th of that month he addressed to the Chief Engineer, General Totten, a letter giving a general description of the bars on the coast. For the rest of the winter and far into the spring he was hard at work. Here is a taste of his experiences, taken from a letter dated Corpus Christi, March 9, 1853:—"I left here on the 22d of February, one of the most beautiful mornings I ever saw, bright, clear, and mild, with a nice breeze just in the right direction. I congratulated myself on the fine start I made, and felt in fine spirits. Things went on finely for an hour or so. Then the breeze became so strong that I had to double-reef all my sails, and on we went, still handsomely. But presently the breeze changed into the most violent gale of the winter. The sea ran in young mountains. Down we brought the mainsail; and if ever a boat did run under a foresail, I rather think mine did that day. How it did blow! The spray dashed in your face like hail. The boat is a magnificent sailer, and a splendid sea-boat: so we still kept on beautifully, though it was slightly humid. Just as we were about to anchor, before reaching the mud-flats, we lost the way; for the spray flew so that we could not see, and the first thing we knew we were driven about four hundred yards up on one of the aforesaid flats, and rather halted. Nothing could be done: so we turned in as best we could, and waited for morning. When morning came, there was not an inch of water within three hundred yards,—could not even float the skiff. A sand island some six hundred yards off was the nearest dry place, and in walking to it you would sink over the knee in mud. In that delightful place my boat remained about ten days. After the first three, I went on board the Government steamer at Aranzas, some four miles off, and went to work at the bar in her whale-boat. When I got through, I found there was no use in waiting for the water to rise: so I took the steamer's crew and dug a canal, through which, after two days' hard work, we floated the Alice into deep water. I then at once ran down, by the outside passage, the Gulf, to Corpus Christi Pass, satisfied myself very quickly of its utter worthlessness, and came here, with flying colors, yesterday. I have finished this harbor and its two passes: by the end of the month I shall have completed the Brazos survey, and will then run up towards Indianola, finishing the inland channel and the San Antonio and Guadalupe Rivers by the end of April, if I have any thing like ordinary good luck. In May I shall finish Paso Cavallo Harbor, and hope to finish the field-work by the end of that month at furthest. Then I shall sell out my boats, and go to Galveston and make out my reports and maps."

On the 18th of April, Captain McClellan addressed to General Totten a report of the result of the surveys on the coast of Texas, as far as they had then been completed. It embraces the bars along the coast from Paso Cavallo to the mouth of the Rio Grande, the harbors of Brazos Santiago, Corpus Christi, Aranzas, and Paso Cavallo, and the inland channel from Matagorda Bay to Aranzas Bay. It is printed in the Executive Documents of the first session of the Thirty-Third Congress, —a brief and business-like document, containing plans and suggestions for improving the harbors designated, with estimates of the probable expenses.

But before the date of his Report he had received information of his having been assigned to a more congenial field of duty; for in a letter to his brother, dated Indianola, April 7, 1853, he tells him that he has been offered the charge of a portion of one of the Pacific Railroad surveys recently authorized by Congress, to start from Puget Sound and to go through the Cascade Mountains to St. Paul on the Mississippi, and adds, "As the results of the surveys are to be presented to Congress during the ensuing February, the time will be limited; and I can never have a better opportunity of seeing California and Oregon: so I did not hesitate a moment in determining to accept the position. I am told that 'the exploration is arduous, and will bring reputation.' Hard work and reputation will carry me a long way."

The expedition to which he was attached was under the general supervision of Governor Isaac I. Stevens, of Washington Territory, formerly of the army, who, to the great loss of his country, met a glorious death in the battle near Chantilly, Fairfax county, Virginia, September 1, 1862. It was charged with the duty of examining the lines of the forty-seventh and forty-ninth parallels of north latitude; and the special object of the exploration was the determination of a railroad-route from the head-waters of the Mississippi to Puget Sound. One party, under the immediate direction of Governor Stevens, was to proceed from the Mississippi westward, survey the intermediate country, and examine the passes of the Rocky Mountains. Captain McClellan, at the head of a separate party, was to explore the Cascade Range of mountains.

Immediately on receiving official news of his appointment, he set out for the Pacific coast, *via* the Isthmus, arrived at Fort Vancouver on the 27th of June, began to make preparations for the expedition, and started on the 24th of July. His party consisted of Lieutenant Duncan, Third Artillery, astronomer, topographer, and draughtsman; Lieutenant Hodges, Fourth Infantry, quartermaster and commissary; Lieutenant Mowry, Third Artillery, meteorologist; Mr. George Gibbs, ethnologist and geologist; Mr. J. F. Minter, assistant engineer, in charge of courses and distances; five assistants in observations, carrying instruments, &c.; two sergeants, two corporals, and twenty-four privates of the Fourth Infantry. Two chief packers, three hunters and herders, and twenty packers, completed the party. There were one hundred and seventy-three animals with the command,—seventy-three for the saddle, one hundred for packing.

The field of Captain McClellan's exploration lies in the western part of Washington Territory. The river Columbia from Fort Okinakane, at about the forty-eighth degree of north latitude, flows in a southerly direction, a little inclining to the east, till it reaches Fort Walla-Walla. Then it makes a sudden turn to the west, and runs to the Pacific in a course nearly at right angles to its former current. The space enclosed between these two arms of the river on the south and east respectively, and the ocean on the west, is partly filled up by the Cascade Mountains, a continuation of the Sierra Nevada Range in California, and deriving their name from the fact that the Columbia breaks through them in a series of falls in its passage to the ocean. Captain McClellan's course from Fort Vancouver was in a northeasterly direction, along the dividing line between the stream flowing westwardly into the Pacific and eastwardly to form the Yakima, which is an affluent of the Columbia.

The party, starting from Fort Vancouver July 24, as has been said, reached the river Wenass on the 20th of August, having travelled one hundred and sixty-two miles. Here a pause of some days was made. Lieutenant Hodges was despatched to Fort Steilacoom, to procure provisions, exchange their pack-horses for mules, if possible, and examine the intermediate route. Lieutenant Duncan was directed to cross to the main Yakima, examine the upper part of that valley, and obtain all possible information in relation to the surrounding country, especially towards the north. Mr. Gibbs was instructed to examine the valley of the Yakima to its junction with the Columbia. Captain McClellan himself, with Mr. Minter and six men, made an examination of the Nahchéss Pass. Lieutenant Mowry was left in charge of the camp at Wenass.

By the 31st of August all these separate parties, except that under Lieutenant Hodges, had accomplished their tasks and returned to the camp. Here Captain McClellan determined to reduce the number of his party; and, accordingly, on the 2d of September Lieutenant Mowry was sent back to the Dalles, on Columbia River, with seventeen men, of whom but two were to return with him. He took with him the collections made up to this time, and every thing that could be dispensed with.

On the 3d of September the depot camp was moved from the Wenass to Ketetas, on the main Yakima. On the 4th, Captain McClellan left the camp, with Mr. Gibbs, Mr. Minter, and six men, to examine the pass at the head of the main Yakima, and returned to the camp on the 12th. While on this separate examination, he wrote a letter to his mother, dated September 11, from which an extract is here made, giving an account of his movements for the previous fortnight:—

"On about the 23d of August I started from the main camp on the Wenass River, to examine what is called the Nahchéss Pass, having on the previous day sent in some fifty pack-animals by the same pass to Steilacoom, for provisions, so that I might start from this vicinity (after examining the passes) with three months' provisions. I took with me my assistant, Minter, three hunters, one packer, one of my Texas men to carry the barometer, and my Mexican boy Jim. The first day's work was of no particular interest: we travelled some six miles up the valley in which we were camped, and struck over the *divide* to the southwest into the valley of the Nahchéss, where we camped, after a hot march of some eighteen miles over a rough, mountainous country,—the last fifteen without water. Next day we travelled about seventeen miles up the valley of the Nahchéss,—that is, wherever there was any valley; for the stream, frequently running through cañons, often threw us back into the mountains, where the trail was very rough, stony, and steep. These cañons are generally through masses of basaltic rock, varying in height from fifty to five hundred feet, and generally perfectly vertical,—the whole width occupied by the bed of the stream. The scenery here is singularly wild and bold. Most of the hills and mountains, being of volcanic rocks, have the sharp, bold outlines peculiar to the formation. Our next march, of about equal length, and over a rather worse country, brought us to the *divide*,—that is, the point where the waters run in one direction towards the Sound, in the other towards the Columbia above Walla-Walla. By ascending a high, bare mountain, called by the Indians Aiqz, we had a fine view of the mountains. The range had now become exceedingly rough, and the mountains large. We were but a short distance from Mount

Ranier,—a magnificent snow peak,—and could count around us some thirty mountains, with more or less snow upon them. We remained one day at the *divide*, examining the country on foot, and then returned by about the same route we had before taken. The day after I reached the main camp I received an express from the officer I had sent into Steilacoom, informing me that most of his animals (horses) had broken down, and that there were no mules at Steilacoom to replace them. Therefore I at once determined to reduce the size of the party. I sent in the whole escort, and others the next day, so as to reduce the number from sixty-nine to thirty. I have mules enough to carry ninety days' provisions for this number, and can now travel much more rapidly. The day after the escort left, I moved camp from the Wenass River to the main Yakima,—about fourteen miles northward,—and started the next day, with the same party as before (with the addition of Mr. Gibbs), to examine the Sinahomis Pass. Our first two marches were of no peculiar interest,—passing through a rather wide valley covered with an open growth of pines. In the third march we struck the mountains (the valley giving out), and had a terrible road, much obstructed by fallen timber and brush, and with some very respectable mountains to pass over. We passed by the foot of a beautiful lake (Kitchelas) in which this river heads: it is some four or five miles long, and about one mile wide, surrounded by very lofty mountains. About two-thirds of the way up the last mountain we ascended, we passed between two small lakes, and, looking down from the top, saw at our feet, some one thousand feet below us, still another,—Willailootzas. We passed over the mountain and encamped some distance down on the farther side, in the bed of an old lake. You may imagine what kind of weather there is among the mountains, when I tell you that nearly every morning at sunrise the thermometer stands at 32°. We remained at this mountain one day, trudging around on foot. Next day I sent the animals back by the trail, and started on foot to examine the *divide* and Willailootzas. I had a very rough climb for some six hours, discovered another small and very pretty lake, from which the water runs both ways, and found my mule waiting for me on the trail at about two o'clock.

A ride of about sixteen miles, over a horrible trail, brought me into camp just before dark and fully prepared for a respectable cup of coffee. Next day we went back about three miles on the trail, and then struck off to visit the largest lake of all,—Kahchéss,—about eight miles long. It is very beautiful, situated, like the others, in the midst of the mountains. Yesterday we travelled about sixteen miles, to visit another large and beautiful lake,—Kleallum. These are all in the mountains, and on the heads of different branches of the main Sahawa, —most of them fully as beautiful and picturesque as many celebrated in the fashionable world. I doubt whether any whites ever saw any of them before: certainly they were unknown to the settlers. Whether steamboats will ever run on them, or Saratogas be established in their vicinity, is with me a matter of exceeding doubt. The only things we have seen of much interest are the mountains and the lakes,—both fine in their way, but rather hard to get at. To-morrow I shall go into the main camp, and hope to find things about ready for me to start into the town incognito to the northward. I shall send an express in a day or two with reports to the Secretary of War, and this at the same time. I hope to reach Mt. Baker in about twenty days from here. Where I will go to then, circumstances must determine,—I think to Colville,—perhaps thence to the Rocky Mountains."

Lieutenant Mowry had returned from the Dalles on the 2d of September, and on the 16th Lieutenant

Hodges arrived from Steilacoom, bringing twenty-nine pack-horses loaded with provisions. Preparations were now made to move northward: thirty-two broken-down horses were sent back, under charge of three men, to the Dalles, and the command was reduced to thirty-six persons, with forty-two riding-animals and fifty-two pack-animals. They started on the 20th, and moved in a north-easterly direction. On the 9th of October they reached their most northerly camp, about thirteen miles south of the "Great Lake," in latitude 49° 26′. They then moved west to the Columbia River, which they crossed at Fort Colville. Thence they proceeded southerly across the Great Plain of the Columbia River, and arrived at Walla-Walla on the 7th of November, at Fort Dalles on the 15th. From Fort Dalles they went down by water to Fort Vancouver, which they reached on the 18th. An extract from a letter to his brother, dated November 28, may be here appropriately introduced:—

"From that place [the Yakima valley] we crossed a rather high mountain-ridge (running nearly east and west), and struck the Columbia not far above Buckland's Rapids, and a little distance below the mouth of the Pischas. My journal written that night says, 'Soon, descending a little, you arrive at the edge of the sudden, precipitous descent that borders the valley of the Columbia. Words can hardly convey an idea of the view from this mountain. Somewhat to the north of west is a handsome snow peak, part of a long snow ridge. This has no name, and is probably seen by whites for the first time. To the north of that the Cascade Range is in full view, the main range coming directly to the Columbia, and crossing it, until it sinks towards the east into a vast, elevated table-land. In the distance, to the north, is seen a long blue range, at the foot of which the Columbia runs from Colville to Okonogan. To the northeast and east, as far as the eye can reach, extends the *beau-idéal* of the sublimity of desolation, a vast plain (as it appears from the height and distance), without one indication of water, one spot of green to please the eye. It is generally of a dead yellowish hue, with large "clouds" of black blending into the general tinge. It must be a sage-desert, with dry burnt grass and outcroppings of basalt. Not a tree or bush is to be seen upon it. The valley of the Columbia is very deep and exceedingly narrow: it is connected with the great plain by steps of basaltic rock,—most of them narrow ledges, and varying in height from fifty to three hundred or four hundred feet. The great river looks like a narrow blue thread or ribbon. It seems as if our only means of travelling farther to the north would be to follow the valley of the river until it leaves the mountains. Forward we must go: the means will perhaps present themselves when we reach the valley.' Sure enough, we were obliged to follow the valley six days, at the end of which we reached Okonogan. During this time we had some very bad and dangerous places to pass over. On one occasion we made but one and three-quarter miles from morning till night,—had two mules instantly killed by falling off a precipice, and two others badly hurt.

"Mt. Okonogan (Okinakane) is delightfully situated on a gravel flat, without a blade of grass or any thing else for some distance from it. A little Frenchman is the only apology for a white man there. He was very kind to us; and he and I misunderstood each other most beautifully in all our conversations. From there I went westward into the mountains, in vain hopes of finding another pass, and finally returned to Okonogan, whence I went as far north as the Great Lake Okonogan. There is little or no timber in the valley: small parts of it are tolerably good, but the greater part worthless. From the forks up to the Great Lake it is, in fact, nothing but a series of lakes of different sizes. The Great Lake is some two miles wide and about seventy in length. The scenery around it is more remarkable for its desolation than its beauty. In fact, the whole of this region has something very lonely and dispiriting about it: you see a very few miserably squalid Indians, and no other signs of animal life: an occasional wolf, with now and then a lonely badger, are all you see. From the forks we struck over to the Colville River, and followed it down to the Columbia opposite Fort Colville. The valley of this little river was about the prettiest we saw,--fine larch timber, and a good deal of yellow pine, the valley very narrow, the stream a bold and pretty one; no Indians; and not even any salmon in it. At Colville we crossed the Columbia, swimming the animals, and ferrying ourselves and 'traps' in canoes."

At Fort Vancouver the party was broken up, and the portion required for office-work was sent to Olympia, where Captain McClellan arrived on the 16th of December. On the 23d he started with a small party to endeavor to complete the barometrical profile of the main Yakima Pass and examine the approaches on the western side; but he was obliged to return without having accomplished his purpose, mainly on account of the great depth of snow and the impossibility of procuring Indian guides.

Some weeks were spent in office-work at Olympia. From that place, on the 8th of February, 1854, Captain McClellan addressed to Governor Stevens a brief report on the railroad-practicability of the passes examined by him; and his general report, sent to the Secretary of War, bears the date of February 25. Both of these reports appear in the first volume of the official publications on the Pacific Railroad route, made by order of Congress. His general conclusions were that between the parallels of 45° 30′ and 49° north latitude there are but two passes through the range practicable for a railroad,—that of the Columbia River and that of the Yakima River; that the latter was barely practicable, and that only at a high cost of time, labor, and money, while the former was not only undoubtedly practicable, but remarkably favorable.

The Secretary of War, in his report to Congress, dated February 27, 1855, says, "The examination of the approaches and passes of the Cascade Mountains, made by Captain McClellan, of the Corps of Engineers, presents a reconnoissance of great value, and, though performed under adverse circumstances, exhibits all the information necessary to determine the practicability of this portion of the route, and reflects the highest credit on the capacity and resources of that officer."

In addition to his duties upon the railroad-survey, Captain McClellan had been directed by the Secretary of War to superintend the construction of the military road from Walla-Walla to Steilacoom. This road was built after he had left the Pacific region; but the contracts and arrangements were made by him before his departure.

He returned home in the spring of 1854. In the

summer of that year he was sent on a secret expedition to the West Indies, the object of which was to select a harbor and procure a site suitable for a coaling-station. It was a service of some danger, as it exposed him to the influences of a tropical climate in the hottest season of the year. He went out in a United States vessel under the command of Lieutenant Renshaw, a gallant and excellent officer, who was killed at Galveston, January 1, 1863, by the blowing up of the Westfield. Captain McClellan selected the bay and promontory of Samaná, on the northeast coast of the island of Hayti, as the most desirable site for the object proposed. It is a spot of much historical interest. Columbus, returning to Spain after his first discovery of the New World, anchored in this bay, having first sailed round the promontory and given names to two of its headlands. Here some of his crew had an affray with the natives, in the course of which, much to the grief of the great navigator, two of the latter were wounded,—the first time that native blood was shed by white men in the New World. At a later period, the peninsula,—which in the old maps is laid down as an island,—as well as the rocky islets in the harbor, of which there were several, became haunts of the buccaneers. On one of these islets, or cays, Jack Banister, a celebrated English pirate, at the close of the seventeenth century, defended himself successfully against two English frigates sent to capture him,—in consequence of which the name of Banister Cays was given to the group. Upon the promontory are some negro villages, occupied by the descendants and survivors of a colony of free colored persons who went from New Jersey under Boyer's administration.*

---

* Part of the information in the text is taken from a memoir on the peninsula and bay of Samaná in the "Journal of the London Geographical Society" for 1853, by Sir R. H. Schomburgk, H. B. M. Consul at the Dominican Republic. The concluding paragraphs are as follows:—

"I have purposely dwelt long and in detail upon this narrow strip of land, called the Peninsula of Samaná, and upon its adjacent magnificent bay. In its *geographical position* its greatest importance is centred. The fertile soil is fit for the cultivation of all tropical productions; its spacious bays and anchoring-places offer a shelter to the navies of the world; and its creeks afford facilities for the erection of arsenals and docks, while the adjacent forests yield the requisite woods for naval architecture: still, its chief importance does not consist in these advantages alone, but in its *geographical position*, forming, as it does, one of the principal keys to the isthmus of Central America and to the adjacent Gulf of Mexico. Mr. Lepelletier de Saint-Remy says, 'Samaná is one of those maritime positions not often met with in a survey of the map of the world. Samaná is to the Gulf of Mexico what Mayotta is to the Indian Ocean. It is not only the military, but also the commercial, key of the Gulf; but the latter is of infinitely greater importance, under the pacific tendencies of European politics.'

"The Bay of Samaná being placed to the windward of Jamaica, Cuba, and the Gulf of Mexico, and lying, moreover, almost due northeast of the great isthmus which now so powerfully attracts the attention of the world, the French author just quoted may well call it '*la tête-du-pont*' to the highway from the Atlantic to the Pacific."

Captain McClellan had never seen or heard of this memoir at the date of his visit to the West Indi s; and it is creditable

Captain McClellan drew up two reports, one on the harbor and its defences, and one forming a general memoir on the island. They have never been printed, and are probably still on file in the archives of the War Department. Our Government entered into negotiations with the Dominican Republic for the cession of the bay and peninsula; but they were not crowned with success. It may be surmised that the influence of France and England, exerted through their representatives, may have prevented it.

After returning home from the West Indies, Captain McClellan was stationed at Washington, employed on duties connected with the Pacific Railroad surveys. In the autumn of 1854, he drew up a very elaborate memoir on various practical points relating to the construction and management of railways, which was published in the same volume with the reports of his explorations. The Secretary of War remarks upon it as follows:—"Captain McClellan, of the Corps of Engineers, after the completion of his field-operations, was directed to visit various railroads, and to collect information of facts established in the construction and working of existing roads, to serve as data in determining the practicability of constructing and working roads over the several routes explored. The results of his inquiries will be found in a very valuable memoir, herewith submitted."

---

to his sagacity to have selected, as the result of his own unaided observation, a site which so competent an authority as Sir Robert H. Schomburgk speaks of in such terms as the above.

In the spring of 1855, Captain McClellan received the appointment of captain in the First Cavalry Regiment, then under the command of Colonel Sumner.

CHAPTER III.

IN the spring of 1855, while the Crimean War was raging, the Government of the United States determined to send a military commission to Europe, to observe the warlike operations then in progress, to examine the military systems of the great Powers of Europe, and to report such plans and suggestions for improving the organization and discipline of our own army as they might derive from such observation. The officers selected for this trust were Major—now Colonel—Delafield, of the Engineers, Major Mordecai, of the Ordnance, and Captain McClellan. The last was by some years the youngest of the three, Colonel Delafield having been graduated at West Point in 1818, and Major Mordecai in 1823. The selection of so young a man for such a trust is a proof of the high reputation he had made for himself in the judgment of those by whom the choice was made; and it may be here mentioned that he was in the first instance designated for the commission by President Pierce himself, who had had an opportunity in the Mexican War to observe what manner of soldier and man he was. Of the three officers, he, too, was the only one who had seen actual service in the field.

The exact nature of the duties assigned to the commission may be learned from the letter of the Secretary of War, the essential parts of which are as follows:—

"WAR DEPARTMENT, WASHINGTON, April 2, 1855.

"GENTLEMEN:—You have been selected to form a commission to visit Europe, for the purpose of obtaining information with regard to the military service in general, and especially the practical working of the changes which have been introduced of late years into the military systems of the principal nations of Europe.

"Some of the subjects to which it is peculiarly desirable to direct your attention may be indicated as follows:—

"The organization of armies and of the departments for furnishing supplies of all kinds to the troops, especially in field-service. The manner of distributing supplies.

"The fitting up of vessels for transporting men and horses, and the arrangements for embarking and disembarking them.

"The medical and hospital arrangements, both in permanent hospitals and in the field. The kind of ambulances, or other means, used for transporting the sick and wounded.

"The kind of clothing and camp equipage used for service in the field.

"The kind of arms, ammunition, and accoutrements used in equipping troops for the various branches of service, and their adaptation to the purposes intended. In this respect, the arms and equipments of cavalry of all kinds will claim your particular attention.

"The practical advantages and disadvantages attending the use of the various kinds of rifle arms which have been lately introduced extensively in European warfare.

"The nature and efficiency of ordnance and ammunition employed for field and siege operations, and the practical effect of the late changes partially made in the French field artillery.

"The construction of permanent fortifications, the arrangement of new systems of sea-coast and land defences, and the kind of ordnance used in the armament of them, —the Lancaster gun, and other rifle cannon, if any are used.

"The composition of trains for siege-operations, the kind and quantity of ordnance, the engineering operations of a siege in all its branches, both of attack and defence.

"The composition of bridge-trains, kinds of boats, wagons, &c.

"The construction of casemated forts, and the effects produced on them in attacks by land and water. The use of camels for transportation, and their adaptation to cold and mountainous countries.

* * * * * * *

"Very respectfully, your obedient servant,

"JEFFERSON DAVIS.

"Major R. DELAFIELD,
"Major A. MORDECAI,
"Captain G. B. McCLELLAN,
"*United States Army.*"

The officers composing the commission sailed from Boston on the 11th of April. On arriving in England, they were courteously received by Lord Clarendon, Secretary of State for the Foreign Department,—Lord Panmure, the Secretary of War, being disabled by illness,—and furnished with letters of introduction to Lord Raglan, Sir Edward Lyons, the admiral of the Baltic fleet, and the officers in command at Constantinople. In France a difficulty arose on account of an imperative rule in the French military service that no foreign officer could be permitted to go into their camp and afterwards to pass into that of the enemy, and that, therefore, it would be necessary for the members of the commission to give a promise that they would not go from the French camp to any other part of the Crimea, even although they might first go to St. Petersburg. This pledge the commission were not prepared to give, and the matter remained for some time in abeyance. But the most ample facilities were extended to them for visiting such military and naval establishments as they desired to inspect.

On the 28th of May, the commission left Paris, intending to proceed to the Russian camp in the Crimea by the way of Prussia, starting first for Berlin, in order to confer with the Russian Minister in that city, Baron de Budberg, to whom the Russian Minister at Washington had given them a letter. Their object was to go from Berlin to the Crimea by the way of Warsaw and Kiev, on the Danube; and Baron de Budberg gave them passports and letters to Baron Krusentein, a Russian official at Warsaw. But on arriving at Warsaw they learned that no person there—not even the veteran hero Paskievitch, with whom they had an interview, and who treated them with much courtesy—had the power to grant them permission to go from Warsaw direct to the Crimea, and that there was nothing to be done but to proceed to St. Petersburg. During their stay in Warsaw, they examined the fortifications of that city and of Modlin.

It was very annoying to the officers of the commission to find their progress blocked by ceremonials and formalities which they might have escaped if they had been civilians and private citizens and gone direct from Constantinople to Sebastopol, as so many idlers and amateurs had done; but, having presented themselves in an official capacity, they could do no less than bear its burdens and encumbrances; and so they went on to St. Petersburg, where they arrived June 19. A few extracts from a letter written by Captain McClellan to his younger brother—now Captain Arthur McClellan—the day after his arrival in the Russian capital, give some of his first impressions of the country and people:—

"We left Warsaw at six P.M. on the evening of the 13th, and reached here at about the same hour last evening, having travelled constantly day and night, merely stopping a few minutes for meals.

"In Poland the country is either flat or slightly rolling, the soil improving as you approach the Niemen, but in many places very poor. There are no towns of any consequence on the road, which, you will observe, passes near the Prussian frontier, but many villages, which are generally of wood and presenting a dirty, squalid appearance. The villages are mostly inhabited by Jews,—as dirty and wretched a race as you ever saw,—worse than any *you* ever saw. The appearance of the Poles is any thing but favorable; they look like a stupid, degraded race,—are dirty and ugly. It is difficult to imagine how they ever fought as they have done in the past. Ostrolinha was the site of a great battle in the revolution of 1831. It is a small wooden town on the Narew (*Nareff*), which is here a rapid stream some fifty yards wide. A large monument commemorates the victory gained by the Russians. Kouno is a town of good size, mostly built of plastered brick. A portion of it is very old, while the new suburbs are handsome and well built. It presents the appearance of a flourishing place, there being many small vessels in the Niemen, and immense trains of carts constantly arriving here from the interior of Russia. They bring down tallow, hemp, &c., and carry back cotton, groceries, &c. As the Niemen empties in Prussian territory, a glance at the map will show you the importance of this place whilst the Russian ports are blockaded. The Niemen is here two hundred and twenty yards wide,—a bold and rapid stream, crossed by a raft-bridge. It was near and at this place that the great mass of the French army crossed the Niemen in June, 1812; and it was at the gate of this same town that in the retreat Marshal Ney fought so desperately, forming in his own person the rear-guard of the Grand Army. Of course I went to the spot during *the short time we remained here. You now enter the* great forests of Russia. As far as Vilkomir there is but little cultivation, the country being mostly covered by pine and beech forests. I should have mentioned that in the public square of Kouno there is a huge iron monument, bearing in Russian an inscription to the effect that out of seven hundred thousand French who crossed the Niemen in *June*, 1812, but seventy thousand recrossed in *December*. As far as Dunaburg (on the river *Duna*, or, as some of the maps have it, *Dwina*) the country is quite rolling,—almost broken; very different from the idea I had formed of it. You pass through a number of small towns and villages.

"Dunaburg appears to be a small town, presenting nothing of peculiar interest. There are some defensive works here.

"Before reaching Dunaburg, we passed through one town (a small one, perhaps hardly deserving the name of more than a village), called Novo Alexandrowsky, which is remarkably pretty. It is situated on the high banks of a large and handsome lake broken by little green islets. The houses and people were remarkably good-looking.

Rigitza is also a pretty little place: there is here a ruined castle of long, long ago. Country now not so much rolling as near Dunaburg, but still by no means flat: it is fertile and well cultivated. Ostroff is another handsome little place: the road here crosses the river on a very fine suspension-bridge; and on an island in the river is a very extensive ruined castle, perhaps of some of the Teutonic knights. Pscov, near which we passed, seems to be especially blessed with churches, the gilded domes of which shone from afar. The country near here, and, in fact, from here to St. Petersburg, is low and level, the soil generally good,—sometimes poor, and sometimes very fertile.

"Pscov is the capital of a province, and at the head of a large lake. Near Ploosa is a swampy district of considerable extent, and many large lakes. Nothing of very great interest until one reaches Gatchina, where is the hunting-palace of the Emperor: it seems to be a very grand establishment. From there to this city the country is very flat, the soil not very good, but settlements increasing as you draw near.

"The general appearance of the portion of Russia I have seen is much superior to that of Poland; and I like the appearance of the people very much.

* * * * * * *

"This is truly a most magnificent city,—wide streets, fine private houses, magnificent public buildings. Thus far I have, of course, merely had a glance at the exterior of things, and will not pretend to describe any thing, more than to say that it fully equals my expectations. We are very comfortably fixed at the Hotel de Russie,—good rooms, good meals, plenty of ice, &c.

"The road from Warsaw here is truly a magnificent one, —especially the portion of it in Poland. It is all macadamized; and they are now hard at work *improving* the Russian part, so that in a couple of months it will be throughout as fine a road as any in the world. Think of the immense length,—one thousand and seventy-four versts, or seven hundred and sixteen miles!

"So great is the traffic upon it at present that it is literally covered from one end to the other with trains of wagons passing in both directions. The trade which formerly passed down the Baltic now seeks its outlet into Prussia by this route.

"So great is this now that it seems hardly possible that Russia can feel the effect of the blockade very sensibly. New channels are opened, and immense additional numbers of men, animals, and capital are now employed in the land-transportation.

* * * * *

"*June* 20 *and* 21, *Midnight.*—I write this paragraph in my room by the natural light,—no candle or any thing whatever: you may imagine the *darkness* of the night here."

During their residence at St. Petersburg, the officers of the commission were treated with much courtesy by the civil and military authorities, and all possible facilities were afforded to them for examining the various military establishments in the vicinity. They were presented to the Emperor, at his request, and graciously received by him. But they did not succeed in obtaining permission to go to Sebastopol, because the officers in command there had requested that no strangers should be permitted to come there, as such visits occasioned them a great deal of embarrassment; and though the Emperor, of course, might overrule such objections, yet he felt bound to defer to the strongly-expressed wishes of officers placed in such responsible positions. Nothing could be urged in reply to this; and, disappointed as they were, they could not, as military men, fail to respect the Emperor's deference to the views of his subordinates.

On the 19th of July the commission proceeded to Moscow, and examined whatever was of interest in a military point of view there. Hastening back to St Petersburg, they left that city on the 2d of August, and arrived at Berlin on the 25th, having in the interval observed the fortifications and defences at Königsberg, Dantzig, Posen, and Schwedt. At Berlin the various military establishments in that city and at Spandau were carefully inspected.

From Berlin they determined to go to the Crimea by the way of Dresden, Laybach, Trieste, and Smyrna, and found themselves at last on the line of operations of the allied army at Constantinople, on the 16th of September. To the courtesy of the English naval authorities they were indebted for a passage in the first steamer that sailed for Balaklava, where they arrived on the morning of October 8. Here every possible facility and kindness, official and personal, was extended to them by the officers of the English army, including Sir George Simpson, the commander. It was hoped that the French Government would relax the rule they had laid down in the spring; but the new authorization to visit their camps and army, received at Balaklava, contained substantially the same condition as had been before exacted, and the commission could not avail themselves of the permission to which such terms were attached. The result was that they confined their examination to the camps, depots, parks, workshops, &c. of the English, Sardinian, and Turkish armies, never entering the French camps in the Crimea except on visits of courtesy.

On the 2d of November they left Balaklava in an English steamer, and spent some days in Constantinople and Scutari, inspecting the hospitals and depots of the allies. From Constantinople they proceeded to Vienna, examining on their route the defences of Varna and the remarkable triumphs of civil engineering in the works on the Sœmmering Railroad.

On the 16th of December they reached Vienna, and spent some days in a careful observation of the Austrian military establishments, and, after leaving Vienna, went to Venice, Verona, Mantua, and Milan, examining the military and naval establishments in each place. At Verona they were most kindly received by the veteran hero Marshal Radetzky, who contributed in every way to the attainment of their wishes as well as to their personal gratification. Colonel Delafield—from the introduction to whose Report this account of the movements of the commission is abridged—speaks in the warmest terms of the peculiar and uniform courtesy extended to them by the authorities and functionaries of Austria. That Government seemed to have quite forgotten the Martin Koszta affair.

On the 2d of February, 1856, they arrived at Toulon, and, with the authority previously obtained from the French Government, examined the military and naval defences of that important depot. But the only facility extended to them was that afforded by a printed ticket of admission transmitted from Paris, which did no more than command the services of a porter to conduct them through the buildings, docks, and vessels, and gave them no opportunity to converse with any of the officers. From Toulon they visited in succession Marseilles, Lyons, Belfort, Strasbourg, Rastadt, Coblentz, and Cologne, observing their fortresses and defences,—in the last three places, however, without the advantage of any special authority.

The 24th and 25th of February were spent at Liège, where their time was occupied at the national foundry for artillery and another for small-arms, both on a more extended scale than any corresponding establishments in Europe at that time.

On the 1st of March the commission was at Paris again. Two days were devoted to an examination of the fortress at Vincennes; and several of the military establishments in Paris were also inspected. They were unable, however, to obtain the requisite authority for seeing those relating to the artillery.

On the 18th of March the commission proceeded to Cherbourg and examined the works there. On the 24th of March they arrived at London, and afterwards visited the arsenal and dockyards at Woolwich, the vessels at Portsmouth, and the defences near Yarmouth, on the Isle of Wight, receiving every courtesy and facility they could desire from the military and naval officers at those stations in furthering the object of their visit. On the 19th of April they embarked for home.

The above is a brief record of the labors of a

very busy year, in which, however, much precious time was lost from delay in obtaining the necessary official permissions to inspect military establishments. And it must be added that in many cases the commission failed to receive those facilities which assuredly would have been extended in our country to a similar board sent from any Government in Europe. It may be too much to expect that nations should be governed in their relations towards each other by the precepts of Christian morality, but surely it is not too much to ask that they should conform to the code of courtesy and good breeding recognized among gentlemen in the intercourse of social life.

After their return, each of the officers upon the commission made a report to the Secretary of War of the results of their tour of observation; and these reports were in due time officially published by Congress in a quarto form, and pretty widely distributed. They were recognized by all competent judges as productions of great merit, reflecting the highest credit upon their respective authors, and amply vindicating the sagacity of the Government which selected them. In October, 1861, Captain McClellan's report was republished by the publishers of the present work, in an octavo volume, with illustrations, with the title, "The Armies of Europe: comprising Descriptions in detail of the Military System of England, France, Russia, Prussia, Austria, and Sardinia, adapting their Advantages to all Arms of the United States Service, and embodying the Report of Observations in

Europe during the Crimean War, as Military Commissioner from the United States Government in 1855–56."

Its contents are as follows. The first thirty-five pages are occupied with an able and interesting summary of the warlike operations in the Crimea, in which the plans and movements both of the Russians and the allies are criticized without a touch of arrogance, and yet with a manly decision of tone which reveals a sound military judgment and thorough military training. Its merits can be fully perceived only by a professional reader; but the general reader cannot fail to recognize in it the marks which show the writer to be a man of vigorous understanding and excellent powers of observation, as well as an accomplished officer. The style is simple, perspicuous, and direct, the style of Washington, Collingwood, and Wellington;—in other words, that good style which a man of sense will always write who has something to say and writes on without thinking about his style at all. As the work, from the nature of its contents, can never have been generally read, two extracts from this portion of the volume are here appended,—enough, it is believed, to justify the commendation which has been bestowed upon it. The first is a brief criticism of the defences of Sebastopol:—

"From the preceding hasty and imperfect account of the defences of Sebastopol, it will appear how little foundation there was for the generally received accounts of the stupendous dimensions of the works, and of new systems of fortifications brought into play. The plain truth is that these defences were simple temporary fortifications of rather greater dimensions than usual, and that not a single new principle of engineering was there developed. It is true that there were several novel minor details, such as the rope mantelets, the use of the iron tanks, &c.; but the whole merit consisted in the admirable adaptation of well-known principles to the peculiar locality and circumstances of the case. Neither can it be asserted that the plans of the various works were perfect. On the contrary, there is no impropriety in believing that, if Todtleben were called upon to do the same work over again, he would probably introduce better close-flanking arrangements.

"These remarks are not intended to, nor can they, detract from the reputation of the Russian engineer. His labors and their results will be handed down in history as the most triumphant and enduring monument of the value of fortifications, and his name must ever be placed in the first rank of military engineers. But, in our admiration of the talent and energy of the engineer, it must not be forgotten that the inert masses which he raised would have been useless without the skilful artillery and heroic infantry who defended them. Much stronger places than Sebastopol have often fallen under far less obstinate and well-combined attacks than that to which it was subjected. There can be no danger in expressing the conviction that the siege of Sebastopol called forth the most magnificent defence of fortifications that has ever yet occurred."

The next is a description of the final assault:—

"A few minutes later than the assault upon the Malakoff, the English attacked the Redan. The Russians being now upon the alert, they did not pass over the open space before them without loss; but the mass succeeded in crossing the ditch and gaining the salient of the work.

Finding themselves entirely unsupported, they at once took shelter behind the traverses, whence the example and efforts of their officers did not avail to draw them, in order to occupy the work closing the gorge. Having in vain used every effort, having despatched every officer of his staff to the rear urging that supports should be at once sent up, and seeing that the Russians were now beginning to assemble in force, the commander of the English storming party reluctantly determined to proceed himself to obtain reinforcements. Scarcely had he reached the trenches, and at last obtained authority to move up the required succor, when, upon turning to lead them forward, he saw the party he had left in the work rapidly and hopelessly driven out at the point of the bayonet. No further effort was made to carry the work. It would, in all probability, have failed, and would only have caused a useless sacrifice of men.

"The failure of the English assault may be attributed partly to the fact that their advanced trenches were too small to accommodate the requisite force without confusion, in part to their not being pushed sufficiently near the Redan, but chiefly to that total absence of conduct and skill in the arrangements for the assault which left the storming party entirely without support. Had it been followed at once by strong reinforcements, it is almost certain that the English would have retained possession of the work.

"The two French attacks on the west of the central ravine were probably intended only as feints: at all events, the parties engaged were soon driven back to their trenches with considerable loss, and effected nothing. Their attempts upon the Little Redan, and the works connecting it with the Malakoff, met with even less success than the English assault. The Russians repulsed the French with great loss, meeting with the bayonet the more adventurous men who reached the parapet. Thus, in five points out of six, the defenders were fully victorious; but, unfortunately for them, the sixth was the decisive point.

"In their admirable arrangements for the attack of the Malakoff, the French counted on two things for success:—first, they had ascertained that the Russians were in the habit of relieving the guard of the Malakoff at noon, and that a great part of the old guard marched out before the new one arrived, in order to avoid the loss which would arise from crowding the work with men; in the second place, it was determined to keep up a most violent vertical fire until the very moment of the assault, thus driving the Russians into the bomb-proofs, and enabling the storming party to enter the work with but little opposition. The hour of noon was therefore selected for the assault, and the strong columns intended for the work were at an early hour assembled in the advanced trenches, all in admirable order, and furnished with precise instructions.

"The mortars maintained an unremitting fire until the moment appointed. The very instant the last volley was discharged, the storming party of Zouaves rushed over the thirty paces before them, and were in the work before the astonished Russians knew what had happened. It was stated that this party lost but eleven men in entering the work. Other troops advanced rapidly to the support of the storming party, a bridge was formed by rolling up five ladders with planks lashed to them, a communication was at once commenced between the advanced trench and the bridge, brigade after brigade passed over, the redoubt was at once occupied by the storming party, and thus the Malakoff, and with it Sebastopol, was won. The few Russians remaining in the work made a desperate resistance. Many gallant attempts were made by Russian columns to ascend the steep slope in rear and regain the lost work; but the road was narrow, difficult, and obstructed, the position strong, and the French in force. All their furious efforts were in vain, and the Malakoff remained in the possession of those who had so gallantly and skilfully won it. With regard to the final retreat to the north side, it can only be said that a personal examination of the locality merely confirms its necessity, and the impression so generally entertained that it was the finest operation of the war: so admirably was it carried out that not a straggler remained behind; a few men so severely wounded as to be unfit for rough and hurried transportation were the sole ghastly human trophies that remained to the allies.

"The retreat, being a more difficult operation than the assault, may be worthy of a higher admiration; but the Russian retreat to the north side and the French assault upon the Malakoff must each be regarded as a masterpiece of its kind, deserving the closest study. It is difficult to imagine what point in either can be criticized; for both evinced consummate skill, discipline, coolness, and courage. With regard to the artillery, I would merely remark that the Russian guns were not of unusual calibre, consisting chiefly of twenty-four-, thirty-two-, and forty-two-pounders, and that the termination of the siege was mainly due to the extensive use of mortars finally resorted to by the allies. If they had been employed in the beginning as the main reliance, the siege would have been of shorter duration.

"The causes of the unusual duration of this siege naturally resolve themselves into three classes: the skilful disposition of the Russians, the faults of the allies, and natural causes beyond the control of either party. Among the latter may be mentioned the natural strength of the position and the severity of the winter. In the first class there may be alluded to:—the skill with which the Russian engineers availed themselves of the nature of the ground; the moral courage which induced them to undertake the defence of an open town with a weak garrison; the constant use they made of sorties, among which may properly be classed the battles of Balaklava, Inkermann, and the Tchernaya; the ready ingenuity with which they availed themselves of the resources derived from the fleet; the fine practice of their artillery; their just appreciation of the true use of field-works, and the admirable courage they always evinced in standing to their works, to repel assaults at the point of the bayonet; the employment of rifle-pits on an extensive scale; finally, the constant reinforcements which they soon commenced receiving, and which enabled them to fill the gaps made in their ranks by disease and the projectiles of the allies.

"The evidences of skill on the part of the allies, as well as the apparent faults on all sides, having been already alluded to, it is believed that the means have been furnished to enable any one to draw his own conclusions as to the history of this memorable passage of arms."

Next after the observations on the Crimean War follow twenty pages on the European engineer troops, to which succeed twenty-eight pages on the French, Austrian, Prussian, and Sardinian infantry. A brief description of the French Zouave will be of interest to the reader:—

"The dress of the Zouave is of the Arab pattern: the cap is a loose fez, or skull-cap, of scarlet felt, with a tassel; a turban is worn over this in full dress; a cloth vest and loose jacket, which leave the neck unencumbered by collar, stock, or cravat, cover the upper portion of his body, and allow free movement of the arms; the scarlet pants are of the loose Oriental pattern, and are tucked under gaiters like those of the foot rifles of the guard; the overcoat is a loose cloak, with a hood; the chasseurs wear a similar one. The men say that this dress is the most convenient possible, and prefer it to any other.

"The Zouaves are all French; they are selected from

among the old campaigners for their fine physique and tried courage, and have certainly proved that they are what their appearance would indicate,—the most reckless, self-reliant, and complete infantry that Europe can produce.

"With his graceful dress, soldierly bearing, and vigilant attitude, the Zouave at an outpost is the beau-idéal of a soldier.

"They neglect no opportunity of adding to their personal comforts: if there is a stream in the vicinity, the party marching on picket is sure to be amply supplied with fishing-rods, &c.; if any thing is to be had, the Zouaves are quite certain to obtain it.

"Their movements are the lightest and most graceful I have ever seen; the stride is long, but the foot seems scarcely to touch the ground, and the march is apparently made without effort or fatigue.

"The step of the foot rifles is shorter and quicker, and not so easy and graceful.

"The impression produced by the appearance of the rifles and of the Zouaves is very different: the rifles look like active, energetic little fellows, who would find their best field as skirmishers; but the Zouaves have, combined with all the activity and energy of the others, that solid *ensemble* and reckless dare-devil individuality which would render them alike formidable when attacking in mass, or in defending a position in the most desperate hand-to-hand encounter. Of all the troops that I have ever seen, I should esteem it the greatest honor to assist in defeating the Zouaves. The grenadiers of the guard are all large men, and a fine-looking, soldierly set."

Two hundred and ten pages—nearly one-half of the whole volume, the Appendix included—are next given to the Russian army, its organization, recruiting, rations, &c.

The following is a description of the Russian Cossacks:—

"There are two peculiarities which cannot fail to arrest the attention and command the reflection of the observer of the Russian cavalry: these are, the general division of the cavalry into regulars and irregulars; and the corps of dragoons.

"The irregulars may be comprehended in the general name of Cossacks. Yet their peculiarities of armament, costume, and action are as varied as their origin; while the sources of the latter are as multifarious as the tribes which compose the mass of Russian nationality, and the circumstances which, through centuries of warfare, have finally united into one compact whole a multitude of conflicting and heterogeneous elements. But, with all this diversity, there are important and peculiar characteristics which pervade the mass, and are common to every individual, with as much uniformity and certainty as that with which the firm government of the Czar is now extended over them. These peculiarities are: intelligence, quickness of vision, hearing, and all the senses; individuality; trustworthiness on duty; the power of enduring fatigue, privation, and the extremes of climate; great address in the use of weapons; strong feeling for their common country; caution, united with courage capable of being excited to the highest pitch: in short, the combination of qualities necessary for partisan troops. The events of more than one campaign have proved, besides, that these irregulars can be used successfully in line against the best regular cavalry of Europe.

"Circumstances of geography and climate have given to these men a race of horses in every way adapted to their riders; the Cossack horse is excelled by none in activity and hardiness.

"The Cossack neglects no opportunity of feeding his

horse; during short halts, even under fire, he gives him whatever is to be had; the horse refuses nothing that is offered him, and eats whenever he has the opportunity, for he has not acquired the pernicious habit of eating only at regular hours. Some idea may be formed of the power of endurance of the Cossacks and their horses from the fact that, in a certain expedition against Khiva, there were three thousand five hundred regular Russian troops and twelve hundred Cossacks: of the regulars but one thousand returned, of the Cossacks but sixty perished.

"The tendency of events, during the present century, has been to assimilate the organization of the Cossacks to that of the regulars, to a certain extent: whether the effect of this has been to modify or destroy their valuable individual characteristics may yet remain to be proved in a general war; the events of the campaign of Hungary are said to indicate that more regularity of action has by no means impaired their efficiency.

"This brief description of the qualities of the irregular cavalry indicates at once the use made of them in war: they watch while the regulars repose. All the duty of advanced posts, patrols, reconnoissances, escorting trains, carrying despatches, acting as orderlies, &c., is performed in preference by the Cossacks: the consequence is, that, on the day of battle, the regular cavalry are brought upon the field in full force and undiminished vigor. Under cover of these active irregulars, a Russian army enjoys a degree of repose unknown to any other; while, on the other hand, it is difficult for their antagonists to secure their outposts and foil their stealthy movements.

"The rapidity and length of their marches are almost incredible; a march of forty miles is a common thing: they will make forced marches of seventy miles; in a thickly-settled country they have, in two days, made six marches of ordinary cavalry without being discovered.

"In concluding this subject, it is impossible to repress

the conviction that in many of the tribes of our frontier Indians, such as the Delawares, Kickapoos, &c., we possess the material for the formation of partisan troops fully equal to the Cossacks: in the event of a serious war on this continent, their employment, under the regulations and restrictions necessary to restrain their tendency to unnecessary cruelty, would be productive of most important advantages.

"In our contests with the hostile Indians, bodies of these men, commanded by active and energetic regular officers and supported by regular troops, would undoubtedly be of great service."

The cavalry of Prussia, Austria, France, England, and the United States are next considered, the whole occupying about one hundred pages; and an Appendix, of the same extent, contains a system of regulations for the field service of cavalry in time of war. This arm engages the author's particular attention, naturally enough, as he was a captain of cavalry at the time.

Besides its other merits, the volume is a record of the most faithful and persevering industry, and contains the results of an immense amount of hard work. It embraces accounts of military schools, forts, museums, camps, hospitals, and garrisons. The arms, dress, and accoutrements of the men, and the equipments of the horses, are minutely described, down to the most exact details. It is illustrated with several hundred engravings, making every thing plain to the eye where a visible representation is needed. In short, no one can look at this volume without seeing that the author has one of those happily constituted minds which neither overlooks nor despises details, and yet is not so hampered by them as to be incapable of wide views and sound generalizations. No man can be a great officer who is not infinitely patient of details; for an army is an aggregation of details, a defect in any one of which may destroy or impair the whole. It is a chain of innumerable links; but the whole chain is no stronger than its weakest link.

In January, 1857, Captain McClellan resigned his commission and retired from the army. He had then been fifteen years in the service,—years of busy activity and energetic discharge of professional duty. We may suppose him to have been moved to this step by the consideration that the future held out no promise of congenial employment and seemed to open no adequate sphere to honorable ambition. A dreary life upon some distant frontier, the monotonous discharge of routine duty, a renunciation of all the attractions of civilized life without the excitement of ennobling adventure or heroic struggle, presented an uninviting prospect to a man like him, in the prime of early manhood, and with unworn energies alike physical and intellectual. He thought, too, that in case of war his chances of occupation and promotion would be quite as good in civil life as if he had remained in the army. The rapid growth and material development of the country created a demand for capacities and accomplishments like his; and immediately upon his resignation he was appointed chief engineer of the Illinois Central Railroad, then just opened, and went to Chicago to reside.

In a few weeks he was made vice-president of the corporation, and took general charge of all the business of the road in Illinois. In this capacity he first made the acquaintance of Mr. Lincoln, now President of the United States, then a practising lawyer in Springfield, Illinois, and occasionally employed in the conduct of suits and other professional services on behalf of the company.

In May, 1860, Captain McClellan was married to Miss Ellen Marcy, daughter of General R. B. Marcy, his former commander in Texas, and the chief of his staff during the Peninsular campaign.

In August, 1860, he resigned the vice-presidency of the Illinois Central Road, in order to accept the presidency of the Ohio & Mississippi Railroad, which post he held, residing in Cincinnati, till the war broke out.

CHAPTER IV.

The guns which opened upon Fort Sumter on the memorable 12th of April, 1861, did not merely crumble the walls of that fortress, but they also shattered all hopes of a peaceful solution of the problems which were then before the country. Civil war was now a sad necessity. The President's proclamation of the 15th called forth the militia for objects entirely lawful and constitutional; and it was responded to with a patriotic fervor which melted down all previously existing party lines. This "uprising of a great people," as it was well termed by a foreign writer, was a kindling and noble spectacle. The heart of the whole land throbbed like the heart of one. But we cannot now look back upon that brilliant and burning enthusiasm without a touch of sadness, because there was mingled with it so much ignorance, not merely of the magnitude of the contest before us, but of the nature of war itself. The spirited young men who, at the call of patriotic duty, thronged to swell the ranks of our volunteer force, marched off as gayly as if they had been going to a hunting-party or a picnic excursion. The rebellion was to be put down at once, and by little more than the mere show of the preponderating force of the loyal States; and the task of putting it down was to be attended with no more of danger than was sufficient to give to the enterprise a due flavor of excitement. War was unknown to us except by report: the men of the Revolution had passed away, and even the soldiers of the War of 1812 had become gray-haired veterans. We had read of battles; we had seen something of the pride and pomp of holiday soldiers; but of the grim realities of war we were absolutely ignorant. Indeed, not a few had come to the conclusion that war was a relic of barbarism, which the world had outgrown, and that modern civilization could dispense with the soldier and his sword.

It need hardly be added that we were wholly unprepared for the gigantic struggle that was before us. Our regular army was insignificant in numbers, and scattered over our vast territory or along our Western frontier, so that it was impossible to collect any considerable force together. Our militia system had everywhere fallen into neglect, and in some States had almost ceased to have any real existence. The wits laughed at it, and the platform-orators declaimed against it, to such a degree that it required some moral courage to march through the streets at the head of a company.

The South had been wiser, or, at least, more provident, in this respect. The military spirit had never been discouraged there. Many of the political leaders had long been looking forward to the time when the unhappy sectional contests which were distracting the country would blaze out into civil war, and preparing for it. In some of the States there had been military academies, where a military education had been obtained: so that they had a greater number of trained officers to put into their regiments. This gave them a considerable advantage at the start. Happily for us, graduates of West Point were scattered all over the North: to them the civil authority looked for assistance, and they rendered an assistance which cannot be too highly estimated.

Ohio was as unprepared as other States. There was a small force of militia nominally organized; but the Constitution and laws of the State provided that all its officers should be elected by the men, and the Governor was limited, in his selection of officers in case the militia was called out, to the parties so chosen. In an emergency like this, it was fortunate that Ohio had so efficient a Governor as Mr. William Dennison. He at once turned to Captain McClellan for assistance, and sent a request to Washington that the latter might be restored to his old rank in the army and the duty of organizing the Ohio volunteers assigned to him. To this request no answer was received: indeed, the communications with Washington were generally interrupted, and the several Governors were thus left to their own resources.

Governor Dennison summoned Captain McClellan to Columbus; and he at once applied himself to the work of organizing the numerous regiments offered. A bill was also introduced into the Legislature, and rapidly passed, authorizing the Governor to select officers for the volunteers outside of the State militia. Under this act, on the 23d of April, 1861, Captain McClellan was commissioned major-general of the Ohio "Militia Volunteers."

Under the proclamation of the President of April 15, calling out the militia, thirteen regiments of infantry were demanded from Ohio for three months, and afterwards the same number for three years. To obtain men was then easy enough, but to find suitable officers was exceedingly difficult; and arms and equipments were entirely wanting. A "Department of the Ohio" was formed on the 3d of May, consisting of Ohio, Indiana, and Illinois, and placed under General McClellan's command, who thus had under his charge the forces of two other States besides his own. He organized his troops in spite of all obstacles, and within two months of the time of his leaving his peaceful avocations he took the field for the first campaign of the war.

Secession placed no State in so embarrassing a position as the great Commonwealth of Virginia. Separated from the capital only by a river, and extending from the ocean to the Ohio, it lay midway between the two contending parties, and early promised to be what it has since become,—the Belgium of the war. There is no doubt that the great body of its citizens were opposed to the State's seceding; but they were equally opposed to the coercion of the States which had already seceded, and sympathized with many of their alleged grievances. A State convention at Richmond, on the 17th of April, when it was evident that war must ensue, passed an ordinance of secession. Although this was not to go into force until it had been ratified by the people, the inhabitants of the eastern and southern portions of the State immediately began hostilities.

In the portion of the State lying west of the Alleghany Mountains, and known as Western Virginia, the feelings of the people were very different. They owned but few slaves, and their soil and climate were unfitted for those branches of industry in which slave-labor is profitable. While disapproving of the slavery agitation in the North, they had no particular interest in the extension of that institution, and were strenuously opposed to secession for its sake; and they also had some grievances regarding alleged inequalities of taxation between Eastern and Western Virginia, which had probably caused many of them already to look forward to the organization of a separate State. In this conjuncture, a convention of the people of Western Virginia was called to assemble at Wheeling on the 11th of June, to consider the alarming condition of public affairs.

Early in May, General McClellan received applications for protection from the people of this region, but was not then prepared to accede to their wishes. Afterwards, however, it became evident that the Virginia authorities contemplated occupying this country, and to secure, by so doing, the command of the Baltimore & Ohio Railroad, the importance of which was appreciated by both parties. Governor Letcher had already called out the State militia, and not only Western Virginia, but Southern Ohio also, might soon be invaded by them.

A small body of Virginia militia had actually advanced, and were encamped at Grafton, on the Baltimore & Ohio Railroad. On the 24th of May, the Secretary of War and General Scott telegraphed to General McClellan, informing him of this camp, and asking him whether its influence could not be counteracted. General McClellan replied in the affirmative. This was the sole order which he received from Washington regarding a campaign in Virginia.

General McClellan had formed his principal rendezvous at Camp Dennison, near Cincinnati; while bodies of troops were also at Gallipolis, Bellaire, and Marietta, on the Ohio River, opposite Virginia. At Wheeling the loyalists were organizing a regiment under Colonel B. F. Kelley. The men were wretchedly provided for, having nothing but muskets; but they did good service before the end of summer. On the 26th of May, intelligence was received at Camp Dennison that the enemy were advancing from Grafton upon Wheeling and Parkersburg, for the purpose of destroying the railroad. General McClellan at once telegraphed to Colonel Kelley to move his regiment (since known as the First Virginia) early the next day along the line of railroad towards Fairmount, in order to prevent any further destruction of the bridges and to protect the repair of those already injured. Two Ohio regiments, under Colonels Irwin and Stedman, were also directed to cross over into Virginia, one to co-operate with Colonel Kelley and the other to occupy Parkersburg. On the same day, General McClellan issued the following proclamation and address:—

"HEAD-QUARTERS DEPARTMENT OF THE OHIO,
May 26, 1861.

"*To the Union Men of Western Virginia.*

"VIRGINIANS:—The General Government has long enough endured the machinations of a few factious rebels in your midst. Armed traitors have in vain endeavored to deter you from expressing your loyalty at the polls. Having failed in this infamous attempt to deprive you of the exercise of your dearest rights, they now seek to inaugurate a reign of terror, and thus force you to yield to their schemes and submit to the yoke of the traitorous conspiracy dignified by the name of the Southern Confederacy. They are destroying the property of citizens of your State and ruining your magnificent railways. The General Government has heretofore carefully abstained from sending troops across the Ohio, or even from posting them along its banks, although frequently urged to do so by many of your prominent citizens. It determined to await the result of the late election, desirous that no one might be able to say that the slightest effort had been made from this side to influence the free expression of your opinions, although the many agencies brought to bear upon you by the rebels were well known. You have now shown, under the most adverse circumstances, that the great mass of the people of Western Virginia are true and loyal to that beneficent Government under which we and our fathers have lived so long. As soon as the result of the election was known, the traitors commenced their work of destruction. The General Government cannot close its ears to the demand you have made for assistance. I have ordered troops to cross the Ohio River. They come as your friends and brothers,—as enemies only to the armed rebels who are preying upon you. Your homes, your families, and your property are safe under our protection. All your rights shall be religiously respected, notwithstanding all that has been said by the traitors to induce you to believe that our advent among you will be signalized by interference with your slaves. Understand one thing clearly. Not only will we abstain from all such interference, but we will, on the contrary, with an iron hand, crush any attempt at insurrection on their part. Now that we are in your midst, I call upon you to fly to arms and support the General Government. Sever the connection that binds you to traitors; proclaim to the world that the faith and loyalty so long boasted by the Old Dominion are still preserved in

Western Virginia, and that you remain true to the Stars and Stripes.

"GEO. B. MCCLELLAN,
"*Major-General U. S. A., Com'd'g Dep't.*"

"HEAD-QUARTERS DEPARTMENT OF THE OHIO,
CINCINNATI, May 26, 1861.

"SOLDIERS:—You are ordered to cross the frontier and enter upon the soil of Virginia.

"Your mission is to restore peace and confidence, to protect the majesty of the law, and to rescue our brethren from the grasp of armed traitors. You are to act in concert with Virginia troops, and to support their advance. I place under the safeguard of your honor the persons and property of the Virginians. I know that you will respect their feelings and all their rights.

"Preserve the strictest discipline. Remember that each one of you holds in his keeping the honor of Ohio and the Union. If you are called upon to overcome armed opposition, I know that your courage is equal to the task; but remember that your only foes are the armed traitors,—and show mercy even to them when they are in your power, for many of them are misguided. When, under your protection, the loyal men of Western Virginia have been enabled to organize and arm, they can protect themselves; and you can then return to your homes with the proud satisfaction of having saved a gallant people from destruction.

"GEO. B. MCCLELLAN,
"*Major-General U. S. A., Com'd'g.*"

General McClellan also wrote full particulars to the President of what he had done, but, receiving no reply, inferred that his course was approved of.

Colonel Kelley reached Grafton on the 13th of May. The enemy retreated at his approach, and he repaired the bridge, and established railroad-communications with Wheeling. Soon after, Colonel Stedman occupied Clarksburg, and established communications with Colonel Kelley. The enemy fell back from Grafton upon Philippi, on the high-road from Wheeling to Staunton, in Central Virginia. General McClellan in the mean time had despatched three Indiana regiments, under Brigadier-General Morris, to Grafton. They arrived on the 31st of May; and General Morris at once assumed the chief command. Hardly six weeks had elapsed since Captain McClellan had been first called upon by Governor Dennison for assistance; and in that time he had actually created an army and begun the first campaign!

The first encounter of the war took place at Philippi, a small town two hundred and ten miles from Richmond. On the 2d of June, General Morris determined to endeavor to drive from this town the rebel force there, under Colonel Porterfield. The attacking force consisted of five regiments, formed in two columns,—the first under Colonel Kelley, the second under Colonel Dumont, accompanied by Colonel (afterwards the lamented General) Lander. Colonel Kelley's column moved towards Philippi by way of Thornton, a distance of twenty-seven miles, partly by railroad. The other column moved directly on Philippi in front. This one reached its destination early on the 3d, notwithstanding deep mud and heavy rain, and at once opened fire from two pieces of artillery upon the enemy, who began a retreat, which was turned into a complete rout when Colonel Kelley, (who had been greatly impeded by the state of the roads) came up and joined in the attack. The enemy left behind them their camp-equipage, seven hundred stand of arms, and several horses. They lost about fifteen men killed and wounded. On the Federal side, Colonel Kelley was severely wounded, but recovered.

General McClellan now pushed the Ohio regiments on into Virginia as rapidly as they could be decently equipped. But the great deficiency which still existed in all military necessaries much retarded him. The loyalists, on the 13th of June, formed a provisional government at Wheeling, with the Hon. Francis H. Pierpoint as Governor. But Old Virginia was determined not to lose the fine country beyond the Alleghanies without a struggle. Large reinforcements arrived at Beverly, on the Staunton road, the head-quarters of the enemy; and with them came General Robert Selden Garnett, the former commandant at West Point, and an officer of high reputation, to assume the chief command. Upon learning this, General McClellan thought it time to move; and, his preparations being so far advanced as to justify it, he left Cincinnati on the 20th of June, and arrived at Grafton on the 22d.

He still received no orders from Washington, and was even left ignorant of the plan for the campaign in Eastern Virginia. His own department was very extensive, and the simple administrative cares connected with it extremely arduous. Besides, not only in Virginia, but in Kentucky and Tennessee, the enemy were very active, and it could not be known how soon he might be called upon to plan a campaign for the defence of the Union interests in those States.

The country which now became the scene of operations was that part of Western Virginia lying between the Baltimore & Ohio Railroad on the north, the Ohio River on the west, the Little Kanawha River on the south, and the Cheat River on the east. The region is broken and mountainous, and cut into numerous ravines and valleys by the many little streams which form the head-waters of the Monongahela, Great Kanawha, Little Kanawha, and other rivers. The roads are few in number and very indifferent in quality; the valleys only are cultivated, the rest of the country being covered with dense forests, and a luxuriant growth of bushes which makes the woods almost impassable. A turnpike road runs from Wheeling southeasterly to Staunton, through Philippi, Leedsville, Beverly, and Huttonsville. From Beverly another turnpike runs westerly, at an acute angle with the Wheeling road, to Buckhannon, where it branches off to Clarksburg on the north and Weston on the west. A mountainous ridge crosses the two roads from Beverly to Philippi and Buckhannon; and at the intersection the enemy were strongly intrenched,—General Garnett commanding in person at Laurel Hill, on the Philippi road, a little north of Leedsville and fifteen miles north of Beverly, and Colonel Pegram at Rich Mountain, on the Buckhannon road, five miles west of Beverly. General Garnett's force was about ten thousand men, and Colonel Pegram's about four thousand. Their natural retreat was by way of Beverly and Huttonsville through the Cheat Mountain Pass, as it is called. North of this there is no road over the Alleghanies passable for artillery until the circuitous road running northeasterly from Leedsville through St. George and West Union to Moorfield is reached. If, therefore, by the capture of Beverly the road by Cheat Mountain Pass (and with it any other road south of it) were cut off, this north road was the only retreat open to General Garnett.

General McClellan's plans are best described in his own language. On the 23d of June he wrote a letter to General Scott. "I stated," says he, "that it was now certain that the enemy had a force of some kind near Huttonsville, with a strong advanced party intrenched near Laurel Mountain, between Philippi and Beverly, and that their chief object seemed to me to be to furnish and protect guerrilla parties, which were then doing much mischief; also that the apprehensions which had existed on the part of our people of an attack by this party of the enemy were not well founded; that, as soon as my command was well in hand and my information more full, I proposed moving with all my available force from Clarksburg on Buckhannon, thence on Beverly, to turn entirely the detachment at Laurel Hill, the troops at Philippi to advance in time to follow up the retreat of the enemy in their front. That, after occupying Beverly, I would move on Huttonsville and drive the enemy into the mountains, whither I did not purpose to follow them unless certain of success."

In pursuance of this plan, the main body of his army, numbering about ten thousand men, were transferred to Clarksburg. It consisted of two brigades, under Brigadier-Generals Rosecrans and Schleich, with a small body of cavalry, a company of regular artillery, and two batteries of volunteer artillery. Another body, under General Morris, was stationed at Philippi, and a body of reserve, under Brigadier-General Hill, of the Ohio militia, was stationed at Grafton. Before leaving Grafton, General McClellan issued the following proclamation and address:—

"HEAD-QUARTERS, DEPARTMENT OF THE OHIO,
GRAFTON, VA., June 23, 1861.

"*To the Inhabitants of Western Virginia.*

"The army of this department, headed by Virginia troops, is rapidly occupying all Western Virginia. This is done in co-operation with and in support of such civil authorities of the State as are faithful to the Constitution and laws of the United States. The proclamation issued by me under date of May 26, 1861, will be strictly maintained. Your houses, families, property, and all your rights will be religiously respected: we are enemies to none but armed rebels and those voluntarily giving them aid. All officers of this army will be held responsible for the most prompt and vigorous action in repressing disorder and punishing aggression by those under their command.

"To my great regret, I find that enemies of the United States continue to carry on a system of hostilities prohibited by the laws of war among belligerent nations, and, of course, far more wicked and intolerable when directed against loyal citizens engaged in the defence of the common government of all. Individuals and marauding parties are pursuing a guerrilla warfare,—firing upon sentinels and pickets, burning bridges, insulting, injuring, and even killing citizens because of their Union sentiments, and committing many kindred acts.

"I do now, therefore, make proclamation, and warn all persons, that individuals or parties engaged in this species of warfare,—irregular in every view which can be taken of it,—thus attacking sentinels, pickets, or other soldiers, destroying public or private property, or committing injuries against any of the inhabitants because of Union sentiments or conduct, will be dealt with, in their persons and property, according to the severest rules of military law.

"All persons giving information or aid to the public enemies will be arrested and kept in close custody; and all persons found bearing arms, unless of known loyalty, will be arrested and held for examination.

"GEO. B. McCLELLAN,
"*Major-General U. S. A. Com'd'g.*"

"HEAD-QUARTERS DEPARTMENT OF THE OHIO,
GRAFTON, VA., June 25, 1861.

"*To the Soldiers of the Army of the West.*

"You are here to support the Government of your country, and to protect the lives and liberties of your brethren, threatened by a rebellious and traitorous foe. No higher and nobler duty could devolve upon you; and I expect you to bring to its performance the highest and noblest qualities of soldiers,—discipline, courage, and mercy. I call upon the officers of every grade to enforce *the strictest discipline; and I know that those of all grades,* privates and officers, will display in battle cool heroic courage, and will know how to show mercy to a disarmed enemy.

"Bear in mind that you are in the country of friends, not of enemies,—that you are here to protect, not to destroy. Take nothing, destroy nothing, unless you are ordered to do so by your general officers. Remember that I have pledged my word to the people of Western Virginia that their rights in person and property shall be respected. I ask every one of you to make good this promise in its broadest sense. We come here to save, not to upturn. I do not appeal to the fear of punishment, but to your appreciation of the sacredness of the cause in which we are engaged. Carry with you into battle the conviction that you are right and that God is on your side.

"Your enemies have violated every moral law: neither God nor man can sustain them. They have without cause rebelled against a mild and paternal Government; they have seized upon public and private property; they have outraged the persons of Northern men merely because they came from the North, and of Southern Union men merely because they loved the Union; they have placed themselves beneath contempt, unless they can retrieve some honor on the field of battle. You will pursue a different course. You will be honest, brave, and merciful; you will respect the right of private opinion; you will punish no man for opinion's sake. Show to the world that you differ from our enemies in the points of honor, honesty, and respect for private opinion, and that we inaugurate no reign of terror where we go.

"Soldiers, I have heard that there was danger here. I have come to place myself at your head and to share it with you. I fear now but one thing,—that you will not find foemen worthy of your steel. I know that I can rely upon you.

"GEO. B. MCCLELLAN,
"*Major-General Com'd'g.*"

Buckhannon was occupied on the 30th by General Rosecrans, and a regiment was sent to take possession of Weston. General McClellan and staff and General Schleich's brigade reached Buckhannon on the 2d of July. Before advancing on the enemy, General McClellan had to give directions regarding an independent portion of his department. Generals Wise and Floyd had invaded the country south of the Little Kanawha River, with a large force. To meet these, General McClellan directed Brigadier-General J. Dolson Cox to proceed thither from Ohio with five regiments, and assigned to him the district between the Great and Little Kanawha Rivers.

On the 9th, the main column of the army reached Roaring Fork, beyond Buckhannon, and two miles from Colonel Pegram's intrenchments. A bridge which had been destroyed had to be rebuilt. On the 10th, Lieutenant Poe was sent out with a detachment to reconnoitre the enemy's position. This reconnoissance was pushed within two hundred yards of the enemy's works. Colonel Pegram, it was found, was strongly intrenched near the foot of Rich Mountain and on the west side of it. The position was surrounded by dense forests, and its natural strength had been increased by rough intrenchments and by felling trees.

As an attack in front would be followed by a serious loss of life, and its success with raw troops, to say the least, was doubtful, General McClellan's plan was to turn Colonel Pegram's position to the south, endeavor to cut off his retreat, and, should he succeed in so doing, to push on to Beverly and cut off General Garnett's retreat by Staunton, forcing him to retire by the northeasterly road to Moorfield. The duty of turning the enemy's works was assigned to General Rosecrans. His instructions were to make a circuit to the south and endeavor to reach and occupy the top of the mountain, get command of the turnpike road from Beverly to Buckhannon, and then move on the rear of Pegram's defences. His further order, constantly to communicate with General McClellan, General Rosecrans does not seem to have been able to carry out.

General Rosecrans set out, with a force of eighteen hundred infantry and a small body of cavalry, at four o'clock on the morning of the 11th of July, to execute these orders. After a fatiguing march through a country saturated with rain and covered with dense woods, he reached the summit of Rich Mountain about one o'clock. The enemy had intercepted some letters, and thus obtained intimation of this movement, and had stationed a considerable force, with two pieces of artillery, at the top of the mountain, where some rude intrenchments had been thrown up. Rosecrans formed his command, and had proceeded a short way towards the turnpike, when he came upon a party of skirmishers, who were driven back upon the main body. The enemy now opened fire from their artillery. A spirited attack soon carried the intrenchments, and the rebels retreated in confusion upon Colonel Pegram, leaving their artillery in possession of the Federals. The success of the movement was complete; but his troops, unused to such exertions, being greatly fatigued, General Rosecrans halted.

No communication was received at head-quarters from Rosecrans after eleven o'clock. The firing at Rich Mountain was distinctly heard; but great fears were entertained that the attack had failed. "Soon after the cessation of the distant firing," says General McClellan, "an officer was observed to ride into the intrenchments and address the garrison. We could not distinguish the words he uttered, but his speech was followed by prolonged cheering, which impressed many with the belief that it had fared badly with our detachment."

General McClellan determined to attack the enemy in front, and Lieutenant Poe was sent to select a proper position for the artillery. Upon his reporting one, a party was despatched to cut a road to it. It was now too late in the day to begin an attack; but one was resolved upon early the next morning, in hopes of relieving Rosecrans if he were hard pressed by the enemy. The next morning, however, the pickets reported that Colonel Pegram had deserted his works and fled over the mountains. Leaving Rosecrans at Rich Mountain, General McClellan pushed on to Beverly. He thus effectually cut off General Garnett's communications with Staunton. His despatch was as follows:—

"Rich Mountain, Va., 9 a.m., July 12.

"Colonel E. D. Townsend, *Assistant Adjutant-General:*—

"We are in possession of all the enemy's works up to a point in sight of Beverly. We have taken all his guns, a very large amount of wagons, tents, &c., every thing he had, and also a large number of prisoners, many of whom are wounded, and amongst whom are several officers. They lost many killed. We have lost in all perhaps twenty killed and forty wounded, of whom all but two or three were in the column under Colonel Rosecrans, which turned the position. The mass of the enemy escaped through the woods, entirely disorganized. Among the prisoners is Dr. Taylor, formerly of the army. Colonel Pegram was in command.

"Colonel Rosecrans's column left camp yesterday morning and marched some eight miles through the mountains, reaching the turnpike some two or three miles in the rear of the enemy. He defeated an advanced force, and took a couple of guns. I had a position ready for twelve guns near the main camp, and as the guns were moving up I ascertained that the enemy had retreated. I am now pushing on to Beverly,—a part of Colonel Rosecrans's troops being now within three miles of that place. Our success is complete, and almost bloodless. I doubt whether Wise and Johnston will unite and overpower me. The behavior of our troops in action and towards prisoners was admirable.

"G. B. McCLELLAN,
"*Major-General commanding.*"

On the night of the 11th, General Garnett, learning of the disaster at Rich Mountain, fell back on Beverly; but, finding his retreat that way cut off, he retraced his steps, and took the northern road by St. George and West Union. In accordance with orders, General Morris followed him, and overtook him at Carrick's Ford, on the main fork of Cheat River. The enemy were posted in a tolerably strong position, but did not withstand the attack, led by Captain Bonham, and retreated in confusion.

General Garnett was himself killed while endeavoring to rally his troops. With soldier-like generosity, General Morris directed the remains to be carefully removed, and afterwards forwarded them to the family in Virginia.

The enemy lost in these engagements about two hundred killed, besides wounded and prisoners, seven or eight pieces of artillery, and large military stores. General Hill failed to carry out the directions sent to him to pursue General Garnett's force, and they escaped. Colonel Pegram, however, finding that Garnett had retreated, fell back on Beverly, and was compelled to surrender at discretion, on the 13th, with about six hundred men. General McClellan occupied Huttonsville and the Cheat Mountain Pass, thus gaining the key to Western Virginia. On the 19th of July he issued the following address to the army:—

"Soldiers of the Army of the West:—

"I am more than satisfied with you. You have annihilated two armies, commanded by educated and experienced soldiers, intrenched in mountain-fastnesses, and fortified at their leisure. You have taken five guns, twelve colors, fifteen hundred stand of arms, one thousand prisoners, including more than forty officers. One of the second commanders of the rebels is a prisoner; the other lost his life on the field of battle. You have killed more than two hundred and fifty of the enemy, who has lost all his baggage and camp-equipage. All this has been done with the loss of twenty brave men killed and sixty wounded on your part.

"You have proved that Union men fighting for the preservation of our Government are more than a match for our misguided and erring brothers. More than this, you have shown mercy to the vanquished. You have made long and arduous marches, with insufficient food, frequently exposed to the inclemency of the weather. I have not hesitated to demand this of you, feeling that I could rely on your endurance, patriotism, and courage. In the future I may have still greater demands to make upon you, still greater sacrifices for you to offer. It shall be my care to provide for you to the extent of my ability; but I know now that by your valor and endurance you will accomplish all that is asked.

"Soldiers, I have confidence in you, and I trust you have learned to confide in me. Remember that discipline and subordination are qualities of equal value with courage. I am proud to say that you have gained the highest reward that American troops can receive,—the thanks of Congress and the applause of your fellow-citizens.

"GEO. B. MCCLELLAN, *Major-General.*"

In the mean time, affairs looked perilous in General Cox's department, south of the Little Kanawha River. General McClellan was preparing to take command there in person, when, on the 22d of July, he received orders to hand over his command to General Rosecrans and report at Washington, where a wider field awaited him.

Thus ended the campaign in Western Virginia. It seems insignificant by the side of some of the bloody contests which have since taken place; but its moral effect was remarkable. It was the first trial that the raw troops of the North were put to, and its success was most encouraging. This is shown by the general satisfaction with which, in the midst of the gloom created by the battle of Bull

Run, the intelligence was received that General McClellan was summoned to Washington.

In organizing the Western Army, General McClellan's services were of great value. No preparations had been made beforehand for the struggle; and it is his deserved honor that, finding the West unprepared, he organized the germ of that brave army which has since gained such renown in Kentucky, Tennessee, and Mississippi.

CHAPTER V.

WHEN General McClellan assumed command in Washington, on the 27th of July, the whole number of troops in and around the city was a little over fifty thousand, of whom less than a thousand were cavalry, and about six hundred and fifty were artillery-men, with nine imperfect field-batteries of thirty pieces. They were encamped in places selected without regard to purposes of defence or instruction; the roads were not picketed, and there was no attempt at an organization into brigades. The works of defence were very limited in number and very defective in character. There was nothing to prevent the enemy's shelling the city from heights within easy range, and very little to prevent their occupying those heights had they been so disposed. The streets of Washington were crowded with straggling officers and disorderly men, absent from their stations without authority, whose behavior indicated a general want of discipline, aggravated by the demoralizing influences of the recent disaster at Bull Run, July 21, 1861.

The task of the commanding officer was one of no common magnitude. He had the materials for an army,—and excellent materials, too, but still only materials. He had no more than the block out of which an army was to be carved. There were courage, patriotism, intelligence, physical energy, in abundance; and to these invaluable qualities were to be added discipline, the instinct of obedience, precision of movement, and the power of combination. A tumultuary military assemblage was to be organized into brigades, divisions, and corps, and brought into proper relations with their commanders. An adequate artillery establishment was to be created, and a sufficient force of engineers and topographical engineers was to be provided. The medical department, the quartermaster's, the subsistence, the ordnance, the provost-marshal's departments, were all to be set in movement. A signal corps was to be formed, and instructed in the use of flags by day and lights by night; and, to keep pace with the march of scientific improvement, a body of telegraphic operators could not be forgotten.

To these gigantic labors General McClellan addressed himself with unwearied diligence; and he was ably seconded by a most efficient staff, with numbers increased from time to time as necessity required. The new levies of infantry, upon arriving in Washington, were formed into provisional brigades, and placed in camp in the suburbs of the city for equipment, instruction, and discipline. Cavalry and artillery troops reported to officers designated for that purpose. Order was restored in Washington by a military police bureau, at the head of which were a provost-marshal and a body of efficient assistants. New defensive works were projected and thrown up. Everywhere the hum of active, organized, and harmonious industry was heard. A preliminary organization was made of the troops on hand into twelve brigades. These were all volunteers, except two companies of cavalry and four of artillery; but all the commanding officers had been educated at West Point, with the single exception of Colonel Blenker, who had had a good military training in Europe.

On the 4th of August, 1861, General McClellan addressed to the President of the United States, at his request, a memorandum upon the objects of the war, the principles on which it should be conducted, and the operations by which it might be brought to a speedy and successful termination. As this is an important document in the history of the war, which should be carefully read by all who desire to understand its subsequent course, and still more by those who would do justice to a commanding officer whose military capacity and even whose loyalty and patriotism have been called in question in high places, it is here inserted in full:—

"The object of the present war differs from those in which nations are usually engaged mainly in this: that the purpose of ordinary war is to conquer a peace and make a treaty on advantageous terms; in this contest it has become necessary to crush a population sufficiently numerous, intelligent, and warlike to constitute a nation. We have not only to defeat their armed and organized forces in the field, but to display such an overwhelming strength as will convince all our antagonists, especially those of the governing aristocratic class, of the utter impossibility of resistance. Our late reverses make this course imperative. Had we been successful in the recent battle (Manassas), it is possible that we might have been spared the labor and expense of a great effort.

"Now we have no alternative. Their success will enable the political leaders of the rebels to convince the mass of their people that we are inferior to them in force and courage, and to command all their resources. The contest began with a class; now it is with a people: our military success can alone restore the former issue.

"By thoroughly defeating their armies, taking their strong places, and pursuing a rigidly protective policy as to private property and unarmed persons and a lenient course as to private soldiers, we may well hope for a permanent restoration of a peaceful Union. But in the first instance the authority of the Government must be supported by overwhelming physical force.

"Our foreign relations and financial credit also imperatively demand that the military action of the Government should be prompt and irresistible.

"The rebels have chosen Virginia as their battle-field; and it seems proper for us to make the first great struggle there. But, while thus directing our main efforts, it is necessary to diminish the resistance there offered us, by movements on other points, both by land and water.

"Without entering at present into details, I would advise that a strong movement be made on the Mississippi, and that the rebels be driven out of Missouri.

"As soon as it becomes perfectly clear that Kentucky is cordially united with us, I would advise a movement through that State into Eastern Tennessee, for the purpose of assisting the Union men of that region, and of seizing the railroads leading from Memphis to the East.

"The possession of those roads by us, in connection with the movement on the Mississippi, would go far towards determining the evacuation of Virginia by the rebels. In the mean time, all the passes into Western Virginia from the east should be securely guarded; but I would advise no movement from that quarter towards Richmond, unless the political condition of Kentucky renders it impossible or inexpedient for us to make the movement upon Eastern Tennessee through that State. Every effort should, however, be made to organize, equip, and arm as many troops as possible in Western Virginia, in order to render the Ohio and Indiana regiments available for other operations.

"At as early a day as practicable, it would be well to protect and reopen the Baltimore & Ohio Railroad. Baltimore and Fort Monroe should be occupied by garrisons sufficient to retain them in our possession.

"The importance of Harper's Ferry and the line of the Potomac in the direction of Leesburg will be very materially diminished so soon as our force in this vicinity becomes organized, strong, and efficient; because no capable general will cross the river north of this city, when we have a strong army here ready to cut off his retreat.

"To revert to the West. It is probable that no very large additions to the troops now in Missouri will be necessary to secure that State.

"I presume that the force required for the movement down the Mississippi will be determined by its commander and the President. If Kentucky assumes the right position, not more than twenty thousand troops will be needed, together with those that can be raised in that

State and Eastern Tennessee, to secure the latter region and its railroads, as well as ultimately to occupy Nashville.

"The Western Virginia troops, with not more than five or ten thousand from Ohio and Indiana, should, under proper management, suffice for its protection.

"When we have reorganized our main army here, ten thousand men ought to be enough to protect the Baltimore & Ohio Railroad and the Potomac, five thousand will garrison Baltimore, three thousand Fort Monroe, and not more than twenty thousand will be necessary at the utmost for the defence of Washington.

"For the main army of operations I urge the following composition:—

250 regiments of infantry, say	225,000	men.
100 field-batteries, 600 guns	15,000	"
28 regiments of cavalry	25,500	"
5 regiments engineer troops	7,500	"
Total	273,000	"

"The force must be supplied with the necessary engineer and pontoon trains, and with transportation for every thing save tents. Its general line of operations should be so directed that water-transportation can be availed of from point to point, by means of the ocean and the rivers emptying into it. An essential feature of the plan of operations will be the employment of a strong naval force to protect the movements of a fleet of transports intended to convey a considerable body of troops from point to point of the enemy's sea-coast, thus either creating diversions and rendering it necessary for them to detach largely from their main body in order to protect such of their cities as may be threatened, or else landing and forming establishments on their coast at any favorable places that opportunity might offer. This naval force should also co-operate with the main army in its efforts to seize the important seaboard towns of the rebels.

"It cannot be ignored that the construction of railroads has introduced a new and very important element into war, by the great facilities thus given for concentrating at particular positions large masses of troops from remote sections, and by creating new strategic points and lines of operations.

"It is intended to overcome this difficulty by the partial operations suggested, and such others as the particular case may require. We must endeavor to seize places on the railways in the rear of the enemy's points of concentration, and we must threaten their seaboard cities, in order that each State may be forced, by the necessity of its own defence, to diminish its contingent to the Confederate army.

"The proposed movement down the Mississippi will produce important results in this connection. That advance and the progress of the main army at the East will materially assist each other, by diminishing the resistance to be encountered by each.

"The tendency of the Mississippi movement upon all questions connected with cotton is too well understood by the President and Cabinet to need any illustration from me.

"There is another independent movement that has often been suggested, and which has always recommended itself to my judgment. I refer to a movement from Kansas and Nebraska, through the Indian Territory, upon Red River and Western Texas, for the purpose of protecting and developing the latent Union and free-State sentiment well known to predominate in Western Texas, and which, like a similar sentiment in Western Virginia, will, if protected, ultimately organize that section into a free State. How far it will be possible to support this movement by an advance through New Mexico from California, is a matter which I have not sufficiently examined to be able to express a decided opinion. If at all practicable, it is eminently desirable, as bringing into play the resources and warlike qualities of the Pacific States, as well as identifying them with our cause and cementing the bond of union between them and the General Government.

"If it is not departing too far from my province, I will venture to suggest the policy of an intimate alliance and cordial understanding with Mexico: their sympathies and interests are with us,—their antipathies exclusively against our enemies and their institutions. I think it would not be difficult to obtain from the Mexican Government the right to use, at least during the present contest, the road from Guaymas to New Mexico: this concession would very materially reduce the obstacles of the column moving from the Pacific. A similar permission to use their territory for the passage of troops between the Panuco and the Rio Grande would enable us to throw a column of troops by a good road from Tampico, or some of the small harbors north of it, upon and across the Rio Grande, without risk and scarcely firing a shot.

"To what extent, if any, it would be desirable to take into service and employ Mexican soldiers, is a question entirely political, on which I do not venture to offer an opinion.

"The force I have recommended is large; the expense is great. It is possible that a smaller force might accomplish the object in view; but I understand it to be the purpose of this great nation to re-establish the power of its Government, and to restore peace to its citizens, in the shortest possible time.

"The question to be decided is simply this: shall we crush the rebellion at one blow, terminate the war in one campaign, or shall we leave it for a legacy to our descendants?

"When the extent of the possible line of operations is considered, the force asked for the main army under my command cannot be regarded as unduly large. Every mile we advance carries us farther from our base of operations, and renders detachments necessary to cover our communications, while the enemy will be constantly concentrating as he falls back. I propose, with the force which I have requested, not only to drive the enemy out of Virginia and occupy Richmond, but to occupy Charleston, Savannah, Montgomery, Pensacola, Mobile, and New Orleans; in other words, to move into the heart of the enemy's country and crush out the rebellion in its very heart.

"By seizing and repairing the railroads as we advance, the difficulties of transportation will be materially diminished. It is perhaps unnecessary to state that, in addition to the forces named in this memorandum, strong reserves should be formed, ready to supply any losses that may occur.

"In conclusion, I would submit that the exigencies of the treasury may be lessened by making only partial payments to our troops when in the enemy's country, and by giving the obligations of the United States for such supplies as may there be obtained.

"GEORGE B. MCCLELLAN,
"*Major-General.*"

General McClellan, speaking of this memorandum in his Report, written two years after, says,—

"I do not think the events of the war have proved these views upon the methods and plans of its conduct altogether incorrect. They certainly have not proved my estimate of the number of troops and scope of operations too large. It is probable that I did underestimate the time necessary for the completion of arms and equipments. It was not strange, however, that by many civilians intrusted with authority there should have been an exactly opposite opinion held in both these particulars."

This simple and modest statement is read with melancholy interest by the light of the events which have transpired since the date of the memorandum. And that portion of the American people—we believe, the larger portion—which is willing to hear before it judges, will not fail to recognize in the memorandum itself the sagacious and comprehensive views of a man who has carefully studied the problem before him, and believe that he had found a solution for it. It steers clear of the safe generalities in which mediocrity takes refuge, as well as the wild predictions that rash self-confidence is apt to make. His conclusions are drawn from a wide and patient survey of the field before him. Here is a plan broad in its scope and well considered in its details. It may be that the event might not, under any circumstances, have responded to his expectations; it may be that the soldier might not have had the means to execute what the statesman had conceived: it is enough to know that the opportunity was never given him to try the experiment fairly. When he spoke of the possibility of ending the war by a single campaign, he perhaps underestimated both the moral and material forces arrayed against him; but, in the multitude of predictions as to the duration of the war which have not come to pass, an anticipation like this will not be treasured up against him.

For some weeks after the date of the above memorandum, the work of organizing and arranging the troops went on diligently and uninterruptedly, and on the 15th of October the grand aggregate of the forces in and around Washington was one hundred and fifty-two thousand and fifty-one, of whom one hundred and thirty-three thousand two hundred and one were present and fit for active duty. The infantry was arranged in brigades of four regiments each, and divisions of three brigades each were gradually formed, with artillery and cavalry attached to each division as far as was practicable. The formation into corps was to be postponed until the army had been for some time in the field, as were recommendations for the promotion of officers to the rank of major-generals till actual trial in service had shown who were best fitted for these important posts.

On the 15th of October, the main body of the Army of the Potomac was in the immediate vicinity of Washington, with detachments on the left bank of the river as far down as Liverpool Point and as far up as Williamsport and its vicinity. General Dix was at Baltimore, General Banks at Darnestown, and General Stone at Poolesville.

On the 21st of October, the disastrous engagement at Ball's Bluff took place. Efforts have been made to connect the name of General McClellan with this affair; but the facts in the case, and especially the testimony taken by the Congressional Committee on the Conduct of the War, show that the reconnoissances directed by him had been brought to a close during the preceding day, and that the movements which led to the battle of the 21st were not ordered by him. It is enough to say that the responsibility of the day does not rest upon General McClellan, without going further and inquiring to whom it does belong; but it may be added that the battle of Ball's Bluff is one of the many enterprises of this war which are held to be brilliant if successful, and rash if unsuccessful. The praise in one event and the blame in the other are alike exaggerated. A great stake is played for, but the rule of the stern game of war requires that in such cases a great stake must be laid down.

On the 31st day of October, 1861, Lieutenant-General Scott addressed a letter to the Secretary of War, in which he requested that, on account of his increasing infirmities and the necessity of repose of mind and body, his name might be placed on the list of army officers retired from active service. The letter was laid before a Cabinet meeting, and General Scott was placed on the retired list of the army, with the full pay and allowance of his rank; and on the same day the President, accompanied by the members of the Cabinet, proceeded to his residence and read to him the official order which gave to the decision the force of law. The venerable commander-in-chief expressed his acknowledgments in words and with a manner which betokened strong emotion, and the President answered in appropriate terms. In the official order announcing General Scott's retirement, the President of the United States said, in language the justice and propriety of which were universally felt,—

"The American people will hear with sadness and deep emotion that General Scott has withdrawn from the active control of the army, while the President and unanimous Cabinet express their own and the nation's sympathy in his personal affliction, and their profound sense of the important public services rendered by him to his country during his long and brilliant career, among which will ever be gratefully distinguished his faithful devotion to the Constitution, the Union, and the flag, when assailed by parricidal rebellion."

Upon the retirement of General Scott, General McClellan, by a general order dated November 1, was directed to assume the command of the army of the United States, with his head-quarters at Washington, and on the same day the new commander-in-chief issued the following order:—

"*General Order No.* 19.

"HEAD-QUARTERS OF THE ARMY,
"WASHINGTON, D.C., Nov. 1, 1861.

"In accordance with General Order No. 94, from the War Department, I hereby assume command of the armies of the United States.

"In the midst of the difficulties which encompass and divide the nation, hesitation and self-distrust may well accompany the assumption of so vast a responsibility; but confiding, as I do, in the loyalty, discipline, and courage of our troops, and believing, as I do, that Providence will favor ours as the just cause, I cannot doubt that success will crown our efforts and sacrifices.

"The army will unite with me in the feeling of regret that the weight of many years, and the effect of increasing infirmities, contracted and intensified in his country's service, should just now remove from our head the great soldier of our nation,—the hero who, in his youth, raised high the reputation of his country on the fields of Canada, which he sanctified with his blood; who, in more mature years, proved to the world that American skill and valor could repeat, if not eclipse, the exploits of Cortez in the land of the Montezumas; whose whole life has been devoted to the service of his country; whose whole efforts have been directed to uphold our honor at the smallest sacrifice of life;—a warrior who scorned the selfish glories of the battle-field, when his great qualities as a statesman could be employed more profitably for his country; a citizen who, in his declining years, has given to the world the most shining instance of loyalty in disregarding all ties of birth and clinging to the cause of truth and honor. Such has been the career of Winfield Scott, whom it has long been the delight of the nation to honor as a man and a soldier.

"While we regret his loss, there is one thing we cannot regret,—the bright example he has left for our emulation. Let us all hope and pray that his declining years may be passed in peace and happiness, and that they may be cheered by the success of the country and the cause he has fought for and loved so well. Beyond all that, let us do nothing that can cause him to blush for us. Let no defeat of the army he has so long commanded embitter his last years, but let our victories illuminate the close of a life so grand.

"GEO. B. MCCLELLAN,
"*Major-General commanding, U. S. A.*"

On the next day, November 2, General McClellan received a sword which had been voted to him by the City Councils of Philadelphia, a deputation of which went to Washington and gave the sword to him in person, at his house. In a very brief reply to the complimentary address which accompanied the gift, he said, "I ask in the future forbearance, patience, and confidence. With these we can accomplish all."

On the 7th, 11th, and 12th days of November, 1861, respectively, letters of instruction were addressed by the commander-in-chief to General Buell, in charge of the Department of the Ohio, and General Halleck, in that of the Department of Missouri. These were general in their scope, rather indicating what it was desirable to accomplish, and pointing out certain principles of government and administration, than going into details which had been matters of oral discussion between him and these officers. A brief extract from the letter to General Buell, of the date November 7, will give an impression of their spirit and purpose:—

> "It is possible that the conduct of our political affairs in Kentucky is more important than that of our military operations. I certainly cannot overestimate the importance of the former. You will please constantly to bear in mind the precise issue for which we are fighting: that issue is the preservation of the Union, and the restoration of the full authority of the General Government over all portions of our territory. We shall most readily suppress this rebellion and restore the authority of the Government by religiously respecting the constitutional rights of all. I know that I express the feelings and opinions of the President when I say that we are fighting only to preserve the integrity of the Union and the constitutional authority of the General Government."

These letters of instruction should be read in connection with two others written subsequently by General McClellan, one dated February 14, 1862, addressed to General Sherman, commanding at Port Royal, giving directions as to movements against Fort Pulaski, Fernandina, Savannah, Fort Sumter, and Charleston, and one dated February 23, 1862, addressed to General Butler, containing instructions as to military movements in the Southwest. From this letter an extract is here subjoined:—

"The object of your expedition is one of vital importance,—the capture of New Orleans. The route selected is up the Mississippi River, and the first obstacle to be encountered (perhaps the only one) is in the resistance offered by Forts St. Philip and Jackson. It is expected that the navy can reduce these works: in that case, you will, after their capture, leave a sufficient garrison in them to render them perfectly secure; and it is recommended that, on the upward passage, a few heavy guns and some troops be left at the pilot-station (at the forks of the river), to cover a retreat in the event of a disaster. These troops and guns will, of course, be removed as soon as the forts are captured.

"Should the navy fail to reduce the works, you will land your forces and siege-train, and endeavor to breach the works, silence their fire, and carry them by assault.

"The next resistance will be near the English Bend, where there are some earthen batteries. Here it may be necessary for you to land your troops and co-operate with the naval attack, although it is more than probable that the Navy, unassisted, can accomplish the result. If these works are taken, the city of New Orleans necessarily falls. In that event, it will probably be best to occupy Algiers with the mass of your troops, also the eastern bank of the river above the city. It may be necessary to place some troops in the city to preserve order; but, if there appears to be sufficient Union sentiment to control the city, it may be best, for purposes of discipline, to keep your men out of the city.

"After obtaining possession of New Orleans, it will be necessary to reduce all the works guarding its approaches from the east, and particularly to gain the Manchac Pass.

"Baton Rouge, Berwick Bay, and Fort Livingston will next claim your attention.

"A feint on Galveston may facilitate the objects we have in view. I need not call your attention to the necessity of gaining possession of all the rolling stock you can on the different railways, and of obtaining control of the roads themselves. The occupation of Baton Rouge by a combined naval and land force should be accomplished as soon as possible after you have gained New Orleans. Then endeavor to open your communication with the northern column by the Mississippi, always bearing in mind the necessity of occupying Jackson, Mississippi, as soon as you can safely do so, either after or before you have effected the junction. Allow nothing to divert you from obtaining full possession of *all* the approaches to New Orleans. When that object is accomplished to its fullest extent, it will be necessary to make a combined attack on Mobile, in order to gain possession of the harbor and works, as well as to control the railway terminus at the city. In regard to this, I will send more detailed instructions as the operations of the Northern column develop themselves.

"I may briefly state that the general objects of the expedition are—*first*, the reduction of New Orleans and all its approaches; then Mobile and its defences; then Pensacola, Galveston, &c. It is probable that by the timo New Orleans is reduced, it will be in the power of the

Government to reinforce the land forces sufficiently to accomplish all these objects. In the mean time, you will please give all the assistance in your power to the army and navy commanders in your vicinity, never losing sight of the fact that the great object to be achieved is the capture and firm retention of New Orleans."

The remarkably sagacious foresight shown in the instructions to General Butler as to the mode of attack upon New Orleans can be fully apprehended only after reading in detail the account of the brilliant capture of that city, by the combined military and naval forces of the United States, a few weeks later.

The several letters above referred to are given in full in General McClellan's Report, and, when read together, will be found to indicate a plan which embraced in its scope all the armies of the Union and the whole region occupied by the Confederates. It was the purpose of the commander-in-chief that the various parts of the plan should be carried out simultaneously, as far as was possible, and in co-operation along the whole line of movement. In this general scheme the Army of the Potomac was to bear its part,—a leading part, it is true, but still a part in concert with other forces of the Union. This should be borne in mind in order to explain and justify the delay which was necessary to enable that army to perform its share in the execution of the whole work.

From what has been said, it is easy to see how trying was the position of General McClellan during the closing weeks of the year 1861, and how painful was the weight of responsibility resting upon him. He was a young man, whose name until recently had been unknown to the public, suddenly set at the head of military operations which extended over a space and were upon a scale to tax the strategical skill and vast organizing genius of Napoleon himself. The Army of the Potomac, which was immediately under him, was ten times larger than any army that had ever been under the command of one man upon the soil of the United States since the Revolution; and the difficulty of commanding armies increases in much more than a direct ratio with their numbers,—or, in other words, it does not follow that among ten men fit to command ten thousand men there will always be found one fit to command a hundred thousand. Even the Duke of Wellington never led an army of a hundred thousand men.*

His position was thus in itself one of great responsibility; but there were extrinsic elements which added to its burdens. The American people are easily elated and easily depressed, and they had passed through both of these states of feeling during the eventful year 1861. At the breaking out of the war, amidst the magnificent uprising of the nation to sustain the Government, we had exulted in the confident expectation that the rebellion

* "Napoleon was of the opinion that he and the Archduke Charles were the only men in Europe who could manœuvre one hundred thousand men: he considered it a very difficult thing."—General Heintzelman. (*Report on the Conduct of the War*, Part I. p. 118.)

would at once be crushed and broken into fragments by the irresistible force arrayed against it. But the disastrous battle of Bull Run and the untoward affair of Ball's Bluff had blighted these fervid hopes, and a despondency had taken possession of the public mind which was as unreasonable as the previous assurance had been. This rising and sinking of our spirits had tended to aggravate that impatience which must be admitted to be one of our national traits; and in the autumn of 1861 a strong desire had taken possession of the public mind that some decisive step should be taken, some vigorous blow should be struck. The people murmured and chafed at the delay that clogged the movements of the Army of the Potomac; the press, with its myriad voices, gave utterance to the feeling, and the cry "On to Richmond!" became the symbol and motto of the hour. This was a very natural sentiment, and, to some extent, commendable,—because it caught its warmth in part from the patriotism of the people and their earnest wish to have the Union restored. They desired to see some results commensurate with their efforts and sacrifices. But strong feeling is apt to be unjust, especially when it is general as well as strong; and our ignorance of war—that happy element in our lot—had an influence in the same direction. We had read of armies, but practically we knew nothing about them. The battles of the War of 1812 and of the war with Mexico had been fought with small and manageable bodies of men; but so immense an army as that which was encamped in and around Washington was a wholly new thing to us. We knew nothing of the vast amount of transportation necessary to supply a hundred thousand men with food,—especially on the bountiful scale upon which our troops are fed,—how dependent such a body is, in a country like Eastern Virginia, on its base of operations, and how it must keep up an uninterrupted connection with a navigable stream or a railway. We knew little or nothing of the obstacles presented to the advance of a great army by the nature of the country,—its woods, its swamps, its streams, and its mud. From some of the articles which appeared in the Northern papers, one would have thought that the writers supposed the soldiers had wings and could live without food. Their experience would have been enlarged, and their judgment corrected, had they been required to transport a single battery of siege-guns over the roads of Eastern Virginia in a rainy December.*

* "Again, the public treat the army as a man or a horse, to whom it is only necessary to say 'go' and motion follows. They fancy that a fight can be witnessed from a hill-top, as a boxing-match can be viewed from a third-story window. They forget that this army, say of sixty thousand men only, must eat at least one hundred thousand meals a day, and, if the army is to be kept in prime order, must sleep at least six hours out of the twenty-four. Where there are turnpike roads, artillery can get along very well. Where there are no turnpikes, and the weather is wet, the last carriage of a single company of artillery—the thirteenth—often mires where the first carriage—a gun, technically—has found no difficulty. What, then, must it be when two or three hundred pieces of artillery, each one accompanied by a caisson, or ammunition-wagon,

And it must be admitted that the friends of General McClellan themselves, or some of them, were unwise in the lavish praise they heaped upon him, by which they awakened such wild hopes and impossible expectations. He was commended not for what he had done, but for what he was about to do; and what he did and said, and still more what he was going to do, was paraded before the public gaze in a way that to no one could be more distasteful than to him, an essentially modest man, who knew better than anybody else the weight of the burden that was upon him. The highest kindness to him at that time would have been to let him alone and say as little about him as possible. To a manly and truthful nature, nothing is less welcome than undeserved praise. Undeserved blame is bitter, but undeserved praise is sickening. Besides,

---

and every six with a forge,—making six hundred and fifty carriages that go into a battle,—have to be carried, in wet weather, through a swampy country, like that, for example, on the Chickahominy? This is mere fighting-material; to which add two or three thousand wagons for feeding-purposes, and you begin to have an idea of what has to be moved when an army moves, to say nothing of the cattle by thousands that have to be driven along, and a horde of camp-followers of all kinds. I am not speaking now of a corps of ten or twenty thousand men who start on a foray with nothing but their shirts, pantaloons, and boots to carry, besides their arms, but of an army which, when a victory is gained, is prepared to retain what is won in an enemy's country,—just such an army as McClellan had in the Peninsula."—From "*Three Great Battles*" (a pamphlet printed, but not published), by J. H. B. Latrobe, Esq.

extravagant commendation is sure to produce a reaction, sooner or later.

The newspaper-correspondents who bedaubed him with flattery, who described his person and features with the minuteness of a passport, who chronicled all his movements, who named him the Young Napoleon,—he being of the same age as the Emperor was at the date of the battle of Austerlitz,—were moved by a friendly spirit, mingled with that hero-worship which is so decided an American trait; but they were doing him any thing but a kindness. Indeed, they were playing directly into the hands of his enemies and ill-wishers, political and personal.

Nor was this all. General McClellan was as little of a politician as a citizen of the United States well can be. The subject of politics had never occupied his mind. His time and attention had been wholly given to the duties of his profession while he remained in the army, and afterwards to the duties of his business. It had so happened that he had never but once, since reaching the legal age, been in a position to exercise the right of voting. But he had opinions upon the political issues of the time; and these opinions were not those of the party into whose hands the people had committed the government of the country; and the only time he had ever voted was in the memorable contest in Illinois between Mr. Lincoln and Mr. Douglas, when he had preferred the latter; but in our country, sooner or later, every thing is swept into the gulf of politics; and thus General McClellan's military capacity, his courage, even his patriotism, began to be looked at from a political point of view, and to be called in question by heated political partisans.

When Congress assembled, in December, 1861, President Lincoln announced the appointment of General McClellan to the post of commander of the army, in these terms, which were generally received as expressing no more than the exact truth:—

"With the retirement of General Scott came the executive duty of appointing in his stead a general-in-chief of the army. It is a fortunate circumstance that neither in council nor country was there, so far as I know, *any difference of opinion as to the proper person to be selected.* The retiring chief repeatedly expressed his judgment in favor of General McClellan for the position; and in this the nation seemed to give a unanimous concurrence. The designation of General McClellan is, therefore, in a considerable degree, the selection of the country, as well as of the Executive; and hence there is better reason to hope there will be given him the confidence and cordial support thus, by fair implication, promised, and without which he cannot with so full efficiency serve the country."

Within a few days after the meeting of Congress, the vague discontent and restless impatience of the community found expression in the shape of a Congressional Committee on the Conduct of the War, consisting of three members of the Senate and four members of the House of Representatives. The first motion towards the formation of the committee was made in the Senate on the 9th day of

December, and the first meeting of the committee was held on the 20th of the same month. From that time until the close of April they sat nearly every day; and there were several meetings during the months of May, June, and July. Had the committee confined their inquiries and investigations to past transactions, and considered themselves as charged with the duty of collecting and recording testimony to be used by future historians of the war, their labors might have been of value to the country; but they did not take this limited view of the scope and sphere of their operations. In their judgment, the future as well as the past was committed to their trust. For instance, the very first witness examined before them was General I. B. Richardson, and the second was General S. P. Heintzelman, and both were examined on the same day, December 24. General Richardson's examination was short, and not very important. The first question put to General Heintzelman by the chairman began thus:—"We have inquired a little about the past: now we want to inquire a little about the present and the future, which is, perhaps, more important. As you are a military man of great experience, we want some of your opinions on some matters." As to the "opinions" of the witness which they wanted, one or two questions and answers may suffice to show:—

"*Ques.*—'I would inquire whether there has been any council of war among your officers and the commander-in-chief.'

"*Ans.*—'I have never been consulted upon any military subject.'

* * * * * *

"*Ques.*—'You think a council of war among the chief officers might be beneficial?'

"*Ans.*—'I thought so. Certainly it would be very satisfactory to some of them, I know. We have been very anxious to know what is proposed to be done. I should act with more confidence if I knew.'

"*Ques.*—'Is there any feeling among officers that they are not consulted,—that they are slighted?'

"*Ans.*—'Yes, sir: I suppose there is some,'" &c. &c.*

This particular grievance—the reserve of the commander-in-chief, and his not consulting with his inferior officers—was a frequent point of inquiry on the part of the committee during the winter months, but by no means the only one. The general plan of the campaign, the policy which delayed a forward movement, the organization of the army, the proportion of cavalry to the other arms, the defences about Washington, the number of men requisite to make it secure, were also among the subjects to which the inquiries of the committee were directed. Their investigations were moulded and colored by a spirit not friendly to the commander-in-chief. Day after day, general officers, and sometimes those of inferior rank, were called before them, and invited, not to say encouraged, to give their opinions upon the plans of the commander-in-chief, his military views, and the manner in which he discharged his duties, and thus to

* Report on the Conduct of the War, Part I. pp. 117–121.

enter upon a line of discussion which, if not directly forbidden by the Army Regulations,* was unfavorable to discipline and tended to injure the relations between the commander-in-chief and his subordinates.

---

* The following is the 26th Article of the Revised Regulations for the Army:—

"Deliberations or discussions among any class of military men, having the object of conveying praise or censure or any mark of approbation toward their superiors or others in the military service, . . . are strictly prohibited."

Some of the officers examined seemed conscious of the difficult position in which they stood between their duty as subjects and their duty as officers. General Lander, for instance, was asked this question:—

"'If you will give us your opinion as a military man on that subject [the plan of the campaign], I will be obliged to you.'

"*Ans.*—'It is against the Army Regulations and laws of Congress to discuss the views and plans of your superior officer. In answering this question,'" &c.—*Report on the Conduct of the War*, Part I. p. 160.

General Fitz-John Porter was asked,—

"'Should' the army 'retire into winter quarters, or should it attempt an enterprise to dislodge the enemy?'

"*Ans.*—'That is a question I cannot answer.'

"*Ques.*—'I merely ask your military opinion.'

"*Ans.*—'I decline to give a military opinion on that point. I am in possession of information in regard to intended movements,—rather, a portion of General McClellan's plans, a small portion only; and I decline giving any information whatever in regard to future movements, or what they ought to be. I do not think it my business to do so, and we are forbidden by our regulations to discuss or express opinions on these matters.'"—*Report on the Conduct of the War*, Part I. p. 171.

It is fair to state that at the very first meeting of the committee "it was agreed that, as a matter of honor, none of its members should reveal any thing that transpired in committee until such time as the injunction of secrecy should be removed;" but such a determination, by the cloud of mystery it threw around their proceedings, could only give rise to conjectures probably more injurious in their influence than the truth would have been if fully revealed. Besides, Congressional committees are human, and not hermetically sealed against the transmission of that kind of knowledge which has the charm of being forbidden.

Nor did the committee confine themselves to the task of taking and recording testimony, and the free discussion in their own room of military plans and movements, but, as they say in their Report, "they were in constant communication with the President and his Cabinet, and neglected no opportunity of at once laying before them the information acquired by them in the course of their investigations." It is fair to presume that they gave advice as well as information; and, indeed, the journal of their proceedings shows that they did; and their advice was probably of weight in the conduct of the campaign. The following is an extract from the journal of the committee:—

"February 26, 1862.

"Pursuant to previous arrangement, the committee waited upon the President at eight o'clock on Tuesday evening, February 25. They made known to the President that, having examined many of the highest military officers of the army, their statements of the necessity of dividing the great Army of the Potomac into *corps d'armée* had impressed the committee with the belief that it was essential that such a division of that army should be made,—that it would be dangerous to move upon a formidable enemy with the present organization of the army. The application was enforced by many arguments drawn from the usages in France, and every other military nation in Europe, and the fact that, so far as the committee could learn, all our military officers agreed that our army would not be efficient unless such an organization was had. The President observed that he had never considered the organization of the army into army corps so essential as the committee seemed to represent it to be: still, he had long been in favor of such an organization. General McClellan, however, did not seem to think it so essential, though he had at times expressed himself as favorable to it. The committee informed the President that the Secretary of War had authorized them to say to him that he deemed such an organization necessary.

"General McClellan was in favor of an organization into corps, but only proposed deferring it till time should show what officers were best fitted for corps commanders,—which seems reasonable enough. It was a measure which surely might have been postponed till the army had taken the field, at least."

Whatever may have been the motives of the committee, or however earnest may have been their desire to see the war brought to a speedy and successful termination, it is certain that, in point of fact, they were only aiding the enemy; for the interference of such a body, direct or indirect, with the conduct of the campaign, could have no other effect than to impair the unity of action and concentration of purpose which are so essential to the success of an army.

CHAPTER VI.

WE are now brought to the close of the year 1861 and the opening of 1862. The positions and numbers of the Confederate army in Eastern Virginia were as follows. At Norfolk and Yorktown there was a considerable force,—probably over thirty thousand men. The army before Washington occupied an extended line running from the southeast to the northwest. The left wing was at Leesburg and its vicinity, in force about forty-five hundred; and there were about thirteen thousand in the valley of the Shenandoah. The main body, comprising about eighty thousand men, was at Manassas and Centreville. At these points the positions were naturally very strong, with impassable streams and broken ground, affording ample protection to their flanks, and with lines of intrenchment sweeping all the available approaches. The right was at Brooks's Station, Dumfries, Lower Occoquan and vicinity, numbering about eighteen thousand. This wing of the army formed a support to several batteries on the Lower Potomac, extending from High Point and Cockpit Point to the Chopawampsic Creek. These batteries, greatly obstructing the navigation of the river, and to this extent practically blockading Washington, were a source of great annoyance to the Administration and of mortification to the people, and a strong desire was felt that a movement should be made to destroy them; but General McClellan was of the opinion that such an attempt would be attended with danger, and that the destruction of these batteries by our army would afford but temporary relief unless we were strong enough to hold the entire line of the Potomac. The desired end could be secured either by driving the enemy from Manassas and Acquia Creek by superior force, or by manœuvring to compel him to vacate the position. The latter course was finally adopted, with success.

That an onward movement should be made to Richmond, and the rebellion be there attacked in its heart, was a point on which the public, the Administration, and the commander-in-chief were agreed; but by what route to make the approach—whether by the Lower Potomac and the Peninsula, or by a direct attack upon the positions at Manassas and Centreville—formed a fruitful subject of debate in the newspapers and among military men; and the discussion was all the more animated from the fact that whatever plans General McClellan had formed, or was forming, he did not make them known to others.

Thus far nothing had, apparently, disturbed the relations between General McClellan and the Administration, or changed the friendly feeling which had inspired the paragraph which has been quoted from the President's message. On the 14th day of

January, 1862, Mr. Simon Cameron resigned his position as Secretary of War, and Mr. Edwin M. Stanton was appointed to fill his place. Mr. Stanton had not been in political life, and was known only as a lawyer in large practice, of strong grasp of mind and great capacity for labor. He had been a member of the Democratic party; and the selection of an able and honorable political opponent for such a place, at such a time, seemed an act alike of wisdom and magnanimity, which gave general pleasure. Thus the appointment was hailed with universal favor, and the highest hopes were entertained of an improved administration of the War Department, under a man fresh from the people, unscarred and unstained by political strife. But, in whatever other respects the country may have been a gainer by the introduction into the Cabinet of a man of Mr. Stanton's energy, it is certain that the hands of General McClellan were not strengthened by the change, and that the confidence reposed in him by the Administration was not thereby increased.*

---

* The following is an extract from the journal of the Congressional Committee on the Conduct of the War, under date of January 21, 1862, a few days after Mr. Stanton's appointment:—

"SIR:—I am instructed by the Joint Committee on the Conduct of the present War to inquire of you whether there is such an office as commander-in-chief of the army of the United States, or any grade above that of major-general. If so, by what authority is it created? Does it exist by virtue

General McClellan had been taken ill at Christmas-time, 1861, and was confined to his bed about three weeks. Upon his recovery, in the middle of January, he says in his Report that he found that an excessive anxiety for an immediate movement of the Army of the Potomac had taken possession of the Administration. He had an interview with the new Secretary of War, soon after the appointment of the latter, in which he explained verbally his design as to the part of the campaign to be executed by the Army of the Potomac; and this was, to attack Richmond by the Lower Chesapeake. The Secretary instructed him to develop his plan to the President,—which he did. Unfortunately, it did not meet with the approbation of the latter; and

---

of any law of Congress, or any usage of the Government? Please give us the information asked for, at your convenience.

"I remain, &c.,

"B. F. Wade, *Chairman.*

"Hon. Edwin M. Stanton,

"*Secretary of War.*"

This seems hardly respectful to the President of the United States, after his announcement in his Annual Message that he had appointed General McClellan to the very office which the committee insinuate does not exist; and had Abraham Lincoln been Andrew Jackson, he would have been a bold man who would have addressed such a letter to the Secretary of War. But we may infer that such a communication would not have been sent to Mr. Stanton unless the committee had surmised it would be welcome,—which inference is strengthened by the fact that the committee, on the preceding day, January 20, had had a conference with the Secretary, at his request, of several hours' duration.

from that moment there began on the part of the President an active interference with the movements of the army, frequently without conference with the commander, which much increased the difficulties of the latter, and were most untoward in their influence upon the results of the campaign. The President's course can be shown out of his own mouth to have been unwise; for in his Annual Message of December 3, 1861, he says, immediately after the paragraph which has been already quoted, announcing the appointment of General McClellan as commander-in-chief,—

"It has been said that one bad general is better than two good ones; and the saying is true, if taken to mean no more than that an army is better directed by a single mind, though inferior, than by two superior ones at variance and cross-purposes with each other.

"And the same is true in all joint operations, wherein those engaged can have none but a common end in view, and can differ only as to the choice of means. In a storm at sea, no one on board can wish the ship to sink: and yet, not unfrequently, all go down together, because too many will direct, and no single mind can be allowed to control."

This is well put: it is good sense, enforced by pertinent illustration; and the question naturally rises, why did not the President "reck his own rede"? Without impugning his patriotism, it may be presumed that he yielded his own judgment to the force of that mysterious influence called "pressure,"—"a power behind the throne, greater than th throne,"—which has done so much harm and so little good in the conduct of the war.

The President's practical exercise of his constitutional functions as commander-in-chief began with the issuing of the following order, which, be it always borne in mind, was done without consultation with General McClellan:—

("President's General War Order, No. 1.)

"Executive Mansion,
Washington, January 27, 1862.

"*Ordered*, That the 22d day of February, 1862, be the day for a general movement of the land and naval forces of the United States against the insurgent forces. That especially the army at and about Fortress Monroe, the Army of the Potomac, the Army of Western Virginia, the army near Munfordsville, Kentucky, the army and flotilla at Cairo, and a naval force in the Gulf of Mexico, be ready to move on that day.

"That all other forces, both land and naval, with their respective commanders, obey existing orders for the time, and be ready to obey additional orders when duly given.

"That the heads of departments, and especially the Secretaries of War and of the Navy, with all their subordinates, and the general-in-chief, with all other commanders and subordinates of land and naval forces, will severally be held to their strict and full responsibilities for prompt execution of this order.

"Abraham Lincoln."

The President, as has been said, disapproved of General McClellan's plan of attacking Richmond by the Lower Chesapeake, and substituted one of his own, by a new order, as follows:—

("President's Special War Order, No. 1.)

"EXECUTIVE MANSION,
WASHINGTON, January 31, 1862.

"*Ordered*, That all the disposable force of the Army of the Potomac, after providing safely for the defence of Washington, be formed into an expedition for the immediate object of seizing and occupying a point upon the railroad southwestward of what is known as Manassas Junction, all details to be in the discretion of the commander-in-chief, and the expedition to move before or on the 22d day of February next.

"ABRAHAM LINCOLN."

These two orders should be considered together and carefully pondered by every candid man who desires to form a correct judgment as to the past, irrespective of political prepossessions. The outposts of an army mark the line where the sphere of party politics ends. A general is a good general or a bad general, a cautious general or a rash general; but no military critic will speak of a tory general or a whig general, a Republican general or a Democratic general. The President of the United States is a civilian, without military training or experience; and he is, moreover, of necessity, greatly occupied with important civil duties, and thus unable to give his time and thoughts exclusively to military matters. The second in date of the above orders, by a stroke of the pen, directs that a most momentous campaign should be conducted upon a plan which the commanding officer, charged with the duty and responsibility of carrying it out, had, after great deliberation, decided to be inexpedient. It is easy to see how unequal, under such difference of opinion, is the contest between the President of the United States and the general who acts under peremptory orders to take a certain step, but has the "details" in his own "discretion." Does he succeed? it is because the plan was good; does he fail? it is because the "details" were not zealously and ably executed.*

But the first of these orders deserves more consideration even than the second. The President appoints a certain future day for a general movement of the land and naval forces of the country, as if it were the marshalling of a civic procession or the arranging of a mock battle on the stage. No man can venture to say that a great army shall move or a great fleet shall sail

---

* It may be a consolation for us to know that the interference of civilians in the plans of military commanders has been an evil in other countries besides ours. A respectable English writer, speaking of their Peninsular campaign, says, "We may here observe how hard is the fate of an English general sent out in command of an expedition. With the single exception of the first Earl of Chatham, England never has possessed an able war-minister. Ministers, in general, are far better skilled in parliamentary tactics and political intrigue than in history, geography, and the other sciences connected with war. Yet they will boldly take upon them to plan campaigns, and will even order impossibilities to be performed, and the whole blame of failure is laid upon the unfortunate commander. What, for example, can be conceived more absurd than a Castlereagh, a Canning, or a Frere, directing a Moore or a Wellington? Such things, however, were."—KEIGHTLEY: *History of England*, vol. iii. p. 507.

on a fixed future day, unless he be endowed with the gift of prophecy. And the 22d day of February was named for the combined movement, it may be presumed, simply because it was the birthday of Washington. Thus a sort of melodramatic grace was attempted to be thrown over the stern aspect of war, and the corps of fine writers who were in attendance upon the army were furnished with a theme for a sensation paragraph. It is melancholy to think that the lives and blood of brave men were under the control of those who could be moved by so trumpery a consideration as this.

General McClellan, on receiving the order of January 3, asked the President whether it was to be regarded as final, or whether he could be permitted to submit in writing his objections to the plan of the Executive and his reasons for preferring his own. Permission was granted, and a letter was addressed to the Secretary of War, under date of February 3. But, before it had been submitted to the President, General McClellan received from him the following note:—

"EXECUTIVE MANSION,
WASHINGTON, February 3, 1862.

"MY DEAR SIR:—You and I have distinct and different plans for a movement of the Army of the Potomac,—yours to be done by the Chesapeake, up the Rappahannock to Urbana, and across land to the terminus of the railroad on the York River: mine to move directly to a point on the railroad southwest of Manassas.

"If you will give me satisfactory answers to the following questions, I shall gladly yield my plan to yours:—

"1st. Does not your plan involve a greatly larger expenditure of *time* and *money* than mine?

"2d. Wherein is a victory *more certain* by your plan than mine?

"3d. Wherein is a victory *more valuable* by your plan than mine?

"4th. In fact, would it not be *less* valuable, in this, that it would break no great line of the enemy's communications, while mine would?

"5th. In case of disaster, would not a retreat be more difficult by your plan than mine?

"Yours, truly,

"ABRAHAM LINCOLN.

"Major-General McCLELLAN."

These questions were substantially answered in the letter to the Secretary of War above referred to, which appears in General McClellan's Report; but its length forbids its being copied in full, and only an abstract of its contents can be given.

He begins with a brief statement of the condition of the troops when he assumed the command in July, 1861, and of the defenceless position of the capital at that time, and thus recapitulates what had been accomplished up to the date of writing:—

"The capital is secure against attack; the extensive fortifications erected by the labor of our troops enable a small garrison to hold it against a numerous army; the enemy have been held in check; the State of Maryland is securely in our possession; the detached counties of Virginia are again within the pale of our laws, and all apprehension of trouble in Delaware is at an end; the enemy are confined to the positions they occupied before the disaster of the 21st of July. More than all this, I have now under my command a well-drilled and reliable army, to which the destinies of the country may be confidently committed. This army is young and untried in battle; but it is animated by the highest spirit, and is capable of great deeds.

"That so much has been accomplished and such an army created in so short a time from nothing, will hereafter be regarded as one of the highest glories of the Administration and the nation."

After telling the Secretary that he has not yet under his command such a force as he asked for in his earliest papers submitted to the President, he thus proceeds:—

"When I was placed in command of the armies of the United States, I immediately turned my attention to the whole field of operations, regarding the Army of the Potomac as only one, while the most important, of the masses under my command.

"I confess that I did not then appreciate the total absence of a general plan which had before existed, nor did I know that utter disorganization and want of preparation pervaded the Western armies.

"I took it for granted that they were nearly, if not quite, in condition to move towards the fulfilment of my plans. I acknowledge that I made a great mistake.

"I sent at once—with approval of the Executive—officers I considered competent to command in Kentucky and Missouri. Their instructions looked to prompt movements. I soon found that the labor of creation and organization had to be performed there: transportation, arms, clothing, artillery, discipline, all were wanting. These things required time to procure them.

"The generals in command have done their work most creditably; but we are still delayed. I had hoped that a general advance could be made during the good weather of December: I was mistaken.

"My wish was to gain possession of the Eastern Tennessee Railroad, as a preliminary movement, then to follow it up immediately by an attack on Nashville and Richmond as nearly at the same time as possible.

"I have ever regarded our true policy as being that of fully preparing ourselves, and then seeking for the most decisive results. I do not wish to waste life in useless battles, but prefer to strike at the heart."

He next proceeds to state that two bases of operation presented themselves for the advance of the Army of the Potomac,—first, that of Washington, its present position, involving a direct attack upon the intrenched positions of the enemy at Centreville, Manassas, &c., or else a movement to turn one or both of those positions, or a combination of the two plans. The relative force of the two armies would not justify an attack on both flanks of the enemy; and an attack on his left flank alone would involve a long line of wagon-communication, and could not prevent him from collecting for the decisive battle all the detachments now on his extreme right and left.

He next sets forth in great detail the difficulties and dangers of an attack upon the right flank, by the line of the Occoquan, and a crossing of the Potomac below that river, showing a minute knowledge of the localities of the region, and demonstrating to his correspondent the great advantage possessed by the enemy in the central position he occupied, with roads diverging in every direction, and a strong line of defence, enabling him to await an attack with a small force on one flank, while he concentrates every thing on the other for a decisive action. Among other difficulties, he speaks of "the present unprecedented and impassable condition of the roads." But, supposing the movement in this direction to be successful, the results, he thinks, would be confined to the possession of the field of battle, the evacuation of the line of the Upper Potomac by the enemy, and the moral effect of the victory,—important results, it is true, but not decisive of the war, or securing the destruction of the enemy's main army or the capture of Richmond.

The second base of operations available for the Army of the Potomac is that of the Lower Chesapeake Bay, which affords the shortest possible land-route to Richmond and strikes directly at the heart of the enemy's power in the East. In favor of this plan he thus reasons:—

"The roads in that region are passable at all periods of the year.

"The country now alluded to is much more favorable for offensive operations than that in front of Washington (which is *very* unfavorable),—much more level, more cleared land, the woods less dense, the soil more sandy, and the spring some two or three weeks earlier. A movement in force on that line obliges the enemy to abandon his intrenched position at Manassas in order to hasten to cover Richmond and Norfolk. He *must* do this; for, should he permit us to occupy Richmond, his destruction can be averted only by entirely defeating us in a battle in which he must be the assailant. This movement, if successful, gives us the capital, the communications, the supplies, of the rebels; Norfolk would fall, all the waters of the Chesapeake would be ours, all Virginia would be in our power, and the enemy forced to abandon Tennessee and North Carolina. The alternative presented to the enemy would be to beat us in a position selected by ourselves, disperse, or pass beneath the Caudine forks.

"Should we be beaten in a battle, we have a perfectly secure retreat down the Peninsula upon Fort Monroe, with our flanks perfectly covered by the fleet.

"During the whole movement our left flank is covered by the water. Our right is secure, for the reason that the enemy is too distant to reach us in time: he can only oppose us in front; we bring our fleet into full play.

"After a successful battle, our position would be—Burnside forming our left, Norfolk held securely, our centre connecting Burnside with Buell both by Raleigh and Lynchburg, Buell in Eastern Tennessee and North Alabama, Halleck at Nashville and Memphis.

"The next movement would be to connect with Sherman on the left, by reducing Wilmington and Charleston; to advance our centre into South Carolina and Georgia; to push Buell either towards Montgomery or to unite with the main army in Georgia; to throw Halleck southward to meet the naval expedition from New Orleans.

"We should then be in a condition to reduce at our leisure all the Southern sea-ports, to occupy all the avenues of communication, to use the great outlet of the Mississippi, to re-establish our Government and arms in Arkansas, Louisiana, and Texas, to force the slaves to labor for our subsistence instead of that of the rebels, to bid defiance to all foreign interference. Such is the object I have ever had in view; this is the general plan which I hope to accomplish.

"For many long months I have labored to prepare the Army of the Potomac to play its part in the programme. From the day when I was placed in command of all our armies, I have exerted myself to place all the other armies in such a condition that they too could perform their allotted duties."

He then tells his correspondent that, if it should be determined to operate from the Lower Chesapeake, the best point of landing would be Urbana, on the Lower Rappahannock, and states his reasons for the opinion; but, if circumstances should render it advisable not to land there, either Mobjack Bay or Fort Monroe might be resorted to. A large amount of cheap water transportation would be requisite to move the army to whatever point might be selected as a base of operations; and he gives some details in relation to this important point. The letter thus concludes:—

"The total force to be thrown upon the new line would be, according to circumstances, from one hundred and ten thousand to one hundred and forty thousand. I hope to use the latter number by bringing fresh troops into Washington and still leaving it quite safe. I fully realize that, in all projects offered, time will probably be the most valuable consideration. It is my decided opinion that, in that point of view, the second plan should be adopted. It is possible—nay, highly probable—that the weather and state of the roads may be such as to delay the direct movement from Washington, with its unsatisfactory results and great risks, far beyond the time required to complete the second plan. In the first case, we can fix no definite time for an advance. The roads have gone from bad to worse. Nothing like their present condition was ever known here before: they are impassable at present. We are entirely at the mercy of the weather. It is by no means certain that we can beat them at Manassas. On the other line I regard success as certain by all the chances of war. We demoralize the enemy by forcing him to abandon his prepared position for one which we have chosen, in which all is in our favor and where success must produce immense results.

"My judgment, as a general, is clearly in favor of this project. Nothing is certain in war; but all the chances are in favor of this movement. So much am I in favor of the southern line of operations, that I would prefer the move from Fortress Monroe as a base, as a certain though less brilliant movement than that from Urbana, to an attack upon Manassas.

"I know that his Excellency the President, you, and I, all agree in our wishes, and that these wishes are, to bring this war to a close as promptly as the means in our possession will permit. I believe that the mass of the people have entire confidence in us. I am sure of it. Let us, then, look only to the great result to be accomplished, and disregard every thing else."

This carefully-prepared and well-reasoned letter, and the many verbal conferences which followed it, seem to have induced the President to give up his own "plan;" for the execution of his order was not insisted upon,—though, as it was not revoked so formally as it had been issued, General McClellan stood before the public in the awkward position of a general officer declining to execute an order of the commander-in-chief still apparently in force. But from this time General McClellan's "plan" of attacking Richmond by way of the Peninsula was assented to, or acquiesced in, by the President; and no further conflict of opinion took place between them on this point.

The plan of operations being settled, the next

thing was to devise ways and means to carry it into execution. Secrecy and despatch were to be secured, as far as was practicable. An immense army was to be moved by water from a point or points in the neighborhood of Washington, and the plan of the campaign was to be kept from the knowledge of the enemy till the latest possible moment. Immediate measures were taken to provide a force of steamers and sailing-vessels necessary for the contemplated object.*

---

* In the order of time, the following letter of the Secretary of War may be appropriately introduced here, as showing his feeling towards General McClellan and the Army of the Potomac:—

"WAR DEPARTMENT,
WASHINGTON, February 17, 1862.

"To Brigadier-General F. W. LANDER:—

"The President directs me to say that he has observed with pleasure the activity and enterprise manifested by yourself and the officers and soldiers of your command. You have shown how much may be done, in the worst weather and worst roads, by a spirited officer, at the head of a small force of brave men, unwilling to waste life in camp when the enemies of their country are in reach. Your brilliant success is a happy presage of what may be expected when the Army of the Potomac shall be led to the field by their gallant general.

"EDWIN M. STANTON,
"*Secretary of War.*"

A few days after, the Secretary wrote another letter, addressed to the editor of the New York "Tribune," which is as follows:—

"WASHINGTON, February 20, 1862.

"SIR:—I cannot suffer undue merit to be ascribed to my official action. The glory of our recent victories belongs to

About the 20th of February, measures were taken to secure the reopening of the Baltimore &

---

the gallant officers that fought the battles. No share of it belongs to me.

"Much has been recently said of military combination and organizing victory. I hear such phrases with apprehension. They commenced in infidel France with the Italian campaign, and resulted in Waterloo. Who can organize victory? Who can combine the elements of success on the battle-field? We owe our recent victories to the Spirit of the Lord, that moved our soldiers to dash into battle, and filled the hearts of our enemies with terror and dismay. The inspiration that conquered in battle was in the hearts of the soldiers, and from on high. Patriotic spirit with resolute courage in officers and men is a military combination that never failed.

"We may well rejoice at the recent victories; for they teach us that battles are to be won now and by us in the same and only manner that they were ever won by any people or in any age since the days of Joshua,—by boldly pursuing and striking the foe. What, under the blessing of Providence, I conceive to be the true organization of victory and military combination to end this war, was declared in a few words by General Grant's message to General Buckner:—'I propose to move immediately on your works.'

"Yours, truly,

"EDWIN M. STANTON."

It is difficult to believe that this absurd letter, which no officer in the army could have read without indignation and disgust, could have been written by a Secretary of War. Besides its bad taste and false rhetoric, it involves a contemptuous disparagement of military science, most unbecoming in a man who was at the head of the War Department of a great nation engaged in a momentous war. And there breathes through it a spirit of hostility towards General McClellan, of ominous import to the success of our arms. After reading it, the President of the United States ought at once to have removed either that officer or Mr. Stanton himself.

Ohio Railroad. The whole of General Banks's division, and two brigades of General Sedgwick's division, were thrown across the river at Harper's Ferry on the 26th, superintended by General McClellan in person, who had gone up from Washington for that purpose. Materials had been collected for making a permanent bridge by means of canal-boats; but, on attempting to pass the boats through the left lock, it was found, for the first time, that the lock was too small to permit their passage. This unexpected obstacle deranged the plans; and an order which had been given for the movement of some forces from Washington was countermanded. Every exertion was made to establish, as promptly as possible, depots of forage and subsistence on the Virginia side, to supply the troops. On the 28th, Charlestown was occupied by a strong Federal force; and on the same day General McClellan returned to Washington. In spite of the untoward mischance of the canal-boats,—for which the commander-in-chief could not be responsible,—the design aimed at had been accomplished, and before the 1st of April the railroad was in running order.

With General McClellan's return to Washington on the 28th of February, preparations were begun for carrying out the wishes of the President and Secretary of War in regard to destroying the batteries on the Lower Potomac,—though in giving his hand to this movement General McClellan yielded his own judgment to theirs. He was convinced that this operation would require the movement of the entire army, that the extremely unfavorable condition of the roads was a serious obstacle to be overcome, and that it was unnecessary, because the proposed movement to the Lower Chesapeake would—as it subsequently did—force the enemy to abandon all his positions in front of Washington. But the preparations for a movement towards the Occoquan in order to carry the batteries were advanced as rapidly as the season permitted.

This brings us down to the 8th of March, 1862, —an important day in the history of the war. General McClellan had invited the commanders of divisions to meet at head-quarters on that day, in order to give them instructions and receive their advice and opinion in regard to their commands; but at a very early hour on the morning of that day he was sent for by the President, who expressed his dissatisfaction with the affair of Harper's Ferry and with the plans for the new movement down the Chesapeake. Explanations were made which, apparently, satisfied the President's mind. At a later hour in the day, the meeting of general officers which had been called was held at head-quarters. The officers present (besides General McClellan) were Generals McDowell, Sumner, Heintzelman, Keyes, Franklin, Fitz-John Porter, Andrew Porter, Smith, McCall, Blenker, Negley, and Barnard. The President of the United States was also there. The plans of General McClellan were fully explained to the council, and the general question submitted to them was whether the enemy should be attacked in front at Manassas and Centreville, or whether a movement should be made down to the Lower Chesapeake. After a full discussion, four of the officers—McDowell, Sumner, Heintzelman, and Barnard—approved of the former plan, and the remainder of the latter. The details were not considered as fixed; though it was generally understood that the point of destination and landing was Urbana, on the Rappahannock.

At the close of this council of officers, nothing had transpired to lead General McClellan to suppose that there was any lingering distrust of him in the President's mind; and he was therefore much and painfully surprised to learn that on that very 8th day of March the President, without consulting him, had issued two important military orders. The first of these was as follows:—

("President's General War Order, No. 2.)

"EXECUTIVE MANSION,
WASHINGTON, March 8, 1862.

"*Ordered*, 1st. That the major-general commanding the Army of the Potomac proceed forthwith to organize that part of the said army destined to enter upon active operations (including the reserve, but excluding the troops to be left in the fortifications about Washington) into four army corps, to be commanded, according to seniority of rank, as follows:—

"First Corps to consist of four divisions, and to be commanded by Major-General I. McDowell. Second Corps to consist of three divisions, and to be commanded by Brigadier-General E. V. Sumner. Third Corps to consist of three divisions, and to be commanded by Brigadier-

General S. P. Heintzelman. Fourth Corps to consist of three divisions, and to be commanded by Brigadier-General E. D. Keyes.

"2d. That the divisions now commanded by the officers above assigned to the commands of army corps shall be embraced in and form part of their respective corps.

"3d. The forces left for the defence of Washington will be placed in command of Brigadier-General James Wadsworth, who shall also be Military Governor of the District of Columbia.

"4th. That this order be executed with such promptness and despatch as not to delay the commencement of the operations already directed to be undertaken by the Army of the Potomac.

"5th. A Fifth Army Corps, to be commanded by Major-General N. P. Banks, will be formed from his own and General Shields's (late General Lander's) division.

"ABRAHAM LINCOLN."

This order was probably of no great practical importance, as it simply anticipated General McClellan's purpose. He had always been in favor of an organization into army corps, but preferred deferring its practical execution until some little experience in the coming campaign and on the field of battle should show what general officers were most competent to exercise these high commands, as an incompetent commander of an army corps might cause very serious damage, while an incompetent division commander could do no great harm. These views commend themselves to common sense; but they failed to convince the President's mind, who assumed a responsibility from which General McClellan at that time shrank. The latter at once issued the order necessary to carry out the command of the President.

The second of the orders issued by the President on the 8th of March was as follows:—

("President's General War Order, No. 3.)

"EXECUTIVE MANSION,
WASHINGTON, March 8, 1862.

"*Ordered*, That no change of the base of operations of the Army of the Potomac shall be made without leaving in and about Washington such a force as, in the opinion of the general-in-chief and the commanders of army corps, shall leave said city entirely secure.

"That no more than two army corps (about fifty thousand troops) of said Army of the Potomac shall be moved *en route* for a new base of operations until the navigation of the Potomac from Washington to the Chesapeake Bay shall be freed from enemy's batteries and other obstructions, or until the President shall hereafter give express permission.

"That any movement, as aforesaid, *en route* for a new base of operations which may be ordered by the general-in-chief, and which may be intended to move upon the Chesapeake Bay, shall begin to move upon the bay as early as the 18th of March instant; and the general-in-chief shall be responsible that it so moves as early as that day.

"*Ordered*, That the army and navy co-operate in an immediate effort to capture the enemy's batteries upon the Potomac between Washington and the Chesapeake Bay.

"ABRAHAM LINCOLN.

"L. THOMAS, *Adjutant-General*."

Here it will be seen that the President again assumes to fix a certain day in the future for the beginning of an important military movement.

Whether the army would be prepared to move upon the Bay on the 18th of March depended upon the state of readiness of the transports, the entire control of which had been placed by the Secretary of War in the hands of one of the assistant secretaries. Unless his arrangements had been completed on or before that day, the army could not have moved.

But the record of the important events of the 8th of March is not completed; for on that day the Merrimac appeared in Hampton Roads and destroyed the Cumberland and Congress, and the news, flashed far and wide by the telegraph-wires, filled the whole land with consternation and dismay. But our spirits rose the next day at the opportune arrival and gallant and successful achievement of the Monitor. It is needless to dwell upon the memorable contest between these two vessels, so important in its effects upon the whole science of naval warfare; but it was an event of no inconsiderable moment in the fate and fortunes of the Peninsular campaign. The power of the Monitor had been so satisfactorily demonstrated, and the other naval preparations were so extensive and formidable, that the security of Fortress Monroe as a base of operations was placed beyond a doubt; but, on the other hand, the presence of the Merrimac in the James River closed that river to us, and threw us upon the York River, with its tributaries, as our only line of water-communication with the fortress. The general plan, therefore, remained undisturbed, though less promising in its details than when James River was in our control.

On Sunday, the 9th of March, trustworthy information came to Washington that the enemy was beginning to evacuate his positions at Centreville and Manassas, as well as on the Upper and Lower Potomac. It is not improbable that, in some mysterious way, they had heard of the council of general officers held on the preceding day, and of the conclusions arrived at.*

---

* "We have the right, we think, to say that McClellan never intended to advance upon Centreville. His long-determined purpose was to make Washington safe by means of a strong garrison, and then to use the great navigable waters and immense naval resources of the North to transport the army by sea to a point near Richmond. For weeks—perhaps for months—this plan had been secretly maturing. Secrecy as well as promptness, it will be understood, was indispensable here to success. To keep the secret, it had been necessary to confide it to few persons; and hence had arisen one great cause for jealousy of the general.

"Be this as it may, as the day of action drew near, those who suspected the general's project and were angry at not being informed of it,—those whom his promotion had excited to envy,—his political enemies (who is without them in America?) —in short, all those beneath or beside him who wished him ill,—broke out into a chorus of accusations of slowness, inaction, incapacity. McClellan, with a patriotic courage which I have always admired, disdained these accusations, and made no reply. He satisfied himself with pursuing his preparations in laborious silence. But the moment came in which, notwithstanding the loyal support given him by the President, that functionary could no longer resist the tempest. A council of war of all the divisional generals was held; a plan of campaign,

As soon as the news came, General McClellan determined to cross the river immediately and ascertain by observation whether the intelligence was true, and then determine what course to pursue. Orders were accordingly issued, during the 9th of March, for a general movement of the army the next morning towards Centreville and Manassas, sending in advance two regiments of cavalry as a corps of observation. At noon on the 10th of March the cavalry advance reached the enemy's lines at Centreville, finding there still burning heaps of military

---

not that of McClellan, was proposed and discussed. McClellan was then forced to explain his projects, and the next day they were known to the enemy Informed, no doubt, by one of those thousand female spies who keep up his communications into the domestic circles of the Federal enemy, Johnston evacuated Manassas at once This was a skilful manœuvre. Incapable of assuming the offensive, threatened with attack either at Centreville, where defence would be useless if successful, or at Richmond, the loss of which would be a grave check, and unable to cover both positions at once, Johnston threw his whole force before the latter of the two."

The above is taken from a pamphlet published in New York, in 1863, with the following title:—"The Army of the Potomac: its Organization, its Commander, and its Campaign. By the Prince de Joinville. Translated from the French, with Notes, by William Henry Hurlbert." The original appeared in the number of the "Revue des Deux Mondes" for October 15, 1862. It is there entitled "Campagne de l'Armée du Potomac, Mars–Juillet, 1862," and bears the signature of "A. Trognon." The article has been generally ascribed to the Prince de Joinville; and, as the translation bears his name on the title-page and has been constantly referred to as his, the future extracts from the pamphlet will be cited under his name.

stores and much valuable property. The mass of the army advanced to the vicinity of Fairfax Court-House, and General McClellan himself went to Manassas. The roads were in so impassable a condition that a rapid pursuit of an enemy who burned or broke up all the bridges behind him in his retreat was impossible. The main body of the army was on the 15th of March moved back to the vicinity of Alexandria, to be embarked. It was while General McClellan was absent on this brief reconnoissance in force that the President saw fit to remove him from the position of general-in-chief, by the following order, which appeared in the "National Intelligencer" of March 12, and which General McClellan heard of for the first time at Fairfax Court-House.

("President's War Order, No. 3.)

"EXECUTIVE MANSION,
WASHINGTON, March 11, 1862.

"Major-General McClellan having personally taken the field at the head of the Army of the Potomac, until otherwise ordered, he is relieved from the command of the other military departments, he retaining command of the Department of the Potomac.

"*Ordered, further*, That the departments now under the respective commands of Generals Halleck and Hunter, together with so much of that under General Buell as lies west of a north-and-south line indefinitely drawn through Knoxville, Tennessee, be consolidated, and designated the Department of the Mississippi; and that, until otherwise ordered, Major-General Halleck have command of said department.

"*Ordered, also,* That the country west of the Department of the Potomac and east of the Department of the Mississippi be a military department, to be called the Mountain Department, and that the same be commanded by Major-General Frémont.

"That all the commanders of departments, after the receipt of this order by them, respectively report severally and directly to the Secretary of War, and that prompt, full, and frequent reports will be expected of all and each of them.

"ABRAHAM LINCOLN."

Whatever emotions General McClellan may have felt on reading this order, his sense of duty as a patriotic citizen, and his instincts of obedience as a soldier, taught him to suppress all expression of them; and, in a note addressed by him to the President on the 12th of March, the next day, he said, in language alike distinguished for good feeling and good taste,—

"I believe I said to you, some weeks since, in connection with some Western matters, that no feeling of self-interest or ambition should ever prevent me from devoting myself to the service. I am glad to have the opportunity to prove it; and you will find that, under present circumstances, I shall work just as cheerfully as before, and that no consideration of self will in any manner interfere with the discharge of my public duties."

On the 13th of March a council of war was assembled at Fairfax Court-House, to discuss the military position. The President's order No. 3, of March 8, was considered. As future events made the action of this council of considerable importance, the memorandum of its proceedings is here given in full:—

"HEAD-QUARTERS, ARMY OF THE POTOMAC,
FAIRFAX COURT-HOUSE, March 13, 1862.

"A council of the generals commanding army corps, at the head-quarters of the Army of the Potomac, were of the opinion—

"I. That the enemy having retreated from Manassas to Gordonsville, behind the Rappahannock and Rapidan, it is the opinion of generals commanding army corps that the operations to be carried on will be best undertaken from Old Point Comfort, between the York and James Rivers: *Provided*—

"1st. That the enemy's vessel, Merrimac, can be neutralized.

"2d. That the means of transportation sufficient for an immediate transfer of the force to its new base can be ready at Washington and Alexandria to move down the Potomac; and,

"3d. That a naval auxiliary force can be had to silence, or aid in silencing, the enemy's batteries on the York River.

"4th. That the force to be left to cover Washington shall be such as to give an entire feeling of security for its safety from menace. (Unanimous.)

"II. If the foregoing cannot be, the army should then be moved against the enemy, behind the Rappahannock, at the earliest possible moment, and the means for reconstructing bridges, repairing railroads, and stocking them with materials sufficient for supplying the army should at once be collected for both the Orange & Alexandria and Acquia & Richmond Railroads. (Unanimous.)

"N.B.—That, with the forts on the right bank of the Potomac fully garrisoned, and those on the left bank occupied, a covering force in front of the Virginia line of twenty-five thousand men would suffice. (Keyes, Heintzelman, and McDowell.) A total of forty thousand men for the defence of the city would suffice. (Sumner.)"

This was assented to by General McClellan, and immediately communicated to the War Department; and on the same day the following reply was received:—

"WAR DEPARTMENT, March 13, 1862.

"The President, having considered the plan of operations agreed upon by yourself and the commanders of army corps, makes no objection to the same, but gives the following directions as to its execution:—

"1. Leave such force at Manassas Junction as shall make it entirely certain that the enemy shall not repossess himself of that position and line of communication.

"2. Leave Washington entirely secure.

"3. Move the remainder of the force down the Potomac, choosing a new base at Fortress Monroe, or anywhere between here and there; or, at all events, move such remainder of the army at once in pursuit of the enemy by some route.

"EDWIN M. STANTON,
"*Secretary of War.*

"Major-General GEORGE B. MCCLELLAN."

On the 14th day of March, General McClellan issued the following address to his soldiers:—

"HEAD-QUARTERS, ARMY OF THE POTOMAC,
FAIRFAX COURT-HOUSE, VA., March 14, 1862.

"SOLDIERS OF THE ARMY OF THE POTOMAC:—

"For a long time I have kept you inactive, but not without a purpose. You were to be disciplined, armed, and instructed; the formidable artillery you now have had to be created; other armies were to move and accomplish certain results. I have held you back that you might give the death-blow to the rebellion that has distracted our once happy country. The patience you have shown, and your confidence in your general, are worth a dozen victories. These preliminary results are now accomplished. I feel that the patient labors of many months have produced their fruit: the Army of the Potomac is now a real army, magnificent in material, admirable in discipline and instruction, excellently equipped and armed; your commanders are all that I could wish. The moment for action has arrived, and I know that I can trust in you to save our country. As I ride through your ranks, I see in your faces the sure presage of victory; I feel that you will do whatever I ask of you. The period of inaction has passed. I will bring you now face to face with the rebels, and only pray that God may defend the right. In whatever direction you may move, however strange my actions may appear to you, ever bear in mind that my fate is linked with yours, and that all I do is to bring you, where I know you wish to be, on the decisive battle-field. It is my business to place you there. I am to watch over you as a parent over his children; and you know that your general loves you from the depths of his heart. It shall be my care, as it has ever been, to gain success with the least possible loss; but I know that, if it is necessary, you will willingly follow me to our graves for our righteous cause. God smiles upon us, victory attends us. Yet I would not have you think that our aim is to be attained without a manly struggle. I will not disguise it from you: you have brave foes to encounter, foemen well worthy of the steel that you will use so well. I shall demand of you great, heroic exertions, rapid and long marches, desperate combats, privations perhaps. We will share all these together; and, when this sad war is over, we will return to our homes and feel that we can ask no higher honor than the proud consciousness that we belonged to the Army of the Potomac.

"GEO. B. MCCLELLAN,
"*Major-General commanding.*"

Preparations were immediately begun, in compliance with the directions contained in the letter from the Secretary of War of March 13, above given. On the 16th of March, General McClellan addressed a letter of instructions to General Banks to post his command in the vicinity of Manassas and intrench himself strongly there, for the general object of covering the line of the Potomac and Washington; and on the same day a similar letter of instructions was addressed by him to General Wadsworth, who was in command at Washington, giving him minute and detailed directions as to the military precautions to be taken to keep the capital secure.

The Secretary of War having expressed a desire that General McClellan should communicate to the Departments, in an official form, his designs with regard to the employment of the Army of the Potomac, the latter addressed to the Department a note under date of March 19, in which he unfolds briefly his plan, sets forth its advantages, and states what will be requisite to insure its successful accomplishment. He especially urges the absolute necessity of a full co-operation of the navy in a combined naval and land attack upon Yorktown, as a part of his programme. He enforces this view by many considerations, and thus concludes his communication:—

"It may be summed up in a few words, that for the prompt success of this campaign it is absolutely necessary that the navy should at once throw its whole available force, its most powerful vessels, against Yorktown. There is the most important point,—there the knot to be cut. An immediate decision upon the subject-matter of this communication is highly desirable, and seems called for by the exigencies of the occasion."

In the mean time, the troops destined to form the active army were collected in camps convenient to the points of embarkation, and every preparation was made to despatch them as rapidly as possible when the transports should be ready. While the army was still encamped at Alexandria, a few days before sailing for Fortress Monroe, General McClellan met the President, by appointment, on board a steamer, and was told by the President that he had been strongly pressed to take General Blenker's division from his (General McClellan's) command and give it to General Frémont; but he, however, suggested many considerations in opposition to this step, and frankly and voluntarily avowed his purpose of allowing the division to remain with the Army of the Potomac. The astonishment, therefore, of General McClellan may well be imagined when by the receipt of the following note he learned that the President had changed his mind, and determined upon a measure the inexpediency of which was so obvious to him but a few days before:—

"EXECUTIVE MANSION,
WASHINGTON, March 31, 1862.

"MY DEAR SIR:—This morning I felt constrained to order Blenker's division to Frémont; and I write this to assure you that I did so with great pain, understanding that you would wish it otherwise. If you could know the full pressure of the case, I am confident that you would justify it, even beyond a mere acknowledgment that the commander-in-chief may order what he pleases.

"Yours, very truly,
"A. LINCOLN.

"Major-General McCLELLAN."

The weak and deprecatory tone of this note disarms, or at least alloys with contempt, the indignation justly awakened by the deliberate breach of faith which it confesses; but it is a melancholy fact that at so critical a period the reins of executive power were in hands that held them with so slack a grasp, and that the President, by yielding to unknown and irresponsible advisers in the conduct of a campaign, seemingly acted as if he thought that many bad generals were better than one good one.

General McClellan could only acquiesce in the latest decision of the President, not suppressing some natural expressions of surprise; but he was relieved by the President's positive and emphatic assurance that he might be confident that in no event should any more troops be detached from his command. General Blenker's division consisted of about ten thousand men.

On the 1st of April, General McClellan addressed

another letter of instruction to General Banks, founded upon the retreat of General Jackson up the Valley of the Shenandoah, and the change for the better in the military position of the Federal cause in that region.

In view of events which subsequently occurred, and of questions which were subsequently raised, it becomes of importance here that the reader should understand how far the defence of Washington was provided for before the Army of the Potomac was withdrawn.

In the first place, the city itself was defended by a strong system of fortifications, built under the directions of General Barnard, and sweeping round a line of thirty-three miles in extent. The troops which were assigned to garrison these fortifications were eighteen thousand in number, with thirty-two field-guns. At Manassas there were ten thousand men; on the Lower Potomac, thirteen hundred; in the Valley of the Shenandoah, thirty-five thousand. Thus, without including General Blenker's division, which was at Warrenton, there were about sixty-three thousand men disposed at various points for the protection of Washington, together with eighty-five pieces of light artillery, including the thirty-two above mentioned. There was also a body of troops in New York, over four thousand in number, which General McClellan recommended to have sent to Washington to reinforce the garrison there.

These forces were deemed by him amply adequate to insure the safety of Washington and to give everybody there an entire sense of security,—

a conclusion not to be doubted, as the following facts show.

There was no reason to apprehend an attack by way of Manassas and Centreville; for the enemy in their retreat across the Rappahannock had destroyed all the railroad-bridges behind them. Had they attempted such a movement, their progress must have been very slow; for they must have rebuilt their bridges, and this would have announced their purpose beforehand and afforded ample time to concentrate a large body of forces at Washington.

Nor was there any real ground of apprehension from the Valley of the Shenandoah; because the movement of the army on Richmond would make it impossible for the enemy to leave in that region men enough to overpower the large body of troops we had there. But, in General McClellan's opinion, the way to defend Washington was to attack Richmond; and the greater the force thrown against the rebel capital, the greater the security of our own. Strongly fortified as Washington was, capable of being readily reinforced from the North, it was manifest that the enemy could not afford to detach from his main army a force sufficient to capture it.

Here were solid grounds enough, it would appear, for General McClellan's conclusion that he had left Washington perfectly safe; but, unhappily, fears, panics, and apprehensions take their rise in that part of the mind which is not reached by the voice of reason. Whether Washington were safe or not was a matter of sound military judgment; but as a matter of fact it is certain that from the moment the Army of the Potomac landed upon the Peninsula an uneasy sense of insecurity took possession of the minds of the President, the Cabinet, and the members of Congress. The public in general shared this feeling; and the Northern press encouraged and increased it. All over the loyal States the question of the safety of Washington was discussed, with abundant zeal and very little knowledge. Some of this alarm may have been counterfeited for political effect; but without doubt much of it was real; and this should be borne in mind, when discussing measures subsequently adopted, disastrous in their consequences, but, unquestionably, inspired by an honest but miserable fright. It was destined, in the providence of God, that our cause should suffer alike from unreasonable hopes and extravagant fears.

CHAPTER VII.

ALEXANDRIA was selected as the point of departure, and the embarkation began on the 17th of March. The removal of a large body of troops, including cavalry and artillery, with armaments and supplies, was of necessity a slow work; and more than a fortnight elapsed before the whole force was transported. General McClellan reached Fortress Monroe on the 2d of April. He had in all between fifty and sixty thousand men with him; and others were to follow as fast as means of transportation could be supplied.

It should here be borne in mind, as a matter of mere justice to General McClellan, that for the successful execution of his projected expedition he had required that the whole of the four corps under his command should be employed, with the addition of ten thousand men drawn from the forces in the vicinity of Fortress Monroe,—that position and its dependencies being regarded as amply protected by the naval force in its neighborhood. Before he left Washington, an order had been issued by the War Department, placing Fortress Monroe and its dependencies under his control, and authorizing him to draw from the troops under General Wool a division of about ten thousand men. And, in addition to the land-forces, the co-operation of the navy was deemed essential in order to reduce or silence the strong batteries which the Confederates had erected at Yorktown and Gloucester.

But he had hardly landed upon the Peninsula when he was doomed to taste the bitterness of disappointed hope, and by another experience to have the conviction forced upon him that the Administration was unfaithful to him. During the night of the 3d of April, he received a telegram from the Adjutant-General of the army, stating that, by the President's order, he was deprived of all control over General Wool and the troops under his command, and forbidden, without that officer's sanction, to detach any portion of his force. No causes were assigned, or have ever been assigned, for this order, which was in violation of a deliberate and official engagement, and left the general in command of a most important military movement without any base of operations under his own control, —a situation without parallel, it is believed, in military history.

Nor was this all. The terrible Merrimac lay, "hushed in grim repose," in the James River; and no one knew when she might reappear or in how formidable a guise. Admiral Goldsborough, then in command of the United States squadron in Hampton Roads, felt, and with justice, that it was his paramount duty to watch the Merrimac; and he, consequently, did not venture to detach for the assistance of the army a suitable force to attack the water-batteries at Yorktown and Gloucester. This was contrary to what General McClellan had been led to expect, and a serious derangement of his plans.

In fact, it should be remembered that during the operations against Yorktown the navy was not able to lend the army any material assistance till after the siege-guns had partially silenced the enemy's water-batteries.

But the heaviest blow was yet to come. On the 4th of April the following telegram was received:—

"Adjutant-General's Office, April 4, 1862.

"By direction of the President, General McDowell's army corps has been detached from the force under your immediate command, and the general is ordered to report to the Secretary of War. Letter by mail.

"L. THOMAS,
"*Adjutant-General.*

"General McCLELLAN."

This fell with crushing weight upon General McClellan's hopes. Its effect upon him cannot be better described than in his own simple language,—the force of which could not be increased by any attempt at rhetorical embellishment:—

"The President having promised, in our interview following his order of March 31, withdrawing Blenker's division of ten thousand men from my command, that nothing of the sort should be repeated,—that I might rest assured that the campaign should proceed, with no further deductions from the force upon which its operations had been planned,—I may confess to having been shocked at this order, which, with that of the 31st ultimo and that of the 3d, removed nearly sixty thousand men from my command, and reduced my force by more than one-third, after its task had been assigned, its operations planned, its fighting begun. To me the blow was most discouraging. It frustrated all my plans for impending operations. It fell when I was too deeply committed to withdraw. It left me incapable of continuing operations which had been begun. It compelled the adoption of another, a different and a less effective, plan of campaign. It made rapid and brilliant operations impossible. It was a fatal error."

General McClellan's plan had been, if the works at Yorktown and Williamsburg offered a serious resistance, that General McDowell's corps should land on the left bank of the York, or on the Severn, so as to move upon Gloucester and West Point, in order to take in reverse whatever force the enemy might have on the Peninsula and compel him to abandon his positions. But, since McDowell's corps was withheld, this plan, of course, became impossible, and there was no choice left but to attack the enemy's positions directly in front. And a grave question now rose,—whether these positions should be assaulted or invested. The problem presented was not easy of solution.

From the moment of landing upon the Peninsula, it became obvious that the difficulties in the advance to Richmond were sufficient to task all the resources of the general in command, even if he had been furnished with the entire force promised him,—which he had not been. The nature of the country is very unfavorable to an invading army, and to the same extent favorable to a force which stands upon the defensive. It is a low, flat region, little elevated above the level of the sea, thinly inhabited, and scourged with malaria for many weeks of the year. It is covered with marshy forests; and the roads which traverse it hardly deserve the name. It is everywhere veined with streams and water-courses, which flow lazily along their level beds, and, by the copious rains which fall there, are easily swollen into broad and shallow lakes. The earth was constantly saturated with moisture, and the mud was deep, pitiless, and universal. After a rain, the so-called roads became utterly impracticable for any kind of wheeled vehicle. The wagons stuck hopelessly fast in the tenacious mire; and to transport them it became necessary to construct corduroy roads,—a slow and toilsome process.

And, strange to say, though this was the earliest-settled portion of the whole country and full of historical interest, serious difficulties were encountered from the want of accurate topographical knowledge of the region before them. The common maps were found to be so incorrect as to be of little or no value. Reconnoissances, frequently made at great risk, proved the only trustworthy sources of information.

The progress of our army would have been slow had natural difficulties alone been in their path; but they found themselves met by a foe whose courage and energy they were too brave themselves not to respect. Among the Confederates there were unity of purpose and concerted action towards a common end. They knew that time was on their side, and their great object was to gain time and delay our progress as much as possible. Since leaving Manassas, they had been diligently at work, without the loss of an hour, in strengthening all available points by skilfully constructed works. It was found that Warwick River was controlled by the Confederate gunboats for some distance from its mouth,—that the fords had been destroyed by dams, the approaches to which were generally through dense forests and deep swamps and defended by extensive and formidable works,—and that Yorktown was strongly fortified, armed and garrisoned, and connected with the defences of the Warwick by forts and intrenchments, the ground in front of which was swept by the guns of Yorktown.

After close personal reconnoissance, and after careful reflection and consultation, General McClellan determined not to attempt to carry the lines of Yorktown by immediate assault, but to assail it by the regular operations of a siege. As this decision has been severely criticized by writers who conduct campaigns in their studies and judge of military movements and military men by the light of subsequent events, it may be well to pause for a moment and consider briefly the grounds of his determination.

He had with him at that time—General Franklin's division not having then arrived—but a little over fifty thousand men. The number of the Confederate forces was not known; but General Johnston had reached Yorktown on the 6th of April with heavy reinforcements, and it was believed that the whole force of the enemy was, or soon would be, not less than a hundred thousand men. Our troops were admirable troops, as their subsequent conduct abundantly showed; but they were comparatively new; and nothing tries the temper and nerve of the soldier so much as the assault of a strongly-defended place.

General Barnard, Chief Engineer of the army, whose position entitled his opinion to the highest consideration, expressed his judgment that the works could not with any reasonable degree of certainty be carried by assault. There are copious extracts from his Report embodied in that of

General McClellan. The details are too technical to be fully understood by the general reader; but a single sentence will serve to show what our assaulting force must have been prepared to meet:—

"It will be seen, therefore, that our approaches were swept by the fire of at least forty-nine guns, nearly all of which were heavy, and many of them the most formidable guns known. Besides that, two-thirds of the guns of the water-batteries, and all the guns of Gloucester, bore on our right batteries, though under disadvantageous circumstances."

It is true that General Barnard has since changed his mind, and given it as his opinion that the lines of Yorktown should have been assaulted; but it is clear that General McClellan had an opposite judgment given at the time and on the spot and under the gravest official responsibility.*

---

* This second, or retrospective, Report of General Barnard was made in January, 1863, at a time when General McClellan was living in retirement and out of favor with the Administration. The Congressional Committee on the Conduct of the War copy several of its paragraphs into their Report on the Army of the Potomac; and the whole of it may be found at page 394 of their Proceedings, Part First, appended to General Barnard's testimony. The Report of the Committee has been translated into French, and published, with notes, by Colonel Lecomte, an accomplished Swiss officer who served on General McClellan's staff during the Peninsular campaign. One of General Barnard's paragraphs which the Committee copy is as follows:—"However I may be committed to any expression of professional opinion to the contrary (I certainly did suggest it), my opinion now is that the lines of Yorktown

General McClellan, on the 7th of April, sent a long telegram to the Secretary of War, in which he explained the reasons why an instant assault was

---

should have been assaulted. There is reason to believe that they were not held in strong force when our army appeared before them; and we know that they were far from complete. The prestige of power, the *morale*, were on our side. It was due to ourselves to confirm and sustain it. We should probably have succeeded. But, if we had failed, it may be well doubted whether the shock of an unsuccessful assault would be more demoralizing than the labors of a siege."

Upon the above, Colonel Lecomte remarks, "We are the more astonished at this retrospective confidence of General Barnard, because, on the spot, the engineer officers who were associated with him, and he himself, we believe, repeatedly expressed very different opinions."

General Barnard further says, "The siege having been determined upon, we should have opened our batteries upon the place as fast as they were completed. The effect on our troops would have been inspiring. It would have lightened the siege and shortened our labors; and, besides, we should have had the credit of driving the enemy from Yorktown by force of arms,—whereas, as it was, we only induced him to evacuate for prudential reasons."

Upon which Colonel Lecomte remarks, "This is not certain. On the contrary, nothing discourages an army and inspirits the enemy more than a fire of artillery that begins feebly, without taking into account that in this way the calibre of the pieces is revealed. And as to the 'credit' of taking Yorktown by force of arms, this slight advantage might also have been doubtful; because, unless we had inflicted heavy loss upon the enemy and taken many prisoners at the very moment of evacuation (which was hardly to be expected), they might have pretended that they repulsed us, and only evacuated the place, later, for prudential reasons."

not to be made, prominent among which was the limited amount of force as yet under his control. This was replied to by the President, in a letter dated April 9, in which he restates the grounds on which Blenker's division had been kept back, and shows that his mind was still not free from apprehensions as to the safety of Washington! The concluding paragraphs are as follow:—

"I suppose the whole force which has gone forward for you is with you by this time. And, if so, I think it is the precise time for you to strike a blow. By delay the enemy will relatively gain upon you; that is, he will gain faster by fortifications and reinforcements than you can by reinforcements alone. And once more let me tell you, it is indispensable to you that you strike a blow. I am powerless to help this. You will do me the justice to remember I always insisted that going down the bay in search of a field, instead of fighting at or near Manassas, was only shifting, and not surmounting, a difficulty,—that we would find the same enemy and the same or equal intrenchments at either place. The country will not fail to note--is now noting—that the present hesitation to move upon an intrenched enemy is but the story of Manassas repeated.

"I beg to assure you that I have never written you or spoken to you in greater kindness of feeling than now, nor with a fuller purpose to sustain you, so far as, in my most anxious judgment, I consistently can. But you must act.

"Yours, very truly,

"A. LINCOLN.

"Major-General McCLELLAN."

To these considerations General McClellan replies, in his Report, in a few words, which are here quoted, as they can hardly be improved:—

"His Excellency could not judge of the formidable character of the works before us as well as if he had been on the ground; and, whatever might have been his desire for prompt action (certainly no greater than mine), I feel confident, if he could have made a personal inspection of the enemy's defences, he would have forbidden me risking the safety of the army and the possible successes of the campaign on a sanguinary assault of an advantageous and formidable position, which, even if successful, could not have been followed up to any other or better result than would have been reached by the regular operations of a siege. Still less could I forego the conclusions of my most instructed judgment for the mere sake of avoiding the personal consequences intimated in the President's despatch."

The investment of Yorktown, as it proved, cost a month of valuable time,—which certainly was no inconsiderable gain to the enemy; but, on the other hand, it cost us no loss of life. We got it at last without bloodshed. But suppose General McClellan had assaulted it early in April, as now he is blamed by many for not having done, and, after the frightful carnage which must have been the result of such an attempt,—after thousands of the flower of our population had been mowed down by a tempest of iron hail, as grass falls before the mower's scythe,—the attack had been at last unsuccessful, as was the Duke of Wellington's upon Burgos: what would have been the public feeling,—bearing in mind always that the judgment of the Chief Engineer,

General Barnard, was against an assault? Would not such a storm of indignation have been raised against General McClellan as would have compelled his sacrifice at the hands of an Administration not inclined—perhaps not able—to resist that sweeping power of public opinion which moves and rages with more than "the force of winds and waters pent"?*

On the 22d of April, while the siege of Yorktown was going on, General Franklin's division, forming part of General McDowell's corps, arrived, and reported to General McClellan. These troops were kept on board the transports, and not employed for some days. It was General McClellan's purpose to act on Gloucester by disembarking this division on the north bank of the York River, under the protection of the gunboats, but subsequent events rendered the movement unnecessary.

Our batteries would have been ready to open upon Yorktown on the morning of the 6th of May at latest; but in the nights of the 3d and 4th of May, that position and the Confederate lines of the

* "Many of Lord Wellington's proceedings might be called rash, and others timid and slow, if taken separately: yet, when viewed as parts of a great plan for delivering the whole Peninsula, they will be found discreet or daring, as the circumstances warranted. Nor is there any portion of his campaigns that requires this wide-based consideration more than his early sieges, which, being instituted contrary to the rules of art, and unsuccessful,—or, when successful, attended with a mournful slaughter,—have given occasion for questioning his great military qualities, which were, however, then most signally displayed."—NAPIER.

Warwick River were evacuated. This work was doubtless commenced some days before, and was conducted with skill and energy. On the 3d, with a view of masking their retreat, the fire of their batteries was unusually severe.

The Confederates left behind them all their heavy guns, eighty in number, each piece supplied with seventy-six rounds of ammunition. A large amount of warlike stores of every description was also abandoned or destroyed. The evacuation is said to have been the result of a council of war at which President Davis and Generals Lee and Johnston were present, and to have been very distasteful to General Magruder, the officer in command, who did not like to retire from his works without a fight.

THE BATTLE OF WILLIAMSBURG.

After the evacuation of Yorktown, the next important point before the Federal army was the city of Williamsburg, the Colonial capital of Virginia. It is about ten miles from Yorktown, and is on the narrowest part of the peninsula between the James and York Rivers, being about three miles from the former, and five and a quarter from the latter.

On the 4th of May, immediately after the evacuation of Yorktown, a portion of the army was put in motion to pursue the flying foe, and General Franklin's division was ordered to move by water to the vicinity of West Point, to cut off the enemy's retreat in that direction. General Stoneman led the advance upon Williamsburg with the entire cavalry force and four batteries of horse-artillery, as fast as the muddy condition of the roads would permit, and, on reaching a space where the roads from Yorktown and Warwick Court-House debouch upon the isthmus, he found a large Confederate force in a strongly-defended position. After sustaining and repelling a cavalry charge of the enemy, and gallantly returning with his batteries the fire of their artillery, as he had no infantry to carry the works, he withdrew his command and fell back to a clearing about half a mile distant.

By this time night was falling. The Federal infantry had come up slowly, retarded by the bad state of the roads, and it was completely dark before they arrived in full force; and, though General Sumner, who had come up and assumed the command, desired to make an attempt to carry the works that night, it was impossible to do so, owing to the late hour and the darkness. The troops bivouacked in the woods, and, unfortunately, a heavy rain set in, and continued for thirty hours, converting the country into a vast lake and the roads into channels of liquid mud. The battle of the next day cannot be better described than in the clear and graphic language of the Prince de Joinville, besides which his account contains the criticism of a candid and intelligent observer upon a defect in the organization of our armies, which is the more worthy of our consideration because offered in so kindly a spirit.

"Next day the battle began again, but, of course, in circumstances unfavorable to the Federals. The two roads leading to Williamsburg were crowded with troops. Upon that to the left from Lee's Mill were the divisions of Hooker and Kearney, belonging to Heintzelman's corps; but they were separated from each other by an enormous multitude of wagons loaded down with baggage and for the most part fast in the mud. Upon that to the right, two other divisions were moving forward with still greater difficulty. Such was the condition of the ground that the cannon sank over the axle into the mud. This medley of men and baggage thrown pellmell into narrow and flooded roads had fallen into considerable disorder. In the United States there is no such thing as a corps of the general staff. The American system of 'every man for himself,' individually applied by the officers and soldiers of each corps to one another, is also applied by the corps themselves to their reciprocal relations. There is no special branch of the service whose duty it is to regulate, centralize, and direct the movements of the army. In such a case as this of which we are speaking, we should have seen the general staff officers of a French army taking care that nothing should impede the advance of the troops, stopping a file of wagons here and ordering it out of the road to clear the way, sending on a detail of men there to repair the roadway or to draw a cannon out of the mire, in order to communicate to every corps-commander the orders of the general-in-chief.

"Here, nothing of the sort is done. The functions of the adjutant-general are limited to the transmission of the orders of the general. He has nothing to do with seeing that they are executed. The general has no one to bear his orders but aides-de-camp, who have the best intentions in the world, and are excellent at repeating mechanically a verbal order, but to whom nobody pays much attention if they undertake to exercise any initiative whatever. Down to the present moment, although this want of a general staff had been often felt, its consequences had not been serious. We had the telegraph, which followed the army everywhere and kept up communications between the different corps: the generals could converse together and inform each other of any thing that it was important to know. But, once on the march, this resource was lost to us, and so farewell to our communications!

"The want of a general staff was not less severely felt in obtaining and transmitting the information necessary at the moment of an impending action. No one knew the country; the maps were so defective that they were useless. Little was known about the fortified battle-field on which the army was about to be engaged. Yet this battle-field had been seen and reconnoitred the day before by the troops which had taken part in Stoneman's skirmish. Enough was surely known of it for us to combine a plan of attack and assign to every commander his own part in the work. No! this was not so. Every one kept his observations to himself,—not from ill will, but because it was nobody's special duty to do this general work. It was a defect in the organization; and, with the best elements in the world, an army which is not organized cannot expect great success. It is fortunate if it escape great disaster.

"Thanks to this constitutional defect of the Federal armies, Hooker's division, which led the column on the left-hand road, and had received, the day before, a general order to march upon Williamsburg, came out on the morning of the 5th upon the scene of Stoneman's cavalry-fight, without the least knowledge of what it was to meet there. Received, as soon as it appeared, with a steady fire from the hostile works, it deployed resolutely in the abatis and went into action. But it came up little by little and alone,—whilst the defence was carried on by from fifteen to twenty thousand men strongly intrenched. The odds were too great.

"Hooker, who is an admirable soldier, held his own for some time; but he had to give way and fall back, leaving in the woods and in these terrible abatis some two thousand of his men killed and wounded, with several of his guns which he could not bring off. The enemy followed him as he fell back. The division of General Kearney, having passed the crowded road, and marching upon the guns at the *pas de course*, re-established the battle. The fight had now rolled from the edges of the plain into the forest; and it was sharp, for the enemy was strongly reinforced. The Federals fought not less firmly, encouraged by their chiefs, Hooker, Heintzelman, and Kearney. Kearney in especial, who lost an arm in Mexico, and fought with the French at the Muzaia and at Solferino, had displayed the finest courage.* All his

* "The general acceded to his urgent request, and immediately ordered up Kearney's division to his aid. He could not have sent a better man. Kearney was of that chivalrous character so often to be met with in the French army. He had lost an arm in the Mexican War, and he afterwards joined the French army as a volunteer aide-de-camp in the Italian campaign, greatly distinguishing himself at both Solferino and Magenta. Kearney brought up his men at the double quick to support Hooker, although the execrable state of the roads somewhat retarded him; but he eventually reached the hard-pressed division. It was a fine sight to see Kearney lead on his men, eager for the fight as they were. He seemed to be ubiquitous,—now leading on his centre, now ordering up a battery, in another moment charging at the head of his troops. His striking, manly form was prominent wherever the fight was thickest, setting a noble example to his soldiers. The opposing troops were soon intermingled in a regular *mêlée*, and both sides fought desperately. Owing to the state of the ground, our cavalry was not serviceable, much to the regret of its officers: it was also very diffi-

aides had fallen around him, and, left alone, he had electrified his men by his intrepidity. During all this time the part of the army massed on the road to the right remained passive. A single division only had come up, and the generals in command could not resolve to throw it into the engagement without seeing its supports. These supports were delayed by the swollen streams, the encumbered roads, the shattered wagons sticking in the mud.

"But all the while the sound of Hooker's musketry was in our ears. His division was cut up and falling back. His guns had been heard at first in front, then on one side, and they were receding still. The balls and the shells began to whistle and shatter the trees over the fresh division, as it stood immovable and expectant.

"It was now three o'clock, and the generals resolved to act. One division passed through the woods to flank the regiments which were driving Hooker, while to the extreme right a brigade passed the creek on an old mill-bridge, which the enemy had failed to secure, and debouched upon the flank of the Williamsburg works. The Confederates did not expect this attack, which, if successful, must sweep every thing before it. They despatched two brigades, which advanced resolutely through the corn-fields to drive back the Federals. The latter coolly allowed their foes to come up, and received them with a tremendous fire of artillery. The Confederates,

---

cult for the artillery to manœuvre. The struggle, which had commenced at the verge of a wood, was gradually drawn into the forest itself, and here, under the cracking branches of venerable trees, amidst the roar of the artillery, many desperate hand-to-hand encounters took place, such as have seldom been witnessed in other wars."—*Estvan's War-Pictures from the South*, p. 277.

The author of the above work was a Prussian officer, serving in the Confederate army.

unshaken, pushed on within thirty yards of the cannon's mouth, shouting, 'Bull Run! Bull Run!' as the Swiss used to shout, 'Granson! Granson!' There, however, they wavered, and the Federal General Hancock, seizing the moment, cried to his soldiers, as he waved his cap, 'Now, gentlemen! the bayonet!' and charged with his brigade. The enemy could not withstand the shock, broke and fled, strewing the field with his dead. At this very moment General McClellan, who had been detained at Yorktown, appeared on the field. It was dusk: the night was coming on, the rain still falling in torrents. On three sides of the plateau on which the general was, the cannon and the musketry were rattling uninterruptedly. The success of Hancock had been decisive, and the reserves brought up by the general-in-chief, charging upon the field, settled the affair. Then it was that I saw General McClellan, passing in front of the Sixth Cavalry, give his hand to Major Williams, with a few words on his brilliant charge of the day before. The regiment did not hear what he said; but it knew what he meant, and from every heart went up one of those masculine, terrible shouts which are only to be heard on the field of battle.* These shouts, taken up along the whole

* "Suddenly a shout of a thousand voices broke upon the air, like the rushing of a mighty wind from the wood. What did this portend? There was little time left for us to speculate. Charge after charge was made upon our men, and the news then spread that General McClellan, with the main body of his army, had arrived on the field of battle. This explained the loud cheers from the wood. Our men could no longer stand their ground. McClellan, in person, led on his troops into the midst of the fire. Magruder now, finding that the battle was lost, ordered a retreat to be sounded, and directed Hill's division, which had just come up, to cover the movement. All the wounded and a great portion of the baggage were

line, struck terror to the enemy. We saw them come upon the parapets and look out in silence and motionless upon the scene. Then the firing died away, and night fell on the combat which in America is called 'the battle of Williamsburg.'"

Our loss in the battle of Williamsburg—the greater part of which was sustained by General Hooker's division—was as follows: Killed, four hundred and fifty-six; wounded, fourteen hundred; missing, three hundred and seventy-two: total, two thousand two hundred and twenty-eight. The engagement had been fought under the disadvantage on our part of not knowing the numbers of the enemy or the strength of his positions; and we became involved in a serious battle, with a large force powerfully intrenched, when we had expected to do no more than attack the rear-guard of a retreating army. This explains the want of concert among the officers on the field, and the failure to send support, in all cases, to the place and at the time when most needed. General McClellan, during the forenoon of the day, was at Yorktown, engaged in making arrangements for the forwarding of General Franklin's division to West Point, and in consultation with the naval commanders, as well as with the other duties incident to his position. It

---

left in the enemy's hands. The shades of night put an end to the fight; a heavy rain, too, began to fall; and these circumstances, fortunately, prevented the enemy from completely overwhelming us. Tired and worn out, our troops returned to Williamsburg, where the excitement had become intense."—*Estvan's War-Pictures from the South*, p. 279.

was not until about one o'clock that he heard from his aides that every thing was not going on favorably in front,—upon which he hurried up as rapidly as possible, arriving there between four and five in the afternoon.

General Keyes, in his examination before the Congressional Committee on the Conduct of the War, says, "The battle of Williamsburg was gained by our side, but at a very great loss in Hooker's division and considerable loss in Hancock's and Peck's brigades. The victory, for the reasons I have stated, was nothing like as decisive as it should have been, nor gained so early in the day. In fact, the victory was not what, in military language, is generally called a perfect victory, because we were not able to sleep in the enemy's camp except in part."*

---

* Upon the battle of Williamsburg, General Barnard says, "We fought, we lost several thousand men, and we gained nothing. If we had not fought, the next day a battle would, in all probability, have been unnecessary. But, if it had been necessary, we should have had time to have brought up our resources, reconnoitred the position, and delivered our attack in such a way that some result would have flowed from it."

Upon this Colonel Lecomte remarks, "We gained there at least the credit of having carried a position by force of arms, which General Barnard regrets so much we did not do at Yorktown. But this is not the only contradiction into which the honorable general falls. He would not have feared, for instance, assaults, however fruitless, upon the strongly-fortified line of Yorktown and Warwick, and he is inconsolable at the losses caused by success."

However imperfect the victory may have been, the battle had been entirely satisfactory so far as the courage and conduct of the men were concerned. They had behaved admirably, regulars and volunteers alike, and given to their commanding officer abundant proof that he might depend alike upon their bravery and their steadiness,—their power to attack and their power to resist attack. That the operations of the army and the course of its commander had thus far been approved by the public sentiment of the country may be inferred from the following resolutions, offered by Mr. Lovejoy, and unanimously adopted by the House of Representatives, on the 5th of May:—

"*Resolved*, That it is with feelings of profound gratitude to Almighty God that the House of Representatives, from time to time, hear of the triumphs of the Union armies in the great struggle for the supremacy of the Constitution and the integrity of the Union.

"*Resolved*, That we receive with profound satisfaction intelligence of the recent victories achieved by the armies of the Potomac, associated from their localities with those of the Revolution, and that the sincere thanks of the House are hereby tendered to Major-General George B. McClellan for the display of those high military qualities which secure important results with but little sacrifice to human life."

On the morning after the battle, finding the enemy's position abandoned, we occupied Fort Magruder and the town of Williamsburg, which was filled with the enemy's wounded, to whose assistance eighteen of their surgeons were sent by General Johnston. Our troops were greatly exhausted by their toilsome march through the mud from their positions in front of Yorktown, and by the protracted battle they had fought; and the roads were in such a state, after thirty-six hours of continuous rain, that it was almost impossible to pass even empty wagons over them. Under these circumstances, an immediate pursuit of the enemy was out of the question.

The divisions of Franklin, Sedgwick, Porter, and Richardson were sent from Yorktown, by water, to the right bank of the Pamunkey, in the vicinity of West Point. Early on the morning of May 7, General Franklin had completed the disembarkation of his division. Between ten and eleven o'clock he was assailed by a large force of the enemy, but, after a spirited engagement of three or four hours, the Confederates retired, all their attacks having been repulsed. The gunboats were very efficient, and contributed materially to the success of the day.

As soon as supplies had been received, and the condition of the roads had somewhat improved, the army turned its face towards Richmond, moving slowly along the left bank of the Pamunkey, one of the two affluents forming the York River, and navigable from its junction with the latter river as far as White House. The head-quarters of the army reached this place on the 16th of May. So bad were the roads that the train of one division took thirty-six hours to get to White House from Cumberland, a distance of only five miles.*

* "Nothing could be more picturesque than this military march along the banks of a fine stream through a magnificent country arrayed in all the wealth of spring vegetation. The winding course of the Pamunkey, through a valley in which meadows of the brightest green alternated with wooded hills, offered a perpetual scene of enchantment to our eyes. Flowers bloomed everywhere, especially on the river-banks, which abounded in magnolias, Virginia jessamines, azaleas, and blue lupines. Humming-birds, snakes, and strange birds of every hue sported in the branches and about the trunks of the trees. Occasionally we passed a stately habitation which recalled the old mansions of rural France, with its large windows in the roof,—around it a handsome garden, and behind it the slave-cabins.

"As the army was descried in the distance, the inhabitants would hang out a white flag. One of the provost-marshal's horsemen would dismount at the door, and, reassured by his presence, the ladies, in their long muslin dresses, surrounded by a troop of little negresses with frizzled hair and bare legs, would come out upon the veranda and watch the passage of the troops. They were often accompanied by old men with strongly-marked faces, long white locks, and broad-brimmed hats,—never by young men. All the men capable of bearing arms had been carried off, willy-nilly, by the Government, to join in the general defence.

"So from point to point we moved along the river. The gunboats went first and explored the country before us; then came the topographical officers, moving through the woods with an escort of cavalry, reconnoitring the country, and sketching by the eye and the compass provisional maps, which were photographed at head-quarters for the use of the generals. The next day, with the help of these maps, the army would get into motion, mingled in masses with its immense team of wagons. About one-fourth of each regiment was occupied in

At White House the Pamunkey ceases to be navigable. The York River Railroad, which runs from Richmond to West Point, crosses the river here by a bridge which the enemy had destroyed. Some of the rails also had been removed from the track, and the rolling stock had been carried off; but the rails were soon relaid, and new cars and locomotives took the place of those that had been taken away. A great depot was established at White House, under the protection of the gunboats. The army began its march to Richmond, following the

---

escorting the *matériel* of the corps, piled up—provisions, ammunition, tents, and furniture—on wagons, at the rate of ten to a battalion. But for the absence of women, we might have been taken for an armed emigration rather than for soldiers on the march.

"On May 16, we reached White House, a fine building, once the property of Washington, and now of his descendants, the Lee family. The head of this family, General Lee, was one of the chief officers of the Confederate Army; one of his nephews was in the Federal ranks. General McClellan, always careful to insist upon respect for private property, stationed sentinels around the residence of the hostile general, forbade any one to enter it, and would not enter it himself. He planted his tent in a neighboring meadow. This respect for Southern property has been made a reproach to the general in Congress: the opinion of the army did not take this direction; it endorsed the delicate feeling of its leader. This feeling was pushed so far that when a general's servants found one day, in an abandoned house, a basket of champagne, the general sent it back again conspicuously the next by an aide-de-camp. We may smile at this puritanical austerity, to which we are not accustomed in Europe. For my own part, I admit that I always admired it."—Prince de Joinville."

line of the railroad, upon which it was dependent for its daily supplies. On the 20th of May, our advanced light troops reached the banks of Chickahominy River, about eight miles from Richmond.

Meanwhile, important events had been going on in the Southern Confederacy. The abandonment of Yorktown without waiting for an assault was the result of a determination on the part of the Southern leaders to transfer the scene of struggle and resistance from the Peninsula to the neighborhood of Richmond. The same policy which counselled a withdrawal from Yorktown required the giving up of Norfolk; for General Huger and his garrison of eighteen thousand men were wanted elsewhere. Orders were, accordingly, given him to evacuate the place, which he did early in May, after destroying a large amount of public property; and on the 10th of May Norfolk was taken possession of by our troops under General Wool.

But a more painful sacrifice yet was exacted at the hands of the Confederates,—the sacrifice of the Merrimac, which had done them such substantial service, and of whose achievements they were so justly proud. About four o'clock on the morning of the 11th of May, a brilliant light was seen from Fortress Monroe, in the direction of Craney Island; and at half-past four an explosion was heard which shook the earth far and wide. This was caused by the blowing up of the Merrimac, which had been abandoned by her officers and crew and set on fire. The reasons for destroying her were simply these: she was wholly unfitted for ocean navigation, and must have gone down in the first storm she met; and her draught of water was such that she could not get far enough up the James River to be out of the reach of the Federal navy, to which the river was now opened, and which at any cost would have avenged upon the Merrimac the loss of the Cumberland and Congress. She must either be destroyed or fall into our hands. This now seems obvious enough; but the sacrifice of the Merrimac—the Virginia, as they called her—was a bitter draught for the Southern people to swallow. It wounded them in their sectional pride, where the Southern mind has always been so sensitive. The newspapers were loud and general in lamenting and denouncing it; and even the court of inquiry which was summoned to investigate the subject reported that her destruction was unnecessary at the time and place at which it was effected. But, for all this, the sacrifice of the Merrimac was a necessary result of the policy of defence which, after great deliberation, was adopted; and that the policy was sound, subsequent events have proved beyond a doubt. It may be not without profit to pause here a moment, and consider in what spirit and with what measures the Confederate States prepared themselves for the conflict before them.

The whole military resources of the Confederates at that time were under the control of three men, President Davis, General Robert E. Lee, and General Joseph E. Johnston,—all of them trained soldiers, and one of them also a trained statesman. There was entire confidence and perfect harmony of action between them. That fatal apple of discord, the Presidency, never made any one of them the rival of any other. They acted together for one object; and that was success in the military contest. They resolved to transfer the scene of decisive conflict from the Peninsula to the neighborhood of Richmond; and that this was a wise determination is shown by a glance at the map. The Peninsula has York River on one side and James River on the other; these rivers must sooner or later have been commanded by our gunboats, and then their forces would have been turned and defeated. The surrender of Norfolk was a source of mortification; but it was a judicious step. The garrison was wanted at Richmond much more than at Norfolk; and as the Confederates had no navy, and their entire coast was or soon would be blockaded, the possession of Norfolk, though it gratified their pride, was of no substantial advantage to them.

The loss of the Merrimac was a more painful sacrifice still: it was indeed a blow upon the naked heart; but it was a judicious, nay, an inevitable, step, and, as such, it was at last acquiesced in.

In the political contests which have ended in the present civil war, it was often said by Northern writers and speakers that the South was an oligarchy, and that though their political forms were democratic their institutions were aristocratic. The remark is, to some extent, true. In the Southern States the mass of the people have always been content to follow the lead of a comparatively few persons who have practised politics as a profession.

This relation between the many and the few, whatever objections may be urged to it in time of peace, is no disadvantange in the conduct of a war.

The Confederate Congress had passed in April a very strong and sweeping conscription-law, which included every able-bodied man between eighteen and thirty-five, and it was everywhere enforced by a powerful public sentiment: so that early in June their army began to be steadily recruited from this source. The work upon the defences around Richmond, which had been planned some time before, was prosecuted as rapidly as possible.

The destruction of the Merrimac opened the James River to our gunboats, but not until the Confederates had had time to protect Richmond against a naval attack. On the 15th of May, a fleet of five of our gunboats, under Captain John Rodgers, steamed up the James, running aground several times, but meeting no artificial impediments till they came to Ward's Bluff, about eight miles from Richmond, where they encountered a heavy battery, called Fort Darling, and two separate barriers, formed of piles, steamers, and sail-vessels. The stream was here very narrow, being only twice as wide as the Galena, the leading gunboat, was long. The banks of the river were lined with rifle-pits, from which sharpshooters annoyed the men at the guns and rendered a removal of the obstructions impossible. The battery was on a bluff one hundred and fifty feet high, bristling with guns of long range and heavy calibre, the shot from which fell with crushing weight upon our gallant little fleet. A rifled hundred-pound Parrott gun on board one of the gunboats, the Naugatuck, burst during the fight, and disabled the vessel. The great height of the bluff put it out of the range of many of our guns; and after a fight of between three and four hours, in which officers and men fully sustained the high character of the American navy, Commodore Rodgers gave the signal to discontinue the action.

One word more, in conclusion, upon the Merrimac, or Virginia, and the lessons her career teaches. Her first appearance upon the stage of the world was on the 8th day of March, and the drama closed with the flames of her funeral pyre on the morning of the 11th of May; and certainly never was there any mortal craft that within the short space of two months played a more important part or led a more eventful life. She was originally a United States steam screw frigate of fifty guns, and, being at Gosport when the rebellion broke out, was, like many of her consorts, partly burned and sunk when it became certain that Norfolk must fall into the hands of the seceding State of Virginia. After a while the Confederates fished her up, and it was found that the bottom of the hull, the boilers, and the essential parts of the engine were little injured. It was proposed to make this wreck the nucleus of a casemated vessel with inclined iron-plated sides and submerged ends. This ingenious suggestion was carried out with skill and energy. The peculiar feature of the Merrimac was that her ends and the eaves of her casemate were submerged. The inclined roof, covered with railroad-iron, was pierced with port-holes for ten guns of very heavy calibre. The inclination of her plates, and their thickness and form, were determined by actual experiment. Her bow was armed with a strong projecting prow or beak of steel. When completed, she looked something like the roof of a house floating upon the water.

On the morning of the 8th of March, this strange, uncouth fabric is seen paddling along the calm waters of Hampton Roads, like some huge animal of the turtle-kind, making not more than five knots an hour. There the Cumberland and the Congress, two old-fashioned wooden frigates, were lying at anchor; and not far from them were the Minnesota and Roanoke, screw frigates, and the St. Lawrence, an old sailing-frigate. The Merrimac crawls by the Congress, delivering a broadside as she passes, and makes straight for the Cumberland. The sailors on board the latter vessel greet her with jokes and laughter; but the officers note with surprise and uneasiness that the shot of their heaviest broadsides rattle off the roof of the ominous craft like so many India-rubber balls, without making the slightest impression upon her iron ribs. In a few moments she crashes into the Cumberland, head on, drives her projecting prow into the starboard bow below the water-line, and knocks a hole in her side as big as a hogshead. The gallant frigate reels and shivers in every limb under the death-stroke, settles by the head, and begins at once to sink, carrying with her two hundred of her dauntless crew, before they had fairly recovered from the surprise of the portentous shock.

The Merrimac next approaches the Congress; but she has probably broken or displaced her prow in running into the Cumberland, and she attacks the Congress, therefore, by shot and shells. But before her tremendous armament the Congress proves as powerless as was the Cumberland before her beak. Her colors are hauled down; she is run ashore, and set on fire by the Merrimac's battery.

Of the other three vessels which have been mentioned, the Minnesota was the only one which could have been of any service; and she, unfortunately, ran aground. The Merrimac, after firing a few shots at her, deeming her a sure prey for the next day, turns aside to shell the camp and batteries at Newport News,—but with very little effect. In the night the gallant little Monitor arrives,—as opportunely as one of Homer's gods coming down from Olympus to share in a mortal fray,—attacks the Merrimac the next morning, and, after a contest resembling a fight between a swordfish and a whale, drives away her gigantic adversary, baffled and disabled, thus rendering us a service cheaply estimated at her weight in gold.

On the 11th of April, the Merrimac again appears in Hampton Roads, attended by five small vessels. As soon as she is discerned, a large fleet of transports and sailing-vessels in the upper roads scuds away to a place of safety, like a flock of "tame villatic fowl" that seeks a sheltering covert when the hawk is seen in the air. Aided by her attendant spirits, she captures three sailing-vessels under the eye of our own fleet, among which was the Monitor herself. After this, the Merrimac slowly moves to and fro across the mouth of Elizabeth River, seemingly inviting a champion to come out and try conclusions with her; but her defiance is not accepted, and she retires with her prizes, unmolested. To make the sting of our mortification a little sharper, all this was done under the bows of two foreign frigates,—one French and one English.

Thus, the destruction of two frigates and the capture of three small vessels make up the list of the Merrimac's material triumphs and trophies; but these were by no means all the services she rendered the Confederates, nor all the harm she did to us. In the first place, she controlled the James River so long as she lived. This rendered it impossible for us to make use of that river as the base of our operations; and this was the best base for a movement upon Richmond, and that one which, unquestionably, we should have adopted but for her presence. And, in the second place, the necessity of watching the Merrimac rendered it impossible to detach from the squadron at Hampton Roads a suitable force to attack the enemy's water-batteries at Yorktown and Gloucester; and this delayed the army before the lines of Yorktown, and gave the Confederates—what they so much wanted—time. Thus the whole current of the Peninsular campaign was turned aside, and the course of the war itself materially influenced, by this single vessel. Never was there a greater apparent disproportion between cause and effect.

And the lesson which the Merrimac teaches is, that in war no chance should be thrown away, no advantage should be foregone; that counsel never should be taken of distrust and despondency; that the game of war is never wholly lost and never wholly won, and that in desperate straits there is nothing that ingenuity can suggest which is not worth trying. A sudden and unexpected charge by Kellermann, at the head of eight hundred cavalry, turned the adverse tide of battle at Marengo into a victory. The little fort of Bard, in the valley of Aosta, a few weeks earlier, checked, and, had not the garrison been over-confident and under-vigilant, would have turned back, the whole French army.* And the Merrimac may have saved the city of Richmond from capture.

It is curious to reflect, after all the inventions by which the force and destructiveness of projectiles have been increased, that in the Merrimac we came back to the point from which naval architecture, as applied to war, started. The Merrimac's beak was nothing more nor less than the *rostrum* of a Roman galley, enlarged and strengthened.

During the march from Yorktown to the banks of the Chickahominy, besides the weighty cares and heavy responsibilities of a commanding general at the head of a great expedition, the mind of General

* See the account in Alison's "History of the French Revolution," chap. xxx.

McClellan was constantly burdened with a conviction that his troops were not numerous enough for the work in hand, and that reinforcements were essential to success. He had carried with him to the Peninsula about eighty-five thousand men, and Franklin's division, which had subsequently joined him, amounted to ten thousand more; but some of his troops had been killed or disabled in battle, some had died from disease, and garrisons had been left at Yorktown, Williamsburg, and Gloucester, so that now he could not confidently rely upon more than eighty thousand men. But time, which was thinning his ranks, was swelling those of the enemy; and the task before him was that of taking a city strongly defended, before which was an army larger than his own. On the 10th of May, from a camp three miles from Williamsburg, he sent a brief telegram to the Secretary of War, setting forth his position, and urging the necessity of reinforcing him without delay with all the disposable troops in Eastern Virginia. He assures the Secretary that the rebels will not abandon Richmond without a struggle, and adds that unless he is reinforced it is probable he shall be obliged to fight nearly double his numbers, strongly intrenched.

On the 14th of May, he sent a telegram to the President in the same strain, stating that the time had come for striking a fatal blow at the enemies of the Constitution, and entreating him that he would cause the Army of the Peninsula to be reinforced without delay by all the disposable troops of the Government. To this, on the 18th, an answer was received from the Secretary of War, the material portions of which are as follows:—

"The President is not willing to uncover the capital entirely; and it is believed that, even if this were prudent, it would require more time to effect a junction between your army and that of the Rappahannock, by the way of the Potomac and York Rivers, than by a land march. In order, therefore, to increase the strength of the attack upon Richmond at the earliest moment, General McDowell has been ordered to march upon that city by the shortest route. He is ordered, keeping himself always in position to save the capital from all possible attack, so to operate as to put his left wing in communication with your right wing; and you are instructed to co-operate so as to establish this communication as soon as possible, by extending your right wing to the north of Richmond.

* * * * *

"When General McDowell is in position on your right, his supplies must be drawn from West Point; and you will instruct your staff officers to be prepared to supply him by that route.

"The President desires that General McDowell retain the command of the Department of the Rappahannock, and of the forces with which he moves forward."

It will be borne in mind that General McClellan wished and had advised that reinforcements should be sent to him by water, as their arrival would have been more certain. Now that the James River was open, they might have been sent by that route, in which event our left flank would have rested upon that river and been protected by it. Richmond could have been approached by the James, and we should have escaped the losses and delays incurred by bridging the Chickahominy, and should have had the army massed in one body instead of being necessarily divided by that stream. This judicious military plan, which in all probability would have resulted in the capture of Richmond, could not be carried out, because to the President's distempered fancy Washington was not safe unless it was covered by McDowell's division in a direct line between that city and Richmond. Under the circumstances of the case, an attack upon Washington by a Confederate force strong enough to carry its defences was about as probable an event as an inundation of the city by an overflow of the Potomac.

By these orders it will be also noticed that General McClellan was commanded to extend his right wing to the north of Richmond, in order to establish the communication between himself and General McDowell. This was running a great risk in case General McDowell should not come, because it exposed our right in a way that no prudent officer would have done; and, as General McDowell did not come, the enemy did not fail to take advantage of the opportunity thus afforded them.

The Secretary's communication of the 18th was accompanied by a copy of the instructions which had been sent to General McDowell on the previous day, of which the following is the substance:—

"WAR DEPARTMENT,
WASHINGTON, May 17, 1862.

"GENERAL:—Upon being joined by General Shields's division, you will move upon Richmond by the general route of the Richmond & Fredericksburg Railroad, co-operating with the forces under General McClellan, now threatening Richmond from the line of the Pamunkey and York Rivers.

"While seeking to establish as soon as possible a communication between your left wing and the right wing of General McClellan, you will hold yourself always in such position as to cover the capital of the nation against a sudden dash of any large body of the rebel forces."

General McDowell had with him forty thousand men and ninety pieces of artillery.

On the 21st of May, General McClellan sent another despatch, of some length, to the President. He explains to him the position of the army, and earnestly and respectfully expresses his regret at the delay of McDowell's advance. He tells the President frankly that the march of McDowell's column upon Richmond by the shortest land route will uncover Washington as completely as its movement by water; that the enemy cannot advance by Fredericksburg, and that if they attempt a movement, which to him seems utterly improbable, their route would be by Gordonsville and Manassas. In conclusion, he desires that the extent of his authority over General McDowell may be clearly defined, and suggests that the dangers of a divided command can only be surely guarded against by explicitly placing General McDowell under his orders in the usual way.

On the 24th he received from the President a reply to the above, in which he suggests a plan of military movement against General Anderson in concert with General McDowell, assures him that

McDowell's division, strengthened by Shields's command, would begin to move on Monday, the 26th, and tells him that McDowell, after joining him, would be under his command.

This, of course, was highly satisfactory, as it gave General McClellan assurance that he would soon be reinforced by at least fifty thousand men, and thus be made sufficiently strong to overpower the large army confronting him. But his astonishment, his agony of disappointment, may well be imagined when all these confident expectations were broken to pieces by the crushing despatch received at a later hour of the same day, which ran thus:—

"May 24, 1862,
From WASHINGTON, 4 P.M.

"In consequence of General Banks's critical position, I have been compelled to suspend General McDowell's movements to join you. The enemy are making a desperate push upon Harper's Ferry; and we are trying to throw General Frémont's force, and part of General McDowell's, in their rear.

"A. LINCOLN, *President.*

"Major-General GEO. B. McCLELLAN."

It is necessary to go back a little and state the events which occasioned this last despatch.

It will be remembered that the State of Virginia, contrary to sound military maxims, and certainly for reasons other than military, had been parcelled out into five separate commands. General Frémont was west of the mountains, General Banks was in the Valley of the Shenandoah, General McDowell was on the Rappahannock, and General Wool was at Fortress Monroe. During the preceding autumn and winter the Confederate General Jackson had been at or near Winchester with a body of raw troops, which he had been engaged in drilling and disciplining. The campaign opened in the valley early in March. On the 23d of that month a battle was fought near Winchester between General Shields and General Jackson, in which the latter was defeated. This battle, by revealing the presence of a considerable force of the enemy in that region, was probably the reason why McDowell's corps was not sent to the Peninsula with McClellan. After the battle of Winchester, Jackson had retreated up the valley to Harrisonburg, and then struck off to the west. On the 8th of May, he fought a battle of not very decisive results with the Federal forces under Milroy and Schenck, at a place called McDowell, near Bull Pasture Mountain. From this point he marched to Harrisonburg, thence to New Market, where a junction was effected with Ewell's division, which had come from Elk Run Valley. Their united forces amounted to at least fifteen thousand men.

About the middle of May, an order was issued from the War Department at Washington for General Shields to move with his command from the Valley of the Shenandoah and join General McDowell at Fredericksburg. This left General Banks with only five or six thousand men at Strasburg. The Government was warned of the danger of leaving him with so small a force when so active and vigilant an officer as Jackson was in the valley; but it was all to no purpose. It is a mistake to suppose that General Jackson had been planning and executing movements of his own, and upon his own responsibility, all this time: he had been under the control of the commander-in-chief at Richmond, and all his marches and battles had reference to one sole object,—the defence of that city. The Confederate authorities knew how important it was for General McClellan that he should be reinforced by General McDowell, and they also knew that it was an apprehension for the safety of Washington that had thus far prevented the junction; and they, of course, reasoned that by keeping up and increasing this alarm they might postpone indefinitely a combination of forces which would be fatal to them. The time had come, now that General Banks was left so exposed, when a decisive blow might be struck towards the end; and the opportunity was not neglected.

After the battle at McDowell, General Jackson had contrived to conceal his movements from the observation of our forces. General Banks, as has been said, was at Strasburg. At Front Royal, twelve miles in advance, Colonel Kenley was stationed, with a Maryland regiment and a few companies,—about twelve hundred in all, rank and file. On Friday, the 23d, at noon, this little handful of men was suddenly and unexpectedly assailed by General Jackson at the head of a force at least ten times as large as its own. Though taken by surprise, and with such immense odds against him,

Colonel Kenley and his men fought gallantly and obstinately for three or four hours, and thus retarded the Confederate advance; but they were at last overpowered by superior numbers, and nearly all cut to pieces or taken prisoners.

The startling news reached General Banks at nightfall, and, after a little reflection, he determined to move upon Winchester as rapidly as possible. Accordingly, at a very early hour the next morning he began his march. His column was attacked in flank while on the way, and a portion of the rear-guard turned back to Strasburg. At four o'clock in the afternoon the advance-guard arrived at Winchester. The whole force General Banks had with him was less than five thousand men, while that of the enemy was fifteen thousand at least. At Winchester General Banks determined to try the strength of the Confederates by actual collision; and preparations were made accordingly during the night. The engagement began early the next morning, and held the enemy in check for five hours. Our soldiers fought well, and were well handled; but it was in vain to contend against such odds, and orders were given to withdraw. The pursuit by the enemy was prompt and vigorous, and the retreat rapid and without serious loss. A halt of two hours and a half was made at Martinsburg; and the rear-guard finally reached the Potomac at sunset on the 25th. This was forty-eight hours after the first news of the attack on Front Royal. It was a march of fifty-three miles, thirty-five of which were performed in one day. The river was crossed the next day; "and," says General Banks, in his official report, "there never were more grateful hearts in the same number of men than when, at mid-day on the 26th, we stood on the opposite shore."

General Banks throughout these two disastrous days behaved with energy and self-possession; and there is nothing disparaging to his military reputation in the fact that he retreated, because he did it in good order against a force three or four times as great as his own, saving all his guns, and losing only fifty-five wagons out of five hundred.

On the part of the enemy it must be admitted that this expedition, as a move upon the great chess-board of war, demands the highest praise. It was admirably planned and skilfully and successfully executed. The loss of men on our side was not great; that of army and medical stores was more considerable; but the indirect, the moral, advantages it secured to the enemy were of infinitely greater moment. To drive General Banks from Strasburg across the Potomac was in itself a play not worth the candle; but the real object of the expedition was to prevent General McDowell's division from being sent to reinforce General McClellan; and it unfortunately succeeded.

When news of the attack on Colonel Kenley's command at Front Royal, on the 23d, reached General Geary, who was at Rectortown with a force charged with the protection of the Manassas Gap Railroad, he immediately began to move to

Manassas Junction. His troops, alarmed by exaggerated reports of the fate of the regiment at Front Royal, burnt their tents and destroyed a quantity of arms. The contagion of panic spread to Catlett's Station, where was General Duryea with four regiments. He hastened to Centreville, and telegraphed to Washington for help. The rumors were swelled and magnified on their way to the capital: the authorities there were thrown into a most unnecessary fright, and telegraphic despatches, pale with the hue of fear, were sent on the wings of lightning all over the land. Of these the following is a specimen:—

"WASHINGTON, May 25, 1862.

"*To the Governor of Massachusetts.*

"Intelligence from various quarters leaves no doubt that the enemy, in great force, are marching on Washington. You will please organize and forward immediately all the militia and volunteer force in your State.

"EDWIN M. STANTON,
"*Secretary of War.*"

It was under the influence of the apprehensions occasioned by the report of General Jackson's movements that the President had telegraphed to General McClellan, on the 24th of May, as we have before stated, that General McDowell's division would not join him. On the same day, an order was sent by the President to General McDowell, directing him to lay aside at present the movement on Richmond, and put twenty thousand men in motion at once for the Shenandoah, in order to capture the force of Jackson and Ewell, either in co-operation with General Frémont, or alone. General McDowell's clear military judgment saw at once the injudiciousness of this order, which turned him from a point where he was greatly needed to a quarter where he could be of no use; and he instantly telegraphed back to the President's order the following reply, addressed to the Secretary of War:—

"The President's order has been received, and is in process of execution. This is a crushing blow to us."

To this the President responded as follows, still on the same 24th of May:—

"I am highly gratified by your alacrity in obeying my orders. The change was as painful to me as it can possibly be to you or to any one. Every thing now depends upon the celerity and vigor of your movements."

To this General McDowell made a reply in writing, of which the principal and material portion is as follows:—

"HEAD-QUARTERS, DEPARTMENT OF THE RAPPAHANNOCK,
"OPPOSITE FREDERICKSBURG, May 24, 1862.

"*His Excellency the President:*—

"I obeyed your order immediately, for it was positive and urgent; and perhaps, as a subordinate, there I ought to stop; but I trust I may be allowed to say something in relation to the subject, especially in view of your remark that every thing depends upon the celerity and vigor of my movements. I beg to say that co-operation between General Frémont and myself, to cut off Jackson and Ewell, is not to be counted upon, even if it is not a practical impossibility; next, that I am entirely beyond helping-distance of General Banks, and no celerity or vigor will be available as far as he is concerned; next, that by a glance at the map it will be seen that the line of retreat of the enemy's forces up the valley is shorter than mine to go against him. It will take a week or ten days for the force to get to the valley by the route which will give it food and forage, and by that time the enemy will have retreated. I shall gain nothing for you there, and lose much for you here. It is, therefore, not only on personal grounds that I have a heavy heart in the matter, but I feel that it throws us all back, and from Richmond north we shall have all our large mass paralyzed, and shall have to repeat what we have just accomplished."

It will be observed that on the 24th of May the President directed General McDowell to march to the Shenandoah, to cut off the retreating division of Jackson, and that on the next day the Secretary of War telegraphed the Governor of Massachusetts that the "enemy, in great force," meaning of course Jackson's command, were marching on Washington. This difference of opinion between two high functionaries as to an enemy's movements is rather a curious fact, and only to be explained on the ground that they were acting independently and without consultation or conference.

What generous mind will refuse to sympathize with General McDowell's suffering and sadness of spirit in obeying an order which he perceives to be most unwise at the very moment he prepares to execute it!

The silent and incommunicative Jackson—a man

who never let his left hand know what his right hand was doing, who rarely spoke and rarely smiled—would have been amused if he had known into what a fright he had thrown the authorities at Washington and no small portion of the Northern people. He had no more idea of going to Washington than of going to Boston: such a diversion of his force would have been an act of madness. Having done all that he desired and proposed to do, his next thought was to get back again; and he accordingly began his retreat up the Valley of the Shenandoah, which he conducted bravely and skilfully. He had a great advantage in his perfect knowledge of the country he was traversing. He contrived to slip through the Federal forces which were pressing upon him from the west and the east. On the 8th of June, he fought a battle with General Frémont, at Cross Keys, on the left bank of the Shenandoah, by which he secured the passage of his army over the bridge at Port Republic, a few miles distant, and the next day engaged a portion of General Shields's command near the latter place. After a hard fight, our forces fell back, and General Jackson continued his retreat, to secure which had been his object in both engagements.

Thus ended General Jackson's memorable campaign in the Valley of the Shenandoah, which had begun on the 11th of March, in which that officer gave evidence of the highest military qualities—vigor, celerity, skill in masking his designs from the enemy, and ability in handling his men—and fully vindicated his title to the enthusiastic admiration with which he was regarded by his people during the remainder of his brief career.

It may be added that, had all the military threads that united at Richmond been held in the hand of General McClellan, as they should have been, he would never have left General Banks exposed with so small a command at an indefensible point. That this statement is not matter of opinion merely may be seen by a careful reading of General McClellan's instructions to General Banks of March 16, to General Wadsworth of the same date, and his letter of April 1 to the Adjutant-General,—all which appear in full in his Report.

We now return to Richmond, where we left General McClellan with the President's second despatch fallen like a stone upon his heart. It was already certain that General McDowell's movements to join him were suspended, and for an indefinite period; and there was nothing for him to do but to address himself to the work before him with such means as he could command, and doubtless with a sadness of spirit like that of the Roman gladiators when they saluted the emperor, "*Morituri te salutamus.*"

The disposition of our forces around Richmond was controlled by two elements, one artificial and one natural,—the former being the Richmond & York River Railroad, and the latter the Chickahominy River. The railroad ran in a direction nearly easterly from Richmond to White House, at which latter place was our depot of supplies. It is difficult for a civilian to form an adequate notion of the immense amount of these supplies which must be furnished every day for the support of an army of seventy thousand men, including forage for horses, cavalry and artillery. The communication between such an army and its base of supplies cannot be for a moment interrupted or even endangered. It was therefore a point of paramount importance to guard this railroad from flank movements on both sides. The Chickahominy River flows in a southeasterly direction, and is crossed both by the Richmond & York River Railroad and the Virginia Central Railroad, which runs northerly,—the river and the portions of the two railroads south of it forming an isosceles triangle, with the apex towards the east. Place the right hand on a table with the palm down, the fingers close together, and the thumb stretched back as far as possible; let the thumb represent the course of the Virginia Central Road, and the forefinger that of the Richmond & York. Richmond will then be in the hollow at the bottom of the thumb, and a line drawn from the ball of the thumb to the first joint of the forefinger will indicate the course of the Chickahominy

In order to keep the railroad entirely secure, the course of the river made it necessary to divide our forces and place part of them on one side of the stream and part on the other. This is not usually deemed a prudent disposition of an army; but there was an imperative necessity for it in this case. Besides, General McClellan had been directed to extend his right wing so as to form a junction with General McDowell; and the order for his co-operation being simply suspended, not revoked, General McClellan was not at liberty to abandon the northern approach.

On the 25th of May he received a telegraphic despatch from the President, at considerable length, detailing the enemy's movements as far as they were known up to its date, stating that twenty thousand of McDowell's forces were moving back to Front Royal, that one more of his brigades was ordered to Harper's Ferry through Washington, and that the rest of his forces were to remain for the present at Fredericksburg, adding that if McDowell's force was beyond their reach they (in Washington) should be entirely helpless. At a later hour on the same day, the President sent him another despatch, indicating apprehensions for the safety of Washington, saying, "I think the time is near when you must either attack Richmond or give up the job and come to the defence of Washington."*

* Upon the President's first despatch of May 25, in which he says that apprehensions for the safety of Washington, and nothing else, prevented McDowell's being sent to the Peninsula, Colonel Lecomte remarks, "We have full faith in the sincerity of the frank and honest language of the President; but the Report" (that of the Congressional Committee, which quotes a part of the President's despatch) "perverts entirely the facts relative to Jackson's campaign, and the insane terror it inspired in Washington, which was the true cause of the failure on the Peninsula. On quitting Washington, before having been deprived of a part of his command, General McClellan had given the most exact and judicious instructions for the defence of the capital. He had pointed out Manassas and Front Royal as points forming a good advanced line, and had

On the 26th of May, news came that a considerable force of the enemy was in the neighborhood

---

ordered Banks to intrench himself there. He had distinctly forbidden him to advance farther into Virginia. But as soon as General McClellan's back was turned, they wished to make Banks a rival of him, and, supposing that the Army of the Potomac would attract all the force of the enemy, it was thought that Banks might gather some cheap laurels if he were sent into the upper Valley of the Shenandoah. The Aulic Council at Washington thought they might in this way strike a master-stroke, and cause Richmond to fall before McClellan had time to appear before it. If the Confederates had not been in so much hurry, if they had let Banks advance farther, this brave general would have run great risk of being captured with all his force. Banks having miraculously escaped, it was enough to hold Harper's Ferry strongly on one side, and Centreville on the other, to cover Washington. Jackson might have moved between Warrenton Junction and Winchester; he might have pushed cavalry detachments into Western Maryland; but he could have attempted no serious enterprise.

"Instead of this, it was thought that a good trick might be played upon Jackson, and that he might be 'bagged,' to use an American expression. To form a notion of this plan of the campaign, manufactured at Washington, and the confusion which attended its execution, one should read the series of telegrams by which the President informs General McClellan of the progress of this wise manœuvre. Generals McDowell, Banks, Sigel, and Frémont, each coming from his own position, and all preserving their independent commands, arrived one after another, to be beaten in detail, or to let Jackson escape before their eyes without a fight. But the most unfortunate result was that the corps of McDowell, divided, weakened by forced marches, and transported to another theatre of war, could not take the part which had been assigned to it. For the second time, and definitively, it was detained far from the army of of Hanover Court-House, to the right and rear of our army, and thus threatening our communications; and General Fitz-John Porter's division was ordered to march the next morning at daybreak to dislodge them. They set off in a heavy storm, came up with the enemy in the course of the day, attacked and defeated him, and took and destroyed his camp at Hanover Court-House. The bridges of the Virginia Central Railroad and the Frede-

---

General McClellan, to which for the second time it thus caused great mischief, as a few brief explanations will show.

"After the destruction of the Merrimac, and the taking of Norfolk by the Federals, which opened the James River, Commodore Goldsborough had proposed to General McClellan to take the James River as a base of operations and have it flank his left wing. This change of base, had it then been carried out, would have made the attack upon Richmond easier, through the aid of the gunboats. General McClellan abandoned this obvious advantage, because he had been ordered to extend his right wing towards McDowell, who was coming from Fredericksburg to reinforce the army of the Peninsula as soon as it had reached Richmond. General McClellan expected General McDowell by the railroad from Fredericksburg to Richmond, and had already sent troops in that direction to effect a junction,—when, instead of this reinforcement, he received a telegraphic order to burn the railroad-bridges over the branches of the Pamunkey, and thus to render all communication with McDowell impossible, the latter's outposts having been at that time but twenty-one miles distant from those of McClellan. But this was the period of Banks's defeat; and such was the terror at Washington that they thought the whole Confederate army was marching to the North and that the capital was to be saved by destroying the bridges. The alarm was so great that it was even proposed to General McClellan to re-embark his army and bring it within the lines of Alexandria."

ricksburg & Richmond Railroad, both over the South Ann, were destroyed, as well as a considerable amount of Confederate property at Hanover Court-House and Ashland. General McClellan was much gratified at the way in which this brilliant movement was executed by General Porter, and he deemed its results valuable, because it was thus rendered impossible for the enemy to communicate by rail with Fredericksburg, or with Jackson except by the very circuitous route of Lynchburg. More important still, by the clearing of our right flank and rear, the road was left entirely open for the advance of McDowell, had he been permitted to join the Army of the Potomac. His advanced guard was at this time at Bowling Green, only about fifteen or twenty miles distant from that of Porter: so near did we come to seizing the golden opportunity which Fortune never offers a second time! McDowell's withdrawal towards Front Royal was, as General McClellan observes in his Report, "a serious and fatal error." He was sent to a point where he could do no good, and diverted from a point where his presence was greatly needed and could not have failed to secure important results.

As our army was massed on both sides of the Chickahominy, it was necessary to maintain easy communication between them; and this compelled the building of several bridges, some of which were new, and others were reconstructions of those which the enemy had destroyed. Our troops were very efficient in work of this kind, but they had great difficulties to struggle against. The Chickahominy in this region is a narrow and shallow stream, fringed with a dense growth of heavy forest-trees, and bordered by low marshy bottom-lands, varying from half a mile to a mile in width. A heavy rain would swell the narrow rivulet into a broad and shallow flood, and the work of days would be swept away in a single night. When the waters were low, a child might ford it; when they were high, a horse and his rider might be drowned in it. The labors of our engineers were

> "Quench'd in a boggy syrtis, neither sea
> Nor good dry land."

The elements, too, seemed to have conspired against us. So rainy a season had never been known within the memory of man: the pitiless floods fell upon us without intermission. The petulant and rebel stream seemed to take a perverse pleasure in breaking the fetters with which patriot hands essayed to bind it. And then these rains turned the wretched narrow roads of the Peninsula into tracks of impassable and heart-breaking mire, in which horses sank to their knees and wagons stuck hopelessly fast.*

---

* "Unfortunately, every thing dragged with us. The roads were long in drying, the bridges were long in building. 'Never have we seen so rainy a season,' said the oldest inhabitant. 'Never did we see bridges so difficult to build,' said the engineers. The abominable river laughed at all their efforts. Too narrow for a bridge of boats, too deep and too muddy for piers, here a simple brook some ten yards wide, flowing between two plains of quicksand, in which the horses sank up to the girths, and which offered no bearings,—there divided into a

During all this time our troops were busily employed, besides building bridges, in intrenching themselves, throwing up redoubts, digging rifle-pits, and felling timber in the line of the batteries.

THE BATTLE OF FAIR OAKS.

On the 30th of May, two corps were on the south side of the Chickahominy,—that of Keyes, comprising the divisions of Couch and Casey, and Heintzelman's, comprising those of Hooker and Kearney. Casey's division, numbering about five thousand, was at Fair Oaks, a station on the York River Railroad. A redoubt and rifle-pit had been constructed, and there was also an abatis in front of them. Couch's division, about eight thousand strong, was at Seven Pines, three-quarters of a mile in the rear; while the two divisions of Heintzelman's corps, in all about sixteen thousand, were still farther back. The right flank of Kearney was on the railroad, and the left of Hooker on White Oak Swamp.

During the day and night of May 30, there had been a violent storm, with heavy torrents of rain.

---

thousand tiny rivulets spread over a surface of three hundred yards, and traversing one of those wooded morasses which are peculiar to tropical countries,—changing its level and its bed from day to day, the river, in its capricious and uncertain sway, annulled and undid to-day the labors of yesterday, carried on under a burning sun and often under the fire of the enemy. And so went by days upon days,—precious, irrecoverable days."—Prince de Joinville.

The Confederates, presuming that a rapid rise in the river would follow, resolved to seize the opportunity, throw their whole force upon our left wing, south of the Chickahominy, and cut it to pieces before aid could come from the other side. They supposed that they should have to deal with no other troops than those of Keyes, not being aware of the presence of Heintzelman's corps. Their dispositions were skilfully made. Longstreet and Hill, with thirty-two thousand men, were to advance along the Williamsburg road; Huger, with sixteen thousand, was to move down the Charles City road, which runs southeast from Richmond, to attack our left flank; and Smith, with the same number, was to march north, along the Nine-Mile road, so as to turn our right flank and cover the Confederate left. Had these plans all been successfully executed, we could hardly have escaped an overwhelming defeat.

The columns started at daybreak on the 31st, and Hill, Longstreet, and Smith were in position to begin the attack at eight o'clock; but Huger did not appear at the appointed time and place. Hour after hour rolled away, and brought no tidings of him: his artillery had been immovably fixed in the mud, and the passage of his troops arrested. At noon, Hill and Longstreet resolved to make the attack without waiting for him. Accordingly, at about one o'clock they fell in overwhelming mass upon Casey's division. Some of his troops, thus suddenly assailed by greatly superior numbers, broke and fled in disorder; but the larger part stood their ground manfully, and were nobly sustained by their officers. But it was impossible to resist the force that was hurled against them. Slowly, inch by inch, they gave way; and it was not until after three o'clock that they fell back through Couch's line of battle to the rear, too much exhausted, and their ranks too much thinned, to take further part in the contest as a body.

At four o'clock we had lost nearly a mile of ground, fifteen of our guns had been captured, and the enemy were in possession of Casey's camp. Couch's division was now assailed. His troops stood firm, and the repeated assaults of the enemy were steadily met,—our left being protected by the impenetrable morasses of the White Oak Swamp. Two of Heintzelman's brigades appeared on the field, with the gallant Kearney at their head. The movements of the troops were now directed by General McClellan in person. But a new element of danger intervened. General Couch discovered large masses of the enemy pushing towards our right and crossing the railroad, as well as a heavy column which had been held in reserve and was now making its way towards Fair Oaks Station. This was part of Smith's division, which had come by the Nine-Mile road to attack our right flank. General Couch at once engaged this column with four regiments; but he was overpowered, and the enemy pushed between him and the main body of his division. Our position was now critical; for, if the enemy had succeeded in getting in our rear, we must have been defeated with great loss. "But," says the Prince de Joinville,—

"But exactly at this moment (six o'clock P.M.), new actors come upon the stage. Sumner, who has at last passed the river with Sedgwick's division on the bridge built by his troops, and who, with a soldier's instinct, has marched straight to the cannon through the woods, suddenly appears upon the flank of the hostile column which is trying to cut off Heintzelman and Keyes. He plants in a clearing a battery which he has succeeded in bringing up. His guns are not rifled guns, the rage of the hour, and fit only to be fired in cool blood, and at long range in an open country: they are real fighting guns, old twelve-pound howitzers carrying either a round projectile, which ricochets and rolls, or a good dose of grape. The simple and rapid fire of these pieces makes terrible havoc in the hostile ranks. In vain Johnston sends up his best troops against this battery, the flower of South Carolina, including the Hampton Legion; in vain does he come upon the field in person: nothing can shake the Federal ranks. When night falls, it was the Federals who, bayonet in hand, and gallantly led by Sumner himself, charged furiously upon the foe, and drove him before them, with fearful slaughter, as far as Fair Oaks Station."

Orders had been sent from head-quarters to General Sumner, at two o'clock, to move his division across the river. Two bridges had been built by his men, one opposite General Sedgwick's division, and one opposite General Richardson's,—both corduroy bridges. But the latter was already destroyed by the flood, and the former much injured. The roads, too, were deep and muddy; and it was not until six o'clock, and after great exertions, that General Sedgwick's division, with a single battery (Kirby's), was able to reach the field and exert a favorable influence upon the fortunes of the day.

The opportune arrival of General Sumner was not our only piece of good fortune; for about sunset the Confederate commander-in-chief, General J. E. Johnston, who had accompanied Smith's corps and directed the enemy's movements since four or five o'clock, was struck from his horse, severely wounded, by the fragment of a shell. In consequence of this, utter confusion prevailed for a time upon the Confederate left.

The next morning, at an early hour, the battle was renewed, the enemy making an attack upon General Richardson's division, which had not taken part in the engagement of the previous day, and which was now posted in front. They met it firmly, and returned with effect the enemy's fire, until General Howard's brigade was ordered to the front, when the enemy's line fell back. Other attacks, in other parts of the field, were repulsed; and finally our line advanced with the bayonet, and the enemy retreated, having gained about half a mile of ground in two days' fighting.

In these severely contested battles our loss was five thousand seven hundred and thirty-seven, and that of the enemy six thousand seven hundred and eighty-three: we also lost ten pieces of artillery.*

---

* At the time the battle of Fair Oaks began, General McClellan was confined to his bed by illness. This fact does not

The battle of Fair Oaks, or Seven Pines, as the Confederates call it, has some points of resemblance to that of Waterloo, and, like that, shows how much military movements are controlled by fortune or accident. At Waterloo, Bonaparte's attack upon the British lines was delayed some hours by the rain, and consequent state of the roads. At Fair Oaks, the muddy roads held fast Huger's division, and caused the assault to be postponed four or five

---

appear in his Report, but is stated by him in his evidence before the Congressional Committee on the Conduct of the War. But that committee say in their Report (p. 22), speaking of the second day's fight, "General McClellan was with the main part of the army on the left bank of the Chickahominy. After the fighting was over, he came across to the right bank of the river." This statement is as untrue as it is unjust. General McClellan, enfeebled as he was by illness, immediately got on horseback when he heard the cannon which opened the battle of the 31st, was employed during the remainder of the day in receiving reports and giving orders, spent a portion of the night in conferring with his officers, and early the next morning went over to the right bank of the river, while the fight of June 1st was raging. Colonel Lecomte remarks upon the statement of the committee, that it is "contradicted by many ocular witnesses, and, among others, by one of his aides who was with him the whole day. General McClellan, says this officer, though severely ill with dysentery, had passed the greater part of the night in seeking his generals and conferring with them. About half-past seven in the morning he left the headquarters of General Sumner, and between eight and nine arrived at the place where the latter was engaged. The fight was then at its height: we were in a clearing, and were fighting along the edge of a wood, two hundred metres" (about six hundred and fifty feet) "from the spot where the general himself (Sumner) was directing the battle."

hours. Huger took no part in the battle, contrary to the plans which had been agreed upon: Grouchy did not appear at Waterloo, as was expected. Sumner's arrival upon the field at six is paralleled by that of Blücher at Waterloo at about the same hour.

So much for the points of resemblance between the two battles; but in other respects that of Fair Oaks illustrates the power of fortune over war. Had Huger's corps attacked us on the left flank at the same time that Hill and Longstreet did in front, we could hardly have escaped destruction. Thus the rain which swelled the stream and occasioned the attack also prevented it from being successful, by making impassable the road over which Huger was directed to move. We had also another piece of good fortune. Smith's corps, it will be remembered, was moved along the Nine-Mile road, to be ready to be employed against our right flank. General Johnston, the commander-in-chief, was with this corps, and, of course, directed its movements. He says in his official report that he accompanied this corps, so that he might be on a part of the field where he could observe and be ready to meet any counter-movement which might be made against his centre or left, and then adds, "Owing to some peculiar condition of the atmosphere, the sound of the musketry did not reach us. I consequently deferred giving the signal for General Smith's advance till four o'clock." Thus the advance of Smith's corps was delayed two hours; and precious hours they were to us, because they enabled Sumner to get to the field and save us from being cut to pieces.

20

General Sumner had crossed the river by the upper of the two bridges which he had built, called the Grape-vine bridge; the lower, called the Sunderland bridge, having been carried away. But before the next morning the Grape-vine bridge was also carried away by the rising flood. "This bridge," says the Prince de Joinville, "saved that day the whole Federal army from destruction."

Such are the momentous consequences in war which flow from causes so seemingly trivial as the state of the atmosphere, the rising or falling of a petty stream, a sudden tempest of rain, or the condition of a road over which artillery must be moved. These things should teach civilian critics a wise self-distrust, and a tenderness of judgment towards generals who have had the misfortune not to succeed in winning a battle or taking a fortress.

General McClellan has been blamed for not having followed up the enemy after the battle of Fair Oaks, and, among others, by General Barnard, who says, in his Report, "The repulse of the rebels at Fair Oaks should have been taken advantage of. It was one of those 'occasions' which, if not seized, do not repeat themselves. We now *know* the state of disorganization and dismay in which the rebel army retreated. We now *know* it could have been followed into Richmond." The italics are General Barnard's own. Without repeating the obvious remark that General McClellan should be judged by what was known then, and not by what we know now, it may be stated that there is nothing to justify the assertion that the rebel army retreated in "disorganization" and "dismay," and that when General Barnard says, "we *know* it could have been followed into Richmond," he claims the authority of omniscience. The reasons why the enemy were not pursued are amply and satisfactorily stated in General McClellan's Report. The Grape-vine and Sunderland bridges had been carried away. The approaches to New and Mechanicsville bridges, higher up the stream, were overflowed; and both of them were enfiladed by batteries of the enemy. To have advanced upon Richmond, the troops must have been marched from various points on the left banks of the Chickahominy to Bottom's Bridge, and over the Williamsburg road to Fair Oaks, upwards of twenty miles,—a march which, as the roads then were, could not have been made in less than two days. "In short," as General McClellan says,—

> "The idea of uniting the two wings of the army in time to make a vigorous pursuit of the enemy, with the prospect of overtaking him before he reached Richmond, only five miles distant from the field of battle, is simply absurd, and was, I presume, never for a moment seriously entertained by any one connected with the Army of the Potomac."*

---

* General Barnard, in his testimony before the Committee on the Conduct of the War, says, "By the rise of the Chickahominy the two bridges built by General Sumner became impracticable by the night of the 31st. The bridges at Bottom's Bridge with difficulty were preserved from destruction; but the rising water overflowed the adjacent road, and soon these bridges became useless for wagons or horses. Fortunately, the railroad bridge had been repaired; and by this alone the left

CHAPTER VIII.

For about three weeks after the battle of Fair Oaks nothing of moment took place. By the 2d of June our left was advanced considerably beyond the lines it had occupied before the battle. The position at Fair Oaks was strengthened by a line of intrenchments which protected the troops while they were at work upon the bridges, gave security to the trains, liberated a large fighting-force, and afforded a safer retreat in case of disaster. To form these intrenchments was hard work: redoubts and embankments had to be raised, rifle-pits to be dug, and trees in great numbers to be cut down; and all this under the burning sun of a Virginia June. General McClellan was anxious to assume the offensive; it was his policy to do so, as the enemy were gaining and we were losing by the mere lapse of time. But no general battle could be risked until the two wings of the army were put in full

---

wing of the army was supplied. By means of planks laid between the rails, infantry, and, with some risk, horses, could pass. This, for several days, was the only communication between the two wings of the army."—*Report on the Conduct of the War*, vol. i. p. 401.

The case in defence of General McClellan can hardly be more strongly put than by this statement; but how is it to be reconciled with General Barnard's subsequently-expressed opinion?

communication with each other, and that, too, by bridges strong enough to stand a flood and long enough to stretch across the whole bottom-land of the river. These necessary works were delayed, and the labors and exposures of the men greatly increased, by the incessant rains. General McClellan's communications to the authorities at Washington show how he was tried and baffled by the obstinately bad weather. On the 4th of June he telegraphs to the President, "Terrible rain-storm during the night and morning; not yet cleared off. Chickahominy flooded, bridges in bad condition;" and on the next day he says to the Secretary of War, "Rained most of the night; has now ceased, but it is not clear. The river still very high and troublesome." On the 7th he tells the Secretary,—

> "The whole face of the country is a perfect bog, entirely impassable for artillery, or even cavalry, except directly in the narrow roads, which renders any general movement, either of this or the rebel army, utterly out of the question until we have more favorable weather."

Three days after, in another despatch to the Secretary, he says,—

> "I am completely checked by the weather. The roads and fields are literally impassable for artillery,—almost so for infantry. The Chickahominy is in a dreadful state: we have another rain-storm on our hands.
>
> "I shall attack as soon as the weather and ground will permit; but there will be a delay, the extent of which no one can foresee, for the season is altogether abnormal."

The heat of the weather, the poisonous miasma

which the sun drew up from the saturated soil, and the heavy toils of the men, began to tell sadly upon the general health of the army. And the vigilant and active enemy allowed us no repose. Little skirmishes and affairs of outposts were constantly occurring; showers of shells would sometimes suddenly fall upon the tents; and no one could say whether these demonstrations were not the preludes to serious attacks. Our men were obliged to work at the intrenchments and upon the bridges as the Jews builded on the walls of Jerusalem: "They which builded on the wall, and they that bare burdens, with those that laded, every one with one of his hands wrought in the work, and with the other hand held a weapon. For the builders, every one had his sword girded by his side, and so builded."*

General McClellan saw with nothing less than anguish of mind the golden moments of opportunity slipping away from him unimproved, and his noble army slowly wasting by disease and exposure. From trustworthy sources of information, he had good reason to believe that the enemy were receiving large accessions to their strength; and in the north, like an ominous cloud, loomed up the corps of the indefatigable Jackson, about which frequent rumors began to fly through the air. General McClellan knew his old classmate well enough to know that he was not a man to lose any time, and that, sooner or later, he would be a formidable element of danger on our right flank. His

---

* Nehemiah iv. 17, 18.

communications to the Government at Washington are full of earnest, almost passionate, entreaties for reinforcements, and in them he restates the reasons why he deems it important that his hands should be strengthened. He suggests that portions of the army of General Halleck, then in the Southwest, might be detached for this purpose. The replies of the Secretary of War are friendly and encouraging in tone. On the 11th of June he tells General McClellan that McCall's force, forming part of McDowell's corps, was on its way, and that it was intended to send the rest of McDowell's corps to him as speedily as possible. General McCall's division, numbering about eleven thousand men, arrived on the 12th and 13th; but these were the only reinforcements that General McClellan received till after the retreat to Harrison's Landing.

General McDowell was at this time on the Rappahannock, with about forty thousand men, including McCall's division. He expected to join General McClellan, and was most desirous of doing so; for on the 10th of June he wrote to the latter, saying, "For the third time I am ordered to join you, and hope this time to get through. * * * * I wish to say I go with the greatest satisfaction, and hope to arrive with my main body in time to be of service. McCall goes in advance, by water. I will be with you in ten days with the remainder, by Fredericksburg." On the 12th he wrote again to General McClellan, telling him that he shall not be with him on so early a day as he had previously announced, but still expecting to join him. It would have been an easy four days' march for McDowell's corps to have made the desired junction with the Army of the Potomac; but the junction never was made, and on the 27th of June the corps of McDowell, Frémont, and Banks were consolidated into one body, called the Army of Virginia, and put under the command of General Pope! Whether this disposition of McDowell's force was in consequence of a real and sudden change of opinion in the councils of the War Department, or whether there was never a settled purpose that he should go to Richmond, and General McClellan was only amused with hopes never meant to be realized, is a matter on which it is now useless to speculate. There would be more of contempt in the one case, and more of indignation in the other; but it could make little difference practically with General McClellan whether he was the victim of want of decision or want of frankness. He was entitled to fair dealing, and the country was entitled to consistency and firmness. In the management of great interests like these, caprice expands to the dimensions of crime.

On the 13th of June the rebel General Stuart, with fifteen hundred cavalry and four pieces of artillery, made a sudden dash upon a small cavalry force we had at Hanover Court-House, and overpowered them. They then swept on to Tunstall's Station on the York Railroad, made an attack upon a railway-train, which contrived to escape in spite of obstructions which had been laid upon the track, though the engineer and some of the passengers were killed. A detachment was sent off to White House to destroy stores, and the main body pushed on to New Kent Court-House, where they were soon joined by their friends, and remained some hours. At night they crossed the Chickahominy and made their way into the Confederate lines.

This must be admitted to have been a dashing and brilliant expedition. A continuous sweep was made clear round the Federal forces, a few prisoners were taken, and a considerable amount of valuable stores was destroyed. The material losses were not much; but the moral results were of consequence. It encouraged and exhilarated the enemy; and, above all, it was a startling revelation to General McClellan of the weak points in his position, and of the danger he was in of having his communications cut and his supplies by rail interrupted.

On the 18th of June, General McClellan had made arrangements to have transports, with supplies of provisions and forage, under a convoy of gunboats, sent up James River. They reached Harrison's Landing in time to be of use to the army on its arrival there. Two considerations had led him to adopt this course. First, in case of an advance on Richmond, our communications with the depot at the White House might be severed; and, second, he had already begun to feel that the increasing pressure upon his right might force him to make a flank movement and establish a new base of operations on the James River.

On Wednesday, June 25, the Army of the Potomac was thus placed. The several corps of Keyes, Heintzelman, Sumner, and Franklin, comprising eight divisions, were on the right bank of the Chickahominy. They were disposed in a semicircular line of three miles in length, stretching from White Oak Swamp on the left to Golding's house and the Chickahominy on the right. The front of this line was strengthened by six redoubts, mounting from five to nine guns each, connected by rifle-pits, or barricades, which contained numerous *emplacements* for artillery. Extensive "slashings"* were made in front, wherever the woods approached too near. Head-quarters were at Dr. Trent's house, in rear of the right, and near Sumner's upper bridge.

On the left bank of the river were Porter's corps, comprising two divisions, and McCall's Pennsylvania Reserves. The troops were disposed along a line extending from New Bridge, on the left, to Beaver Dam Creek, on the right. We had an advanced post, composed of a regiment and a battery, on the heights overlooking Mechanicsville; and a line of pickets was stretched along the river between the Mechanicsville and Meadow bridges. Four batteries had been constructed on the left bank, on the ground occupied by Porter; and these batteries mounted six guns each. They were in-

* A "slashing" is a kind of defence made by cutting down trees in front of a position, two or three feet from the ground, and allowing them to fall. Their branches thus form a barrier against the advances of infantry, and a space is opened for the play of artillery.

tended to operate upon the enemy's positions and batteries opposite, or to defend the bridges which connected the two wings of the army.

Some of the bridges built by our troops were of no use to us, because the enemy held the *débouches*, or ground that commanded the road, on the right bank. We could use, on the 25th of June, the following: Bottom's bridge, in rear of our left, and between five and six miles from its front; the railroad bridge; Sumner's upper bridge; Woodbury's, Alexander's, and Duane's bridges. These last afforded a very direct communication between the two wings of the army. As our operations against Richmond were conducted along the roads leading to it from the east and northeast, Bottom's bridge was of little direct service to us. Most of the supplies for the troops on the right bank of the river were brought up by the railroad and over the railroad bridge.

As it was now certain that the army was not to be strengthened by any reinforcements from McDowell, General McClellan resolved to do the best he could with what he had. He had covered the front of his position with defensive works, to enable him to bring the greatest possible numbers into action, and to secure the army against the consequences of unforeseen disaster. As Jackson had kept McDowell from joining him, he hoped that Jackson might also be kept from joining Lee.

THE SEVEN DAYS.

On the 25th of June, a forward movement of the picket-line of the left was ordered, preparatory to a general and final advance. The orders were successfully carried out, and about a mile of ground was gained, with small loss. The advantage thus secured was important, as by it both the corps of Heintzelman and Sumner were placed in a better position for supporting the main attack, which it was intended General Franklin should commence the following day. During this day, June 25, information came that the enemy had received reinforcements from Beauregard's army, and that Jackson was near Hanover Court-House with a large body of troops.

On the next day, Thursday, the 26th, General McClellan had intended to make a final attack; but he was anticipated by the enemy, and assailed on his right by a strong force which crossed the Chickahominy at Meadow bridge and near Mechanicsville. It appears that on the 25th a council of the Confederate generals was held at Richmond, and it was determined that while Jackson was moving upon the right flank of the Federal army a general and simultaneous attack should be made upon the whole line. When the approach of the enemy was discovered on our right, our pickets were called in, and the regiment and battery at Mechanicsville were withdrawn. A strong position was taken by our troops so as to resist the threatened attack. It extended along the left bank of Beaver Dam Creek, a slender tributary of the Chickahominy, which runs nearly north and south. The front line was composed of McCall's division: Seymour's brigade held the left, and Reynolds's the right. Meade's brigade was in reserve. The left of the line was covered by the river, the right by two brigades of Morell's division, deployed for the purpose of protecting that flank. The position had been carefully prepared, and was materially strengthened by "slashings" and rifle-pits. The creek in front, bordered by beautiful catalpa-trees in flower, was crossed by only two roads practicable for artillery. It was to force these roads that the enemy made especial efforts. Their attack began at three P.M. along the whole line, and a determined attempt was made at the same time to carry the upper road. General Reynolds succeeded in resisting this attempt, and the enemy fell back for a while. Our troops then had a breathing-space for a couple of hours,—though the fire of the artillery and the skirmishing did not cease. The passage of the lower road was then attempted; but here also General Seymour was successful. The action ceased as the darkness gathered, and the enemy retired at nine o'clock from the front of a position which it had assailed in vain and with very heavy loss. We had been successful at all points; and the troops that lay that night in front of Richmond will never forget the enthusiasm that ran like wildfire through our lines, from the heights of the upper Chickahominy to the lowlands of White Oak Swamp, when the news of the success was brought to them, and, amid the ringing cheers of men, the bands, long silent by command, filled the air with strains of triumphant music.

In the course of the 26th, the rapid movement of events, and especially the cloud of advancing forces on our right, every moment growing darker and more menacing, determined General McClellan to put into immediate execution that plan of transferring his base of operations to the James River which he had been meditating for some days, and in view of which he had already directed large supplies of forage and provisions to be forwarded. The task was one of no common difficulty. The distance between the points of departure and destination was about seventeen miles. An army of ninety thousand men, including cavalry and artillery, was to be marched this distance; and, what was much more difficult, a boundless procession of four thousand wagons, carrying supplies, must go with it, a large siege-train must be transported, and a herd of twenty-five hundred oxen must be driven. For the wagons, the train, and the cattle there was but one road available: luckily, it was in good condition. But it ran north and south, and between it and Richmond there were several roads going east and west, along which attacks might be expected from an active and vigilant enemy. General McClellan, in short, was attempting one of the most difficult and dangerous enterprises in war,—a flank movement in the face of a superior force. But there was no help for it: it must be done.

Time was now an element of the greatest importance. The design was to be kept concealed from the enemy till the latest possible moment, and every instant of the precious interval was to be profitably employed. Orders were immediately telegraphed to Colonel Ingalls, quartermaster at the White House, to run the cars till the last moment, filling them with provisions and ammunition, to load all his wagons with subsistence and send them to Savage's Station, to forward as many supplies as possible to James River, and to destroy the rest. These commands were all obeyed, and so promptly and skilfully that nearly every thing was saved, and only a comparatively small amount of stores destroyed.*

To begin auspiciously the contemplated movement, it was necessary to keep the enemy in check on the left bank of the river as long as possible, to give time for the removal of the siege-guns and trains. The night following the 26th of June was a busy one on the right of our army, and the work of removal went on till after sunrise; but shortly before daylight it was sufficiently advanced to permit the withdrawal of the troops from Beaver Dam Creek. A new position was taken, in an arc of a circle, covering the approaches to our bridges of communication. The first line was composed of the divisions of Morell and Sykes, the former on

* The Prince de Joinville says that a complete railway train, locomotive, tender, and cars, which had been left on the rails, was sent headlong over the broken bridge into the river. Nothing was left for the enemy but three siege-guns; and these were the only siege-guns he captured.

the left, the latter on the right. The division of McCall was posted in reserve, and fifteen companies of cavalry under General Cooke were in rear of the left. The battle-ground was a rolling country, partly wooded and partly open, extending from the descent to the Chickahominy on the left, and curving around, in rear of Coal Harbor, towards the river again. Our artillery was posted on the commanding ground, and in the intervals between the divisions and brigades; and the slope towards the river, on our left, was also swept by the fire of four batteries, one of them of siege-guns, on the right bank of the river. General Stoneman's movable column, comprising most of our cavalry and some picked troops of the other arms, which had been cut off by the rapid advance of Jackson, fell back on White House, and rendered no assistance during the battle.

Our dispositions were completed about noon of Friday, June 27, and shortly after that hour the skirmishers of the enemy appeared, advancing rapidly, and a general attack was made upon the whole position. The engagement soon became extremely severe, and General Porter asked for reinforcements. At two P.M., Slocum's division of the 6th Corps was ordered to cross the river and support him. By three P.M. the pressure of the superior numbers of the enemy had become so heavy that all the reserves had been moved forward, and our line, thus strengthened, met and resisted repeated and desperate attacks along the whole front. General Slocum's division arrived at half-past three, and was distributed along the weaker portions of our line. Our troops, including this division, numbered about thirty-five thousand men; and it is believed that they were attacked by from sixty to seventy thousand of the enemy. Many of our men were wearied by the fighting of the day before, and most of them by having been under arms for more than two days. The pressure of the superior numbers of the enemy was very hard to bear; but it was borne manfully, and, time after time, on the left and on the right, our troops repulsed the determined attacks of the swarming Confederates, who charged again and again up to their position. Every effort of the enemy failed to break our lines until about seven o'clock, when our left was forced, and the whole position flanked by a furious attack of fresh troops. The battle of Gaines's Mill was lost. Our men fell back to the hill in the rear, overlooking the bridge. Two brigades from the 2d Corps arrived most opportunely at this moment. They checked and drove back the stragglers, and advanced boldly to the front. Their cheers were heard by the enemy; and the knowledge that fresh troops had arrived, the terrible losses they had themselves sustained, and the gathering darkness, prevented them from following up their advantage.

The battle was lost, and with it we lost about nine thousand men and twenty guns; but the object for which it was fought had been attained. The enemy was checked, and the needed time was gained. Our siege-guns and material were saved, and the right wing, under cover of the night, joined the main body of the army on the right bank of the river. The rear-guard crossed at six o'clock in the morning, destroying the bridge behind them.

Saturday, June 28, was for our army a day rather of marching and working than of fighting. The enemy were exhausted by the desperate fight of the previous day: they were also on the left bank of the river, or at least the greater part of them were, and the bridges were destroyed, so that they must either build new bridges in order to cross the river, or else fall back to the Mechanicsville bridge. Thus a few precious hours were gained. In accordance with orders given by General McClellan to his corps commanders, assembled by him at his head-quarters on the evening of the 27th, the execution of his plan for a flank movement to the James River was commenced at once, under his own direction.

General Keyes, with his 4th Corps and its artillery and baggage, crossed the White Oak Swamp bridge, and seized strong positions on the opposite side, to cover the passage of the other troops and trains. General Heintzelman and General Sumner, with the 3d and 2d Corps, remained in the works. General Franklin, while withdrawing his command from their position in the works, was attacked by artillery-firing from three points, and an attempt was made to carry a part of his line. The fighting here was sharp for a little while, and extremely damaging to the enemy, who speedily retired. This was the only fighting of the day. Men were busy loading the wagons with ammunition, provisions, and necessary baggage, and destroying all that could not be carried off. General Porter, with the 5th Corps, began the passage of the White Oak Swamp during the day.

On Sunday, the 29th, the troops of the 4th Corps remained in their position, covering the road through the swamp, until relieved, as will be mentioned, by the arrival of General Slocum; and those of the 5th Corps held their ground beyond the swamp, covering the roads leading from Richmond towards the line of retreat. McCall's division also crossed the swamp, and took a proper position to aid in covering the general movement.

Day broke darkly: clouds and fog hung very low, and a thick mist added to the cheerlessness of the morning. It was a sorry sight to see the empty embrasures, the deserted camps, filled but the night before, and for so many previous days, with guns and fighting-men. But the darkness of the morning was good for troops that desired to steal a march on the enemy, and its coolness was good for men that were to fight.

Slocum's division of the 6th Corps marched straight back to Savage's Station, where it was to be posted as a reserve to the position to be taken by the rear-guard; but, on reaching the Station, it received orders to cross the swamp and relieve the corps of General Keyes. The rear-guard, composed of the 2d and 3d Corps and Smith's division of the 6th Corps, moved from the works at daylight, and marched about half-way to Savage's Station, halting at Allen's farm, where a line was formed on both sides of the railroad, towards Richmond.

About nine o'clock the enemy made an attack with infantry and artillery, and renewed the attempt twice. The firing of both sides was sharp for a while, but the assault was repulsed with ease by the skirmish-line of Summer's corps, supported by artillery, and our loss was very slight. A report that the enemy had repaired the bridges, and crossed the Chickahominy in the rear of our position at Allen's farm, was brought to General Sumner at that place, and he at once fell back to Savage's Station and united his command with Smith's division of the 6th Corps, which General Franklin, by reason of the same report, had already moved thither. The junction took place a little after noon, and General Sumner assumed command of the forces so united.

At Savage's Station a large field extended to the left from the railroad, and the ground sloped steadily downwards towards Richmond. General Sumner formed his line in this field, at right angles to the railroad. The rise in the ground gave our troops an excellent view of the whole position, and was favorable for the posting of artillery. Some regiments were also placed on the right of our position, nearly parallel to the track, so as to watch the apprehended approach of the enemy from the left bank of the river. General Heintzelman, in seeming violation of his orders, withdrew from his position on the left before four o'clock, and marched to the swamp, which he crossed at Brackett's Ford. Thus the rear-guard was weakened by the loss of nearly fifteen thousand men, and the situation of

General Sumner appeared critical. His position, however, was good, and the troops excellent. The whole of the 2d Corps, said to be the only corps in the army which has never to this day lost a gun or a color, was there, with one division of Franklin's corps. About four o'clock the enemy commenced his attack in large force by the Williamsburg road, which here runs nearly parallel to the railroad. The enemy's left was supported by their boasted iron-clad railroad battery, mounted, according to their newspapers, with a rifled thirty-two. The attack was gallantly met. General Burns, commanding the front line, rendered special service. The reserves were successively sent forward, and the action continued with great obstinacy till after eight in the evening, when the enemy were driven from the field and into the woods beyond, where our deployed companies, which were speedily thrown forward, found the ground thickly strewn with the bodies of the sufferers. The position we had gained in this brilliant and picturesque engagement was held till the road in the rear was cleared; and during the ensuing hours of darkness, all the troops crossed the White Oak Swamp bridge, and Sumner's last brigade, commanded by General French, destroyed the bridge at six o'clock in the morning.

During the same night, the 4th Corps, followed by the 5th, was moving towards the river, and on the morning of Monday, June 30, General Keyes had arrived there in safety. He took up a position below Turkey Creek bridge, with his left resting on the river. General Porter posted the 5th Corps so as to prolong Keyes's line to the right and cover the Charles City road to Richmond. General Franklin, with his own corps, Richardson's division of the 2d Corps, and Naglee's brigade, held the passage of White Oak Swamp. The position of the remaining troops was changed at times during the day; but it is enough to say that they were so disposed as to hold the ground in front of the road connecting Franklin's position with Porter's right, so as to cover the movement of the trains in the rear. General McClellan occupied himself in examining the whole line, rectifying the position of the troops, and expediting the passage of the trains.

The fierce battle fought on Monday, June 30, is known by the name of the battle of Glendale, or Nelson's Farm. It is a little difficult to be understood, for two reasons. In the first place, the troops of the 2d and 3d Corps were so divided that the army may be said on that day to have been without its corps organization, and to have been an army of divisions, and those divisions, in several instances, were separated from their usual connection. In the second place, though the sharpest fighting was in or near Glendale, yet there was fighting along a line of about five miles, extending from White Oak Swamp to Malvern Hill, and lasting from noon till after dark.

The first attack was made on Franklin's position, which was assailed by a concentrated fire of artillery. A very fierce and obstinate artillery-combat took place here, and there was also some infantry-fighting. Our men suffered severely; but repeated attempts of the enemy to cross the swamp were unsuccessful, and General Franklin held the position till after dark.

Some two hours after the attack just mentioned was commenced, a strong column moved down the Charles City road, near which, on its right, General Slocum was posted. General Kearney's division of the 3d Corps connected with General Slocum's left. General McCall, with the Pennsylvania Reserves, prolonged our line to the left, crossing the New Market road, and General Hooker's division of the 3d Corps was on the left of McCall. General Sumner, with Sedgwick's division in reserve, was in rear of McCall, on the Quaker road. The first attempt of the enemy was made on Slocum's left; but it was checked by his artillery, and abandoned. Then, passing to their right, the enemy made a fierce onslaught on General McCall. His division speedily gave way, with loss of general officers and guns, and the enemy pressed on so vigorously that their musketry proved fatal on the Quaker road. The centre of our army was nearly pierced, the main road of communication almost in the enemy's power. At this critical moment Sumner hurried to the front some regiments of Sedgwick's division, just returned at the double quick from White Oak Swamp, to which they had been marched in order to support Franklin. A gallant advance was made; Sumner's artillery opened sharply. The advance of the enemy was checked, some ground was regained, and some guns were retaken. Hooker, moving to his right, aided in the repulse. The gap caused by the giving way of McCall's command was speedily closed, and our line of retreat was once more securely held. Another effort was made by the enemy on Kearney's left; but this also was repulsed, with heavy loss. The enemy's attack thus failed at all points; but our success was costly. We lost heavily in killed and wounded, and in guns. All, or nearly all, of McCall's guns were left in the hands of the enemy.

On the same day, at about five P.M., an attack was made on General Porter's left flank, near Malvern Hill. It was met by the concentrated fire of about thirty guns on the hill, by the fire from the gunboats on the river, and by the infantry-fire of Warren's brigade. The enemy was soon forced to retreat, with the loss of two guns. Thus, on the right, in the centre, and on the left, the fierce and persistent efforts of the enemy had failed; but our trains were not yet in safety, and our communications not yet secure, so that more marching and more fighting were still before the brave Army of the Potomac. The troops distributed along the line between White Oak Swamp and Malvern Hill fell back to the latter place during the night, and were posted there, as they arrived, by General Barnard, who received his instructions from the general commanding.

On Tuesday, July 1, the sun rose on a scene such as few but soldiers see, and soldiers rarely. The whole Army of the Potomac was massed on the slopes of Malvern Hill. It is an open plateau, and extends about a mile and a half in width and three-quarters of a mile in depth. On the highest ground there is an old-fashioned Virginia house, of brick, in one story. Trees standing thickly supply it with grateful shade. Behind the house, the ground falls away as abruptly as at the Highlands of the Hudson, and the delighted eye ranges over miles and miles of level country, profusely clothed with an almost tropical vegetation, and watered by the James, the Appomattox, and Turkey Creek. It is a scene of rare loveliness and peace; and gunboats, seemingly sleeping at their moorings on the gleaming river, half seen through the screen of foliage, added on that day to the air of repose which brooded over the whole landscape. But no stronger contrast could be presented than by the scene in front. On those broad slopes, in triple concentric lines, with the guns in the intervals and on the higher ground in the rear, the weary Army of the Potomac was rapidly ranging itself. The general commanding, and other general officers, were making the circuit of the position and superintending the movements of the troops, and, as by magic, the great army came into the order of battle. Cavalry escorts, the lancers with their red pennons fluttering beneath the glittering points of their weapons, gave animation to the scene.

The line taken up by our army was something more than the half of a circle. The left rested on the hill near the river, and the line curved round the hill and backwards, through a wooded country, towards a point below Haxall's, on the James. The flotilla was so moored as to protect our left flank and command the approaches from Richmond. Porter's corps was on the left; next came Couch's division of the 4th Corps, then Heintzelman's corps, then Sumner's, then Franklin's, and, on the extreme right, Keyes, with the remainder of the 4th Corps. The remains of McCall's division were in reserve, and stationed in the rear of Porter and Couch. The right, where the troops were less compact than elsewhere, was strengthened by "slashings" and barricades.

The enemy began to feel along our lines early in the day, and annoyed our troops by artillery-fire from various points. Batteries appeared, and fired, and disappeared only to present themselves again at a new point, and so keep our wearied troops from preparing by rest for the coming struggle. About three o'clock the real battle began. A heavy fire of artillery opened on Couch's division and the left of Kearney's, which was connected with the right of Couch's; and a brisk attack of infantry on Couch's front speedily followed. The enemy, disregarding the fire of our artillery, pressed steadily on till they were within short musket-range. Then Couch's men, who had been lying down, sprang to their feet, and delivered a fire which destroyed the order of the enemy and drove them back in confusion. Their attack thus failed utterly, and the advantage gained was improved by an advance of our men for nearly half a mile, which gave them a better position.

About two hours of comparative quiet followed this discomfiture of the enemy, during which the general surveyed the whole line, and every thing was made ready for the coming attack, and kept so. It was begun at six o'clock; and Porter and Couch received it. The whole artillery of the enemy suddenly opened upon them, and brigade after brigade came rushing forward to carry their position, but only to meet the crushing fire of a determined infantry, and the tempest of grape, canister, and shell that poured upon them from our massed artillery, with the enormous projectiles that came howling over the pleasant woods and fields from the great guns on the river. Until dark—and the battle was when the days are longest—the enemy persisted in their desperate efforts, but to no purpose. It was a day of useless slaughter for them, but of comparatively trifling loss for us. The darkness fell like a curtain, to close and conceal the sublime spectacle of the battle of Malvern Hill.

With the last shots fired by the artillery, after nine o'clock in the evening of this day, the fighting of the "Seven Days" ended. The troops had little rest that night, for a further movement was ordered as soon as the enemy were finally repulsed. By the morning of the following day the whole army was marching rapidly towards Harrison's Landing, on the James River. As there was but one main road, it was necessary to crowd it to its utmost capacity with artillery and cavalry, while the infantry went on each side. A heavy rain soon began to fall,—such a rain as is only felt in the

South: the road first became slippery, then muddy, then deep with mud. Through this clinging soil the weary horses dragged their loads, while on each side the living stream of infantry forced its toilsome way through the thick and dripping underbrush which bordered the road. Fortunately, the distance was not great, and the troops poured rapidly into the vast plain on the river, and sank to rest upon its trampled wheat, their journey ended, their great task accomplished. The woods of the Peninsula were on one side of them, beautiful in their midsummer luxuriance, and perhaps concealing indefatigable enemies; but on the other was the broad river, bearing on its calm waters the powerful gunboats which displayed the flag of our navy, and, thanks to the provident foresight of the general commanding, bearing also countless vessels filled with the ammunition and equipments, the food and the clothing, of which our troops stood so much in need.

Mr. Emil Schalk,—a severe military critic, and chary of praise,—speaking of the retreat from the Chickahominy to the James River, says, "This plan of defence reflects the highest credit and honor on the general who conceived and carried it out."* Such is the opinion, it is believed, of all competent judges, whether soldiers by profession, or civilians who have made the art of war a special subject of study. It was a military movement of great danger and difficulty, extending over several days, marked

---

* Campaigns of 1862 and 1863, p. 179.

throughout by admirable combinations and dispositions,—in which nothing was overlooked, nothing was forgotten, and not a single mistake was made. The sagacious foresight, the calm self-reliance, the thorough professional knowledge, the vigilant eye, of the commanding general formed the power by which the whole breathing mass of courage and endurance was guided and propelled. And the conduct of the army was, to borrow General McClellan's own expression, "superb." The whole retreat was one unbroken strain upon their physical energies and moral force. They had to march all night and fight all day. The nervous exhaustion produced by toil and want of sleep was aggravated by the excessive heat of the weather, by which many a manly frame was prostrated. The enemy were brave, vigilant, well handled, superior in numbers, and confident of success; but only at Gaines's Mill was any decisive advantage gained. At every point, at every moment, the Confederates had met organized courage, disciplined valor, the dauntless front of men who trusted in themselves and trusted in their commander; and at Malvern Hill the closing hours of danger and suffering were illumined by the blaze of victory, like the rich red sunset which ends a day of storm and cloud. And not only had our men fought admirably, but they had toiled patiently and intelligently. Guns were to be removed, wagons and teams were to be helped along, here a piece of road was to be mended, and there trees were to be cut down to obstruct the enemy's passage; and for all these labors the officers found quick faculty, serviceable hands, and a willing spirit. When it is remembered that the carriages and teams belonging to the army, stretched out in one line, would have reached nearly forty miles, we can understand that nothing could have insured their safe removal in the face of an enemy but that universal training of the brain and hand found among a people who are all taught to handle indifferently the pen, the axe, the gun, and the spade.

The general in command, when the James River had been reached, had a right to look around with just pride upon the army now sheltered and safe. On the 28th, in the bitterness of his soul, he had said, in a telegraphic message to the Secretary of War, "If I save this army now, I tell you plainly that I owe no thanks to you, or to any other persons in Washington. You have done your best to sacrifice this army." That army he had saved; and the army was conscious of it. But there was nothing of triumph in his own mind; for their safety had been won at fearful cost. Our killed, wounded, and missing from the 26th of June to the 1st of July reached the mournful aggregate of fifteen thousand. Of the sick and wounded, many had of necessity been left behind, but with a proper complement of surgeons and attendants and a bountiful supply of rations and medical stores.

And there was another consideration which might have deepened the sadness of his mind, if he had allowed his thoughts to dwell upon it at such a moment. He had conducted an important movement with a skill and success which an intelligent military judgment could understand and appreciate; but still that movement was a retreat. This was the great fact present to the public mind. He had been compelled to abandon his position before Richmond; the place was not taken: he was a general in command of a large army, and had failed to accomplish the object of his own hopes. The facts and events which had rendered a retrograde movement necessary required some reflection to make them understood and some candor to make them felt. His knowledge of human nature, and of the bitterness and unscrupulousness of party, was enough to reveal to him the harsh judgments, the misconstructions, the injustice, the cruel insinuations, the calumnious charges, to which he had exposed himself by the crime of failure,—that crime which the public is so slow to forgive. He must have foreseen how the pert phrase-makers of the land—who conduct campaigns so admirably in their arm-chairs, and dispose of brigades and divisions as easily as they fold and label their letters—would strive to mangle him with their pens,—weapons more cruel than the tiger's claw or the serpent's tooth,—and point out what he should have done, and should not have done, to have escaped the shame and disgrace of retreating before a rebel foe. Sir John Moore, dying in the arms of victory at the close of a successful retreat, said, "I hope the people of England will be satisfied: I hope my country will do me justice." His country, in time, did justice to that great man. Sooner or later, the world comes round to see the truth and do the right;

and for the coming of that time General McClellan can afford to wait.

But the saddest of all experiences for a commanding general is to lose the confidence of his army. That cup was never put to General McClellan's lips. His soldiers were intelligent enough to understand what he had done, and generous enough to be grateful to him for it. They had witnessed his toils and exposures, his calm self-reliance, his resolute front, his unaltered brow: they had seen him perplexed but not cast down, anxious but not despairing. The approach of danger, the burden of responsibility, had called forth reserved powers and unrevealed energies. Their common perils, their common labors, the trying scenes they had passed through, the safety they had secured, had created new ties of sympathy between the commanding general and his noble army. No muttered curses fell upon his ear, no sullen, averted countenances met his eye; but, as he rode along their lines, shouts of welcome instead, and faces glowing with honest joy, passed a judgment upon his course that enabled him to meet with composure the sneers of the scoffer, the malice of partisan falsehood, and the rash censures of presumptuous half-knowledge.

CHAPTER IX.

THE history of the Army of the Potomac during the months of July and August, 1862, may be told in a few words. During their retrograde movement to the banks of the James, they had been fearfully weakened by losses in killed, wounded, and prisoners; but they were not in the least demoralized. They had conducted themselves in a way to move the admiration and win the gratitude of their commander; and from a full heart, on the 4th of July, he issued to them the following admirable and heartful address:—

"HEAD-QUARTERS ARMY OF THE POTOMAC,
CAMP NEAR HARRISON'S LANDING, July 4, 1862.

"SOLDIERS OF THE ARMY OF THE POTOMAC:—Your achievements of the last ten days have illustrated the valor and endurance of the American soldier. Attacked by superior forces, and without hope of reinforcements, you have succeeded in changing your base of operations by a flank movement, always regarded as the most hazardous of military expedients. You have saved all your material, all your trains and all your guns, except a few lost in battle, taking in return guns and colors from the enemy. Upon your march, you have been assailed day after day, with desperate fury, by men of the same race and nation, skilfully massed and led. Under every disadvantage of number, and necessarily of position also, you have in every conflict beaten back your foes with enormous slaughter. Your conduct ranks you among the celebrated armies of history. No one will now question that each of you may always with pride say, 'I belong to the Army of the Potomac.' You have reached the new base, complete in organization and unimpaired in spirit. The enemy may at any moment attack you. We are prepared to meet them. I have personally established your lines. Let them come, and we will convert their repulse into a final defeat. Your Government is strengthening you with the resources of a great people. On this, our nation's birthday, we declare to our foes, who are rebels against the best interests of mankind, that this army shall enter the capital of the so-called Confederacy, that our national Constitution shall prevail, and that the Union, which can alone insure internal peace and external security to each State, 'must and shall be preserved,' cost what it may in time, treasure, and blood.

"GEORGE B. McCLELLAN."

The high spirit which breathes through this address, animates also his communications with the Government at Washington. He informs the President, in a despatch of July 7, that his men were in splendid spirits and "anxious to try it again;" and in this anxiety he himself distinctly shared.

Having a brief interval of comparative leisure, he drew up and addressed to the President a letter, under date of July 7, containing certain views regarding the conduct of the war, which, in his judgment, were essential to its objects and success. The letter is as follows:—

"HEAD-QUARTERS ARMY OF THE POTOMAC,
CAMP NEAR HARRISON'S LANDING, VA., July 7, 1862.

"MR. PRESIDENT:—You have been fully informed that the rebel army is in our front, with the purpose of overwhelming us by attacking our position or reducing us by blocking our river-communications. I cannot but regard our condition as critical, and I earnestly desire, in view of possible contingencies, to lay before your Excellency, for your private consideration, my general views concerning the existing state of the rebellion, although they do not strictly relate to the situation of this army or strictly come within the scope of my official duties. These views amount to convictions, and are deeply impressed upon my mind and heart. Our cause must never be abandoned; it is the cause of free institutions and self-government. The Constitution and the Union must be preserved, whatever may be the cost in time, treasure, and blood. If secession is successful, other dissolutions are clearly to be seen in the future. Let neither military disaster, political faction, nor foreign war shake your settled purpose to enforce the equal operation of the laws of the United States upon the people of every State.

"The time has come when the Government must determine upon a civil and military policy covering the whole ground of our national trouble.

"The responsibility of determining, declaring, and supporting such civil and military policy, and of directing the whole course of national affairs in regard to the rebellion, must now be assumed and exercised by you, or our cause will be lost. The Constitution gives you power sufficient even for the present terrible exigency.

"This rebellion has assumed the character of war: as such it should be regarded, and it should be conducted upon the highest principles known to Christian civilization. It should not be a war looking to the subjugation of the people of any State, in any event. It should not be at all a war upon population, but against armed forces and political organizations. Neither confiscation of property, political executions of persons, territorial organization of States, or forcible abolition of slavery, should be contemplated for a moment.

"In prosecuting the war, all private property and unarmed persons should be strictly protected, subject only to the necessity of military operations; all private property taken for military use should be paid or receipted for; pillage and waste should be treated as high crimes, all unnecessary trespass sternly prohibited, and offensive demeanor by the military towards citizens promptly rebuked. Military arrests should not be tolerated, except in places where active hostilities exist; and oaths, not required by enactments constitutionally made, should be neither demanded nor received.

"Military government should be confined to the preservation of public order and the protection of political right. Military power should not be allowed to interfere with the relations of servitude, either by supporting or impairing the authority of the master, except for repressing disorder, as in other cases. Slaves, contraband under the act of Congress, seeking military protection, should receive it. The right of the Government to appropriate permanently to its own service claims to slave-labor should be asserted, and the right of the owner to compensation therefor should be recognized. This principle might be extended, upon grounds of military necessity and security, to all the slaves within a particular State, thus working manumission in such State; and in Missouri, perhaps in Western Virginia also, and possibly even in Maryland, the expediency of such a measure is only a question of time. A system of policy thus constitutional and conservative, and pervaded by the influences of Christianity and freedom, would receive the support of almost all truly loyal men, would deeply impress the rebel masses and all foreign nations, and it might be humbly hoped that it would commend itself to the favor of the Almighty.

"Unless the principles governing the future conduct

of our struggle shall be made known and approved, the effort to obtain requisite forces will be almost hopeless. A declaration of radical views, especially upon slavery, will rapidly disintegrate our present armies. The policy of the Government must be supported by concentrations of military power. The national forces should not be dispersed in expeditions, posts of occupation, and numerous armies, but should be mainly collected into masses and brought to bear upon the armies of the Confederate States. Those armies thoroughly defeated, the political structure which they support would soon cease to exist.

"In carrying out any system of policy which you may form, you will require a commander-in-chief of the army, one who possesses your confidence, understands your views, and who is competent to execute your orders, by directing the military forces of the nation to the accomplishment of the objects by you proposed. I do not ask that place for myself. I am willing to serve you in such position as you may assign me, and I will do so as faithfully as ever subordinate served superior.

"I may be on the brink of eternity; and, as I hope for forgiveness from my Maker, I have written this letter with sincerity towards you and from love for my country.

"Very respectfully, your obedient servant,

"GEORGE B. MCCLELLAN,

"*Major-General commanding.*

"His Excellency A. LINCOLN, *President.*"

In regard to this communication, two questions have arisen. First, Was it proper for General McClellan to write such a letter? This would seem to be answered by the statement that he had previously asked and obtained the President's permission to do so. On the 20th of June he had said, in a despatch, "I would be glad to have permission to lay before your Excellency, by letter or telegraph, my views as to the present state of military affairs throughout the country;" and the next day the President replied, in language marked by that personal kindness which generally characterized his communications, "If it would not divert too much of your time and attention from the army under your immediate command, I would be glad to have your views as to the present state of military affairs throughout the whole country, as you say you would be glad to give them."

Second, Are the views which General McClellan sets forth in his communication sound and wise in point of fact? Upon this question much has been and will be said on both sides; but whatever is said on one side will do but little towards convincing the other. In short, it raises the issues on which the country began to be divided soon after the war broke out, and on which it is now rent in twain. Every man has made up his fagots on these questions and bound them round with the cords of passion and prejudice; and it is useless to attempt to disturb them. Time, which determines all things, will sooner or later determine whether General McClellan was right or wrong.

As to the Army of the Potomac, it was General McClellan's opinion that it ought not to be withdrawn, but that it should be promptly reinforced and thrown again upon Richmond. In his judgment, it was our policy to concentrate here every thing we could spare from less important points, in order to make a successful demonstration against the enemy in his most vital and important point. The Government was undecided in its plans. On the 4th of July the President had informed General McClellan that it was impossible to reinforce him so as to enable him to resume the offensive within a month or six weeks, and that therefore for the present a defensive policy was his only care, —adding, "Save the army, first, where you are, if you can, and, secondly, by removal, if you must."

On the 11th of July, one of the recommendations contained in General McClellan's letter of July 7 to the President was adopted, by the appointment of Major-General Halleck to the post of General-in-Chief of the entire army of the United States. This was the position held by General McClellan before he left Washington to conduct the Peninsular campaign. Its duties had subsequently been performed by the President and Secretary of War; and it was understood that they had a military adviser, in the person of Major-General Hitchcock.

The disposition to be made of the Army of the Potomac was one of the first subjects to which the attention of the general-in-chief was called on his arrival in Washington; and, in order to observe for himself its condition, he made a visit to Harrison's Landing, leaving Washington on the 24th of July and returning on the 27th. The result of this visit was that General Halleck, after full consultation with his officers, came to the conclusion that it would not be possible to strengthen the Army of the Peninsula with the reinforcements which General McClellan required, and he therefore determined to withdraw it to some position where it could unite with that of General Pope, who was now in command of the Army of Virginia. But this decision was not immediately made known to General McClellan, who on the 30th of July received a despatch from General Halleck saying that, in order to enable him to move in any direction, it was necessary to relieve him of his sick, and that arrangements had been made accordingly, adding, "I hope you will send them away as quickly as possible, and advise me of their removal." General McClellan began immediately to execute this order, but pressed the general-in-chief to inform him of the views of the Government in regard to the future disposition of the Army of the Potomac, because if a forward movement were contemplated many of the sick could be of service at the depots, and he could not decide what cases to send off unless he knew what was to be done with the army.

On the 3d of August, Coggin's Point, on the south side of the James, was occupied by our troops, and Colonel Averill, at the head of three hundred cavalry, attacked and dispersed a cavalry force of the enemy four hundred and fifty in number, at Sycamore Church, on the main road from Petersburg to Suffolk, four miles from Cole's House. On the 5th of August, General Hooker attacked a very considerable force of infantry and artillery stationed at Malvern Hill, carried the position, and drove the enemy back to Newmarket, four miles distant; and on the same day Colonel Averill returned from a reconnoissance in the direction of Savage's Station towards Richmond, in the course of which he had encountered the 10th Virginia Cavalry near White Oak Swamp bridge and driven them back some distance towards Richmond. These military demonstrations were made with the expectation, or at least the hope, that an offensive movement upon Richmond would still be the policy of the Government.

On the 3d of August, the decision of the Government was distinctly communicated to General McClellan in a despatch from General Halleck, in which he said, "It is determined to withdraw your army from the Peninsula to Acquia Creek. You will take immediate means to effect this, covering the movement the best you can. Its real object and withdrawal should be concealed even from your own officers." This was a heavy blow to General McClellan; and he earnestly protested against it in a long telegraphic despatch, dated August 4, to which General Halleck replied in a letter dated August 6.

General McClellan's arguments against the removal of the army and in favor of an offensive movement, as presented in his despatch, are briefly as follows. The army was in excellent discipline and condition, and in a favorable position, being only twenty-five miles from Richmond, and they would not be likely to have a battle till they were within ten miles of it.

At Acquia Creek they would be seventy-five

miles from Richmond, with only land-transportation all the way.

The step would demoralize the army, and have a most depressing effect upon the people of the North, and might induce foreign Powers to recognize our adversaries.

The communication concludes thus:—

"It may be said that there are no reinforcements available. I point to Burnside's force,—to that of Pope, not necessary to maintain a strict defensive in front of Washington and Harper's Ferry,—to those portions of the Army of the West not required for a strict defensive there. Here, directly in front of this army, is the heart of the rebellion: it is here that all our resources should be collected to strike the blow which will determine the fate of the nation.

"All points of secondary importance elsewhere should be abandoned, and every available man brought here. A decided victory here, and the military strength of the rebellion is crushed. It matters not what partial reverses we may meet with elsewhere: here is the true defence of Washington; it is here, on the banks of the James, that the fate of the Union should be decided.

"Clear in my convictions of right, strong in the consciousness that I have ever been, and still am, actuated solely by the love of my country, knowing that no ambitious or selfish motives have influenced me from the commencement of this war, I do now what I never did in my life before: I entreat that this order may be rescinded.

"If my counsel does not prevail, I will with a sad heart obey your orders to the utmost of my power, directing to the movement, which I clearly foresee will be one of the utmost delicacy and difficulty, whatever skill I may possess. Whatever the result may be—and may God grant that I am mistaken in my forebodings!—I shall at least have the internal satisfaction that I have written and spoken frankly, and have sought to do the best in my power to avert disaster from my country."

The considerations urged by General Halleck in reply were as follows:—

The enemy's forces in and around Richmond were estimated at two hundred thousand. General Pope's army was only forty thousand; the Army of the Peninsula, effective force, about ninety thousand. The relative position of the enemy towards them was such that his command and that of Pope must be united; and they could not be united by land without exposing both to destruction. It was a military impossibility to send Pope's forces by water to the Peninsula; and thus the only alternative was to send the Army of the Peninsula to Pope.

A simple change of position to a new and by no means distant base would not demoralize an army in excellent discipline, unless the officers themselves should assist in that demoralization,—which he is satisfied they would not.

The political effect of the withdrawal might at first be unfavorable; but the public were beginning to understand the necessity of it, and they would have more confidence in a united army than in its separated fragments.

It would be impossible to furnish the requisite reinforcements under several weeks.

To keep the army in its present position until it could be reinforced would almost destroy it, in the sickly region where it then was. In the mean time,

General Pope's forces would be exposed to the heavy blows of the enemy, without the slightest hope of assistance from General McClellan.

A majority of the highest officers of the Army of the Potomac were decidedly in favor of the movement.

All General McClellan's plans required reinforcements; but reinforcements could not be had.

There was nothing, of course, for General McClellan to do but to submit, and obey the orders of his superior,—which he did with a heavy heart.

In the mean time, the removal of the sick, in compliance with the order of July 30, was going on as rapidly as possible, though somewhat interrupted by another order, of August 6, directing the immediate shipment of a regiment of cavalry and several batteries of artillery to Burnside's command at Acquia Creek. The order of August 3d also required the transportation of a great amount of material. All this was obviously a work of time; but in spite of this, in spite of General McClellan's repeated and emphatic assertions to the contrary, General Halleck's mind became possessed with the notion that the removal of the sick had not been begun when the order was first received, and that the whole business of transportation was not pushed on so rapidly as it should have been. But General McClellan never received from the Administration "that forbearance, patience, and confidence" for which he had asked,—and which every soldier has a right to ask,—but always had a countenance of suspicion and distrust turned towards him. He had now twelve thousand sick and wounded to transport, besides cavalry, artillery, wagons, baggage, and supplies. He was working day and night to speed their removal; he was in a situation that demanded kind consideration, for he was the leader of an enterprise which had failed, whose hopes had been crossed, whose plans for the future had been arrested, who was obeying faithfully orders which he deemed unwise; and surely he did not need at such a moment the further discipline of a despatch like this, under date of August 9:—"Considering the amount of transportation at your disposal, your delay is not satisfactory: you must move with all possible celerity."

The plain statements in General McClellan's Report, and the letters of the Quartermaster and Assistant Quartermaster, which are also to be found there, are sufficient to vindicate him completely from the charge of negligence or delay in transporting his materials and men. Indeed, in an issue like that between him and the commander-in-chief the testimony of General McClellan must be held to be decisive. Here was a certain work to be done, the removal of a certain number of persons, sick and well, and a certain amount of stores, supplies, and warlike materials from one point to another. The time within which the task could be accomplished depended upon several elements which were wholly matters of fact,—such as the number of vessels, their capacity, their speed, the state of the water in the river, and the wharf-accommodations at the points of departure and arrival,—upon all which General McClellan had, and General Halleck had not, the means of being exactly informed. Thus, it was General McClellan's knowledge against General Halleck's surmise or conjecture. General Halleck, sitting in his office at Washington, might have thought that there was unreasonable delay; but General McClellan alone could have known what was the proportion between the work to be done and the means to do it.

General McClellan, happily for his peace of mind and health of body, is not a man of irritable temperament, and so he could possess his soul in patience under the rash expressions of General Halleck's impatience, which, too, may have had the excuse of being prompted by patriotic zeal and professional activity; but this excuse cannot be offered on behalf of a deliberate wrong. In a letter subsequently written to the Secretary of War, General Halleck says, "The evacuation of Harrison's Landing, however, was not commenced till the 14th, eleven days after it was ordered." The authority for this statement—which is neither more nor less than that General McClellan had refused or delayed for eleven days to execute a military order—is a despatch from the latter, under date of August 14, which says,—

"Movement has commenced,—by land and water. All the sick will be away by to-morrow night.* Every thing being done to carry out your orders." At the date of this despatch, nearly all the sick, a

* This would have been absolutely impossible if nearly all of them were not already gone.

large amount of supplies and materials, a regiment of cavalry, and five batteries of artillery had been removed, and the phrase "movement has commenced" referred obviously to the movement of the main army; and yet General Halleck sets his hand and gives his official sanction to a statement which distinctly conveys the impression that none of these things had been done at that time! Comment is unnecessary, as strong facts do not need the aid of strong language.*

---

*A passage between General Halleck and General McClellan is worthy of being preserved in a note, as one of the curiosities of official life. On the 12th of August, General McClellan's head-quarters were at Berkeley, seventy miles from Jamestown Island, the nearest telegraph-office. Being desirous of having more speedy and full explanation of the condition of affairs in the army than he could get by sending a steamer to Jamestown Island and waiting ten hours for a reply, he proposed to go in person to the office, and so informed General Halleck at the close of a despatch of the 12th. He accordingly went to Jamestown Island, but on arriving there found there was an interruption in the electric current, so that he was obliged to continue on to Fortress Monroe and across the Chesapeake Bay to Cherry-Stone Inlet, on the "Eastern Shore." He arrived there late in the evening, and immediately sent the following dispatch:—

"CHERRY-STONE, August 13, 1862, 11.30 P.M.

"Please come to the office; wish to talk to you. What news from Pope? "G. B. MCCLELLAN,
Major-General.

"Major-General H. W. HALLECK,
Washington."

The next day, at half-past twelve, he sent another despatch, as follows:—

On the 16th of August all the troops were in motion by land and water, and late in the afternoon

---

"CHERRY-STONE INLET, August 14, 1862, 12.30 A.M.

"Started to Jamestown Island to talk with you; found cable broken, and came here. Please read my long telegram. All quiet at camp. Enemy burned wharves at City Point yesterday. No rebel pickets within eight (8) miles of Coggin's Point yesterday.

"Richmond prisoners state that large force with guns left Richmond northward on Sunday.

"G. B. McCLELLAN,
"*Major-General.*

"Major-General H. W. HALLECK,
Washington."

To which the following reply was received:—

"WASHINGTON, August 14, 1862, 1.40 A.M.

"I have read your despatch. There is no change of plans. You will send up your troops as rapidly as possible. There is no difficulty in landing them. According to your own accounts, there is now no difficulty in withdrawing your forces. Do so with all possible rapidity.

"H. W. HALLECK,
"*Major-General.*

"Major-General G. B. McCLELLAN."

Before General McClellan had time to decipher and reply to this despatch, the telegraph-operator in Washington informed him that General Halleck had taken his hat and walked out of the office without another word or message! General McClellan then telegraphed thus:—

"CHERRY-STONE INLET, August 14, 1862, 1.40 A.M.

"Your orders will be obeyed. I return at once. I had hoped to have had a longer and fuller conversation with you, after travelling so far for the purpose.

"G. B. McCLELLAN,
"*Major-General.*

"Major-General H. W. HALLECK,
Washington, D. C."

of that day, when the last man had disappeared from the deserted camps, General McClellan followed with his personal staff in the track of the grand Army of the Potomac, "bidding farewell," as he says in his Report, "to the scenes still covered with the marks of its presence, and to be ever memorable in history as the vicinity of its most brilliant exploits." On the 20th the army was at Yorktown, Fortress Monroe, and Newport News, ready to embark for whatever might be its destination.

A brief extract from General McClellan's Report at this point may be here fittingly introduced:—

"As the campaign on the Peninsula terminated here, I cannot close this part of my report without giving an expression of my sincere thanks and gratitude to the officers and men whom I had the honor to command.

"From the commencement to the termination of this most arduous campaign, the Army of the Potomac always evinced the most perfect subordination, zeal, and alacrity in the performance of all the duties required of it.

"The amount of severe labor accomplished by this army in the construction of intrenchments, roads, bridges, &c. was enormous; yet all the work was performed with the most gratifying cheerfulness and devotion to the interests of the service.

"During the campaign ten severely contested and sanguinary battles had been fought, besides numerous small engagements, in which the troops exhibited the most determined enthusiasm and bravery. They submitted to exposure, sickness, and even death, without a murmur. Indeed, they had become veterans in their country's cause, and richly deserved the warm commendation of the Government.

"It was in view of these facts that this seemed to me an appropriate occasion for the general-in-chief to give, in general orders, some appreciative expression of the services of the army while upon the Peninsula. Accordingly, on the 18th, I sent him the following despatch:—

"'HEAD-QUARTERS ARMY OF THE POTOMAC,
August 18, 1862, 11 P.M.

"'Please say a kind word to my army, that I can repeat to them in general orders, in regard to their conduct at Yorktown, Williamsburg, West Point, Hanover Court-House, and on the Chickahominy, as well as in regard to the (7) seven days, and the recent retreat.

"'No one has ever said any thing to cheer them but myself. Say nothing about me. Merely give my men and officers credit for what they have done. It will do you much good, and will strengthen you much with them, if you issue a handsome order to them in regard to what they have accomplished. They deserve it.

"'G. B. MCCLELLAN,
"'*Major-General.*

"'Major-General HALLECK,
"'*Washington, D. C.*'

"As no reply was received to this communication, and no order was issued by the general-in-chief, I conclude that my suggestion did not meet with his approbation."

Immediately on reaching Fortress Monroe, General McClellan gave directions for strengthening the defences of Yorktown, so as to resist any attack from the direction of Richmond, and left General Keyes, with his corps, to perform the work and temporarily to garrison the place. On the evening of the 23d he sailed with his staff for Acquia Creek, where he arrived on the following morning and reported for orders. On the 26th he was ordered to Alexandria, and reached there the same day. In the mean time the corps of Heintzelman and Porter had sailed from Newport News and Yorktown, on the 19th, 20th, and 21st, to join General Pope's army; and those of Franklin and Sumner followed a day or two after.

General McClellan remained at Alexandria till the close of the march. A brisk intercourse by telegraph was kept up between him and the commander-in-chief with reference to General Pope's movements and the defence of Washington; but no specific duty was assigned to him, and his brave army was by parcels detached from him, and sent to take part in movements in regard to which it is easy to see he had the gravest misgivings. Few experiences in life are more trying than to see things going wrong and have no power to prevent it. The following extract from a despatch sent from the camp near Alexandria, on the 30th of August, while the disastrous second battle of Bull Run was going on, shows how much he felt and how much he suppressed:—

"I cannot express to you the pain and mortification I have experienced to-day in listening to the distant sound of the firing of my men. As I can be of no further use here, I respectfully ask that, if there is a probability of the conflict being renewed to-morrow, I may be permitted to go to the scene of battle with my staff, merely to be with my own men, if nothing more: they will fight none the worse for my being with them. If it is not deemed best to intrust me with the command even of my own army, I simply ask to be permitted to share their fate on the field of battle."

On the 30th, the following order was issued from the War Department:—

"WAR DEPARTMENT, August 30, 1862.

"The following are the commanders of the armies operating in Virginia:—

"General Burnside commands his own corps, except those that have been temporarily detached and assigned to General Pope.

"General McClellan commands that portion of the Army of the Potomac that has not been sent forward to General Pope's command.

"General Pope commands the Army of Virginia and all the forces temporarily attached to it. All the forces are under the command of Major-General Halleck, general-in-chief.

"E. D. TOWNSEND,
"*Assistant Adjutant-General.*"

The practical effect of this order was that General McClellan had no control over anybody, except his staff, some hundred men in camp near Alexandria, and a few troops at Fortress Monroe.

CHAPTER X.

THE campaign of General Pope in Virginia was closed with the disastrous battle of August 30, 1862, fought on the ill-omened field of Bull Run, and with that of Chantilly, two days after, in which our success was dearly bought by the loss of two of the best officers in the service, General Stevens and General Kearney. On the 1st of September General McClellan went into Washington, where he had an interview with General Halleck, who instructed him verbally to take command of the defences of the place, with authority expressly limited to the works and their garrisons, and not extending to the troops in front under General Pope.

On the same day General McClellan waited upon the President of the United States, at the house of General Halleck, and in obedience to a message from him. He was then and there told by the President that he had reason to believe that the Army of the Potomac was not cheerfully co-operating with and supporting General Pope, and was asked to use his influence in correcting this state of things. General McClellan replied that the information could not be true, and that the Army of the Potomac, whatever might be their estimate of General Pope, would obey his orders and do their duty. But this did not satisfy the President, who seemed much moved during the interview; and, at his earnest and reiterated request, General McClellan telegraphed to General Porter as follows:—

"WASHINGTON, September 1, 1862.

"I ask of you, for my sake, that of the country, and the old Army of the Potomac, that you and all my friends will lend the fullest and most cordial co-operation to General Pope in all the operations now going on. The destinies of our country, the honor of our army, are at stake, and all depends now upon the cheerful co-operation of all in the field. This week is the crisis of our fate. Say the same thing to my friends in the Army of the Potomac, and that the last request I have to make of them is that, for their country's sake, they will extend to General Pope the same support they ever have to me.

"I am in charge of the defences of Washington, and am doing all I can to render your retreat safe, should that become necessary.

"GEORGE B. McCLELLAN.

"Major-General PORTER."

General Porter sent the following reply: —

"FAIRFAX COURT-HOUSE, 10 A.M., September 2, 1862.

"You may rest assured that all your friends, as well as every lover of his country, will ever give, as they have given, to General Pope their cordial co-operation and constant support in the execution of all orders and plans. Our killed, wounded, and enfeebled troops attest our devoted duty.

"F. J. PORTER, *Major-General.*

"General GEORGE B. McCLELLAN,
"*Washington.*"

It need hardly be said that General McClellan's message, unexplained, is open to the obvious inference that he had some doubt whether General Porter and the troops under him would be faithful in the discharge of their duty to the nation and its cause; but no such impression ever crossed his mind, and what he did was done solely at the President's request.

On the same day, September 2, the roads leading

into Washington from the west began to be filled with the broken fragments of a defeated and demoralized army, like a lee shore strewn with the wreck of a noble fleet. Ambulances moved slowly along with their mournful freight of wounded men. Groups and squads of straggling soldiers appeared, weary and footsore, some slightly hurt, and all dispirited, some sadly silent, and some uttering curses and threats. The emergency of the case required immediate action; and in view of the attachment of the Army of the Potomac to their late commander, and of their unabated confidence in him, the President of the United States did the best and wisest thing he could have done under the circumstances: he turned to General McClellan for help. In a personal interview, he begged of the latter to reassume command of the forces, make provisions for the defence of the capital, and act according to the best of his judgment for the common cause. Not readily, not without a good deal of anxious misgiving, did General McClellan yield; but he did yield at last. He accepted the trust, and instantly began the discharge of its duties with his wonted energy. Aides were sent out to the commanders of divisions, with instructions to move their commands to designated points. On the very day of his reappointment, General McClellan was himself in the saddle, giving personal directions to portions of the advancing army; and the next day he was at Alexandria, rectifying the positions of the troops and issuing necessary orders.

The soldiers of the Army of the Potomac, as soon

as they learned that their beloved commander was to lead them again, took heart once more. Confidence returned. "Hope elevated and joy brightened their crests." Missing men reappeared, the broken fragments of divisions and brigades were reunited, order reigned anew in the lately disordered files, and the shattered and demoralized host began instantly to assume the method and proportions of an army, with "degree, priority, and place." Before the close of that very 2d of September, such dispositions were made as insured the successful defence of Washington against any attack on the south side of the Potomac.*

---

* "To-day, by order of the President, General McClellan has again assumed the supreme command of the army. Immediately after accepting the chief command of all the Union forces in the neighborhood of Washington, General McClellan proceeded to inspect the troops and fortifications on the south side of the river. This occupied him until after midnight. His reception by the officers and soldiers was marked by the most unbounded enthusiasm. In every camp his arrival was greeted by hearty and prolonged cheering, and manifestations of the wildest delight. Many of the soldiers who fought under him in the hardest battles of the war wept with joy at again having for their commander one upon whom they could place implicit reliance. Already his hurried visit to our camps has wrought a remarkable change in the soldiers. His presence seemed to act magically upon them: despondency is replaced by confidence, and all are glad that McClellan will hereafter direct them."—*Ellis's Leaves from the Diary of an Army Surgeon*, p. 214.

"To-night the Union army will all be concentrated in the works around this city, and General McClellan has already assumed the position of commander-in-chief of all the forces in the field

But this was not the intention of the enemy; for on the 3d he had disappeared from the front of Washington, and the information received of his movements induced the belief that he intended to cross the Upper Potomac into Maryland. This made an active campaign necessary in order to cover Baltimore, prevent the invasion of Pennsylvania, and clear Maryland; and measures were immediately taken accordingly. General Banks was left in command of the defences of Washington; and on the 4th of September a forward movement of the army was commenced, and General McClellan himself left the capital and took the field on the 7th. At this time it was known that the mass of the rebel army had passed up the south side of the Potomac, in the direction of Leesburg, and that a portion had crossed into Maryland; but whether they intended to send over their whole force with a view to turn Washington by a flank movement down the north bank of the Potomac, or to move on Baltimore, or to invade Pennsylvania, were matters of uncertainty. This constrained General McClellan to proceed with great caution for a few days, and so move as to keep both Baltimore and Washington covered, and at the same time hold the troops in readiness to follow the enemy if he went into Pennsylvania.

The general course of the march was in a northwesterly direction, the points of destination being the city of Frederick, in Maryland, and its vicinity.

---

in this part of the country. The announcement of this latter fact has been hailed with acclamations of infinite delight by nearly the whole population."—*Same*, p. 218.

The army moved in five columns, stretching across the region embraced between the Baltimore & Ohio Railroad and the Potomac. The left always rested on the river, and the extreme right was as far out as Cooksville. On the 14th of September, Burnside and Sumner, each with two corps, were at South Mountain, Franklin's corps and Couch's division were at Burkettsville, and Sykes's division was at Middletown.

As soon as General McClellan had left Washington, an active intercourse by telegraph-wires began to be kept up between him and the authorities there, especially the President of the United States and the commander-in-chief. The communications sent to General McClellan are tinged with a questioning and complaining spirit, showing that he no more enjoyed the confidence of the Administration than during the campaign in Virginia, and forcing upon him the conviction that his appointment was rather extorted from them in deference to the strong sentiment of the army than as a spontaneous movement of their own. General Halleck's mind was darkened with apprehensions for the safety of the capital, and he feared that General McClellan's movements were too precipitate, and that he was exposing his front and rear. Upon these views of the commander-in-chief, General McClellan remarks, in his Report,—

"The importance of moving with all due caution, so as not to uncover the national capital until the enemy's position and plans were developed, was, I believe, fully appreciated by me; and, as my troops extended from the

Baltimore & Ohio Railroad to the Potomac, with the extreme left flank moving along that stream, and with strong pickets left in rear to watch and guard all the available fords, I did not regard my left or rear as in any degree exposed. But it appears from the foregoing telegrams that the general-in-chief was of a different opinion, and that my movements were, in his judgment, too precipitate not only for the safety of Washington, but also for the security of my left and rear.

"The precise nature of these daily injunctions against a precipitate advance may now be perceived. The general-in-chief, in his testimony before the Committee on the Conduct of the War, says, 'In respect to General McClellan's going too fast, or too far from Washington, there can be found no such telegram from me to him. He has mistaken the meaning of the telegrams I sent him. I telegraphed him that he was going too far, not from Washington, but from the Potomac, leaving General Lee the opportunity to come down the Potomac and get between him and Washington. I thought General McClellan should keep more on the Potomac, and press forward his left rather than his right, so as the more readily to relieve Harper's Ferry.'

"As I can find no telegram from the general-in-chief recommending me to keep my left flank nearer the Potomac, I am compelled to believe that when he gave this testimony he had forgotten the purport of the telegrams above quoted, and had also ceased to remember the fact, well known to him at the time, that my left, from the time I left Washington, always rested on the Potomac, and that my centre was continually in position to reinforce the left or right, as occasion might require. Had I advanced my left flank along the Potomac more rapidly than the other columns marched upon the roads to the right, I should have thrown that flank out of supporting distance of the other troops, and greatly exposed it. And if I had marched the entire army in one column along the banks of the river, instead of upon five different parallel roads, the column, with its trains, would have extended about fifty miles, and the enemy might have defeated the advance before the rear could have reached the scene of action. Moreover, such a movement would have uncovered the communications with Baltimore and Washington on our right, and exposed our left and rear. I presume it will be admitted by every military man that it was necessary to move the army in such order that it could at any time be concentrated for battle; and I am of opinion that this object could not have been accomplished in any other way than the one employed. Any other disposition of our forces would have subjected them to defeat in detached fragments."

In the mean time the Confederate army had crossed the Potomac at two fords near Point of Rocks, entered Maryland, and marched as far as Frederick, which they reached and occupied on the 6th. The main body of the army encamped for some days on a line between Frederick and the Potomac River. Recruiting-offices were opened in the city, and citizens invited to enlist; but very few recruits were obtained. An address was issued to the people of Maryland by General Lee, but no enthusiastic response was made; and the Confederate leaders were much disappointed at the coldness and indifference with which they were received.

On the 10th, General Lee began to evacuate Frederick, and, taking the road to Hagerstown, crossed the Catoctin Mountains, passed through the valley in which Middletown is situated, and drew up his forces along the crest of South Mountain, to await the advance of General McClellan. At the same time he detached a portion of his force, amounting to twenty-five thousand men, and sent them, under command of General Jackson, to Harper's Ferry, by the Williamsport road. On the 13th, the rear-guard of the enemy's army was found in strong position at Turner's Gap of the South Mountain, over which the main road from Frederick to Hagerstown is carried; and preparations were made for an attack the next morning. The position of the Confederates was very strong on the sides and summit of the mountain, both to the right and left of the gap. The battle began on the morning of the 14th, but was some hours merely an artillery duel, with no very decisive results, though, on the whole, with gain to our side. At three, our line of battle was formed, and orders were given to move the whole forward, and take or silence the enemy's batteries. They were executed with enthusiasm and complete success. Our right, centre, and left advanced simultaneously towards the enemy, unbroken by a fire from two pieces of cannon which played upon our columns for upwards of an hour before they were silenced by our batteries. The right wing, where General Hooker was in command, was first engaged, and the left followed at no long interval. The tactics and order of battle were simple, and substantially the same all along the line. Steadily, without pause or wavering, our gallant troops pressed up the slope, and delivered heavy volleys of musketry as they came within range. It was for some time a hot and steady fight of man against man, company against company, regiment against regiment. The woods, the ledges of rock, all the natural lines of attack and defence, were for some time blazing with steady sheets of dazzling flame and ringing with sharp volleys. But our line moved on with the sweeping and irresistible force of a mighty flood, and the Confederates soon began to waver and give way. They were driven up to the top of the mountain, and thence down on the other side. At six o'clock the enemy had been beaten from all their positions, and we held undisturbed possession of the heights.

The battle of South Mountain reflected high honor upon the officers and men who took part in it. The judicious plans of the general commanding were admirably and successfully carried out. Our numbers were probably somewhat larger than the enemy's; but this advantage was more than counterbalanced by his superiority in position, on the crest and sides of a hill, with woods and rocky ledges for shelter and defence, and broken ground everywhere to embarrass the movements of our troops.

Our losses were three hundred and twelve killed, twelve hundred and thirty-four wounded, twenty-two missing. Among the killed was General Reno, a brave and valuable officer, who was General McClellan's classmate at West Point.

At the same time with the battle of South Mountain, an engagement took place at Crampton's Pass, between a division under General Franklin and a portion of the Confederate army. The enemy were found in the rear of Burkettsville, at the base of the mountain, with infantry posted in force on both sides of the road, and artillery in strong positions to defend the approaches to the Pass. They were forced from their positions by a steady charge of our line, and driven up the slope, and at the end of three hours' fighting the crest was carried, and the enemy fled down the mountain on the other side.

On the 12th of September, the Confederate force under General Jackson, which had been detached for the purpose, appeared before Harper's Ferry, and on the 15th the unfortunate and humiliating surrender of that position took place,—the Union cavalry having, on the night of the 14th, cut their way through the enemy's line and reached Greencastle, Pa., in safety the next morning. The untoward surrender of this post awakened a very strong feeling throughout the country, and a court of inquiry was immediately summoned to investigate the circumstances. The court met in Washington on the 25th of September, and their report was published early in November. It gives a detailed narrative of the surrender, and states the conclusion that "the incapacity" of Colonel Miles, the commanding officer (who, happily for him, was killed during the assault), "amounting almost to imbecility, led to the shameful surrender of this important post." The report also strongly reflects upon "the military incapacity" of Colonel Ford, the officer second in command, in consequence of which he was dismissed from the service of the United States.

But the military commission diverges a little

from its legitimate path of inquiry, and lends itself to the persistent hostility with which General McClellan was pursued by the general-in-chief, in the paragraphs following:—

"The commission has remarked freely on Colonel Miles, an old officer, who has been killed in the service of his country; and it cannot, from any motives of delicacy, refrain from censuring those in high command when it thinks such censure deserved.

"The general-in-chief has testified that General McClellan, after having received orders to repel the enemy invading the State of Maryland, marched only six miles per day, on an average, when pursuing this invading enemy.

"The general-in-chief also testifies that, in his opinion, he could and should have relieved and protected Harper's Ferry; and in this opinion the commission fully concur."

Upon these charges General McClellan quietly and pertinently remarks in his Report,—

"I have been greatly surprised that this commission, in its investigations never called upon me, nor upon any officer of my staff, nor, so far as I know, upon any officer of the Army of the Potomac able to give an intelligent statement of the movements of that army. But another paragraph in the same report makes testimony from such sources quite superfluous. It is as follows:—

"'By a reference to the evidence it will be seen that, at the very moment Colonel Ford abandoned Maryland Heights, his little army was in reality relieved by Generals Franklin's and Sumner's corps at Crampton's Gap, within seven miles of his position.'

"The corps of Generals Franklin and Sumner were a part of the army which I at that time had the honor to command, and they were acting under my orders at Crampton's Gap and elsewhere; and if, as the commission states, Colonel Ford's 'little army was in reality relieved' by those officers, it was relieved by me."

It will be observed that the general-in-chief testifies and the commission reports on an issue not then legitimately on trial; and that is, the rate at which the army of General McClellan marched during the Maryland campaign. Good haters should have good memories; and the general-in-chief had apparently forgotten, when he was censuring General McClellan before the commission for moving only six miles a day, that only a short time before he had been apprehensive that the army was going too fast, and was thus uncovering Washington as well as exposing its own front and rear.

Why, in point of fact, the army moved no more than six miles a day may be easily explained.

In the first place, it was not distinctly known where the rebel army was going, and it was necessary to proceed cautiously, so as to keep watch upon it and be ready to anticipate and foil any sudden movement. In the second place, the invading army was well organized, well disciplined, led by a skilful commander, and flushed with victory, whereas our own was demoralized by a recent defeat and by a sudden change in command; and these slow marches were necessary for organization and consolidation, and to establish true relations between the soldiers and their new leader.

But to return to the surrender of Harper's

Ferry. Before General McClellan left Washington, he recommended to the proper authorities that the garrison at Harper's Ferry should be withdrawn by way of Hagerstown to aid in covering the Cumberland Valley, or that, taking up the pontoon bridge and obstructing the railroad bridge, it should fall back to the Maryland Heights and there hold out to the last. This was unquestionably judicious advice; but it was not deemed proper to adopt either of the plans suggested. The garrison was not withdrawn,—as would have been the wiser course, for the position was of no value as a strategic point, as the enemy's troops then stood, —nor were measures taken to protect them from capture.

It was not until the 12th that General McClellan was directed to assume command of the garrison at Harper's Ferry, as soon as he should open communication with that place; but when this order was received, all communication from the direction he was approaching was cut off. Nothing, therefore, was left to be done but to endeavor to relieve the garrison. Artillery was ordered to be fired by our advance, at frequent intervals, as a signal that relief was at hand; and these reports, as was afterwards ascertained, were distinctly heard at Harper's Ferry. It was confidently expected that Colonel Miles would hold out till our forces had carried the mountain-passes and were in a condition to send a detachment to his relief; and this he assuredly might have done, had he been competent to the important command intrusted to him. And it was with a view of relieving the garrison at Harper's Ferry that Franklin's column was ordered to move through Crampton's Pass, in front of Burkettsville, while the centre and right marched upon Turner's Pass in front of Middletown.

On the 14th a verbal message from Colonel Miles reached General McClellan, which was the first authentic intelligence the latter had received as to the condition of things at Harper's Ferry. The messenger reported as to the position of our force there, and stated that Colonel Miles instructed him to say that he could hold out with certainty two days longer. General McClellan directed him to make his way back, if possible, with the information that he was rapidly approaching and felt confident that he could relieve the place. It does not appear that this message ever reached Colonel Miles.

On the afternoon of the 14th, General McClellan addressed a letter to Colonel Miles, giving him instructions and information, assuring him that the centre was making every effort to relieve him, and entreating him to hold out to the last extremity. Three copies of this letter were sent by three different couriers on three different routes, but none of them succeeded in reaching Harper's Ferry.

On the previous day, September 13, General McClellan had sent to General Franklin a letter of detailed instructions as to his movements, and further orders were despatched on the following day.

The results of the battle of South Mountain—

considering Franklin's attack on Crampton's Pass as a part of one general and concerted plan—responded exactly to General McClellan's hopes and wishes; and the close of the action, on the evening of the 14th, found General Franklin's advance within six miles of Harper's Ferry. A despatch was sent to him from head-quarters during the night of the 14th, containing instructions as to his movements in case he should succeed in opening communication with Colonel Miles; and this would have been done had the place held out for twenty-four hours longer. But the surrender was made at eight A.M. on the 15th.

Upon a fair examination of the case, it cannot be maintained that General McClellan is guilty of the charge made by the general-in-chief, and sanctioned by the Committee of Inquiry, that he failed to relieve and protect Harper's Ferry, having the power to do so.

THE BATTLE OF ANTIETAM.

The pursuit of the enemy followed immediately after the battle of South Mountain, and on the 15th they were found strongly posted behind Antietam Creek, near Sharpsburg. Our troops were not up in sufficient force to begin the attack on that day. The ground occupied by the Confederates was a rugged and wooded plateau, descending to the banks of the Antietam, which is here a deep stream, with few fords, and crossed by three stone bridges. On all favorable points the enemy's artillery was posted; and their reserves, hidden from view by the hills on which their line of battle was formed, could manœuvre without being seen by our army, and, from the shortness of their line, could easily reinforce any point which needed strengthening. Their position, stretching across the space included between the Potomac and the Antietam, their flanks and rear protected by these streams, was very strong, and it had the further advantage of masking their numbers from our observation.

On the morning of the 16th it was discovered that the enemy had changed the position of his batteries; and the whole forenoon was spent in reconnoitring, in examining the ground, finding fords, clearing the approaches, and hurrying up the ammunition and supply trains, which had been delayed by the rapid march of the troops. About daylight the enemy opened a heavy fire of artillery on our guns in position, which was promptly returned. Their fire was silenced for the time, but it was frequently renewed during the day.

General McClellan's plan was to attack the enemy's left with the corps of Hooker and Mansfield, supported by Sumner's, and, if necessary, by Franklin's; and, in case of success at this point, to move Burnside's corps against the enemy's extreme right, and, having carried their position, to press along the crest towards our right, and, whenever either of these flank movements should be successful, to advance our centre with all the forces then disposable. The general in command himself occupied a ridge on the centre, where Porter's corps, including Sykes's division, was stationed as a reserve.

About three o'clock, General Hooker crossed the Antietam by the bridge on the Hagerstown road and an adjacent ford, and soon gained the crest of the hill on the right bank of the stream. He then turned to the left, and followed down the ridge, under a sharp fire of musketry, which lasted till dark.

During the night, General Mansfield's corps crossed the Antietam by the same bridge and ford used by Hooker's.

At daylight on the 17th, General Hooker attacked the enemy's forces before him, and drove them from the open field in front of the first line of woods into a second line of woods beyond. But out of this second line a very destructive fire was poured from a body of fresh troops, before which our own forces recoiled. General Mansfield's corps was now ordered up, and came promptly into action; and for about two hours the tide of battle swayed to and fro with varying fortunes. The scene of the heaviest fighting was a piece of ploughed land, nearly enclosed by woods, and entered by a corn-field in the rear, on the crest of the hill. Three or four times this position was taken and lost, and the ground was thickly strewn with the bodies of the dead. Early in the fight, the gallant veteran General Mansfield was mortally wounded. General Hartsuff, of Hooker's corps, and General Crawford, of Mansfield's corps, were both wounded, the former severely. Between nine and ten, General Hooker, who had shown excellent conduct and the most brilliant courage, was shot through the foot, and, after having fainted with pain, was obliged to leave the field.

At this time General Sumner's corps reached this portion of the field, and became hotly engaged; but it suffered severely from a heavy fire of musketry and shell from the enemy's breast-works and batteries, and portions of the line were compelled to withdraw. General Sedgwick and General Dana were seriously wounded, and taken from the field. On the left, General Richardson was mortally wounded, and General Meagher disabled by the fall of his horse, shot under him.

At one o'clock the aspect of affairs on our right flank was not promising. Our troops had suffered severely, and our loss in officers had been frightful. Portions of our force were scattered and demoralized, and the corn-field before mentioned was in the enemy's possession. We were in no condition to assume the offensive, and hardly able to hold the positions we had gained. At this time General Franklin arrived upon the field with fresh troops; and while one of his divisions, under Slocum, was sent forward on the left to the support of French and Richardson, another, under Smith, was ordered to retake the woods and corn-fields which had been so hotly contested during the day. This order was executed in the most gallant style, and in ten minutes the enemy were driven out and our troops were in undisturbed possession of the whole field.

This was substantially the close of the battle on our right, though the artillery on both sides maintained a fire for some time longer. It was not deemed safe for Franklin's corps to push on any farther, because the rest of our troops had suffered too severely to be relied upon as an efficient reserve. The battle had been fought with desperate courage on both sides, but the advantage, on the whole, was with us. But we had lost too many men, and were too much exhausted, to make any new attack, and the enemy were not able to assume the offensive.

Meanwhile, Burnside had been engaged on the extreme left of the Federal position in attempting to cross the lower stone bridge,—a structure strongly defended by infantry and artillery. After two unsuccessful attacks, it was finally carried by assault, and the Confederates driven to a range of hills in the rear, where their batteries played upon our troops with damaging effect. A halt was then made until three o'clock, when urgent orders were sent from head-quarters to General Burnside to push forward his force and carry these heights at any cost. The advance was then gallantly resumed, the enemy driven from his guns, and the heights carried. By this time it was nearly dark, and strong reinforcements having just then reached the enemy from Harper's Ferry, attacked Burnside's troops on the left flank, and forced them to retire to a lower line of hills nearer the bridge. During this movement General Rodman was mortally wounded.

All day long General Porter's reserve corps filled the interval between the right wing and General

Burnside's command, guarding the main approach from the enemy's position to our trains of supply. It had been necessary to maintain this part of our line in strong force, lest the enemy, taking advantage of an exhibition of weakness there, should pierce our centre, gain our rear, and capture or destroy our supply-trains. General Burnside, at the close of the day, hotly pressed by the enemy, had sent an urgent request for reinforcements; but they could not be had, and he was ordered to hold his ground, or at least the bridge, till dark. At one moment, about the middle of the afternoon, the position on our right was so critical that two brigades from Porter's corps were ordered to reinforce our troops on that wing; but, after conference with General Sumner, the order was countermanded while in the course of execution.

Our entire force engaged at Antietam was about eighty-seven thousand men. That of the Confederates was less at the beginning, but they were reinforced during the day by Jackson's command from Harper's Ferry; and during the afternoon the numbers were probably about equal. Our loss in killed, wounded, and missing was twelve thousand four hundred and nine; that of the Confederates was at least as great.

Thirteen guns, thirty-nine colors, upwards of fifteen thousand stand of small arms, and more than six thousand prisoners were our trophies of success in the battles of South Mountain and Antietam. Not a gun or a color was lost by our army.

Early on the 18th the Confederates sent in a flag of truce, asking permission to bury their dead who had fallen between the lines of the two armies. The request was granted. General McClellan says, in his Report, after a detailed account of the battle,—

"Night closed the long and desperately-contested battle of the 17th. Nearly two hundred thousand men and five hundred pieces of artillery were for fourteen hours engaged in this memorable battle. We had attacked the enemy in a position selected by the experienced engineer then in person directing their operations. We had driven them from their line on one flank, and secured a footing within it on the other. The Army of the Potomac, notwithstanding the moral effect incident to previous reverses, had achieved a victory over an adversary invested with the prestige of recent success. Our soldiers slept that night conquerors on a field won by their valor and covered with the dead and wounded of the enemy.

"The night, however, brought with it grave responsibilities. Whether to renew the attack on the 18th or to defer it, even with the risk of the enemy's retirement, was the question before me.

"After a night of anxious deliberation, and a full and careful survey of the situation and condition of our army, and the strength and position of the enemy, I concluded that the success of an attack on the 18th was not certain. I am aware of the fact that, under ordinary circumstances, a general is expected to risk a battle if he has a reasonable prospect of success; but at this critical juncture I should have had a narrow view of the condition of the country had I been willing to hazard another battle with less than an absolute assurance of success. At that moment—Virginia lost, Washington menaced, Maryland invaded—the national cause could afford no risks of defeat. One battle lost, and almost all would have been lost. Lee's army might then have marched as it pleased on Washington, Baltimore, Philadelphia, or New York. It could have levied its supplies from a fertile and undevastated country, extorted tribute from wealthy and populous cities, and nowhere east of the Alleghanies was there another organized force able to arrest its march."

He then proceeds to set forth some of the considerations which led him to doubt the certainty of success in attacking before the 19th.

The troops were greatly overcome by the exhaustion of the recent battles, and the long day and night marches of the previous three days.

The supply-trains were in the rear, and many of the troops had suffered from hunger. They required rest and refreshment.

One division of Sumner's and all of Hooker's corps, on the right, after fighting valiantly for many hours, had been driven back in disorder, and were somewhat demoralized.

Our losses had been very heavy.

Many of our heaviest batteries had consumed all their ammunition, and they could not be supplied till late on the 18th.

Large reinforcements which were immediately expected had not arrived.

Supplies of forage had to be brought up and issued, and infantry-ammunition distributed.

The 18th was, therefore, spent in collecting the dispersed, giving rest to the fatigued, burying the dead, and the necessary preparations for a renewal of the battle. Orders were given for an attack at daylight on the 19th. But during the night of the 18th the enemy abandoned their position, and crossed the Potomac into Virginia, just two weeks from the day they had entered Maryland. As their line was near the river, the evacuation presented little difficulty, and was effected before daylight.

On the 19th, General McClellan sent to the commander-in-chief a telegraphic report as follows:—

"I have the honor to report that Maryland is entirely freed from the presence of the enemy, who has been driven across the Potomac. No fears need now be entertained for the safety of Pennsylvania. I shall at once occupy Harper's Ferry."

On the following day this despatch was received:—

"WASHINGTON, September 20, 1862, 2 P.M.

"We are still left entirely in the dark in regard to your own movements and those of the enemy. This should not be so. You should keep me advised of both, so far as you know them.

"H. W. HALLECK,
"*General-in-Chief.*

"Major-General G. B. McCLELLAN."

In reply to this curt and ungracious message, General McClellan, after giving the information sought, as far as it was in his power to do, said,—

"I regret that you find it necessary to couch every despatch I have the honor to receive from you in the spirit of fault-finding, and that you have not yet found leisure to say one word in commendation of the recent achievements of this army, or even to allude to them."

On the same 19th of September, in the midst of his onerous cares and labors, General McClellan found time to send another despatch to the commander-in-chief, as an act of prompt justice to a brave officer. It was as follows :—

"HEAD-QUARTERS ARMY OF THE POTOMAC, September 19.

"As an act of justice to the merits of that most excellent officer, Major-General Joseph Hooker, who was eminently conspicuous for his gallantry and ability as a leader in several hard-fought battles in Virginia, and who in the battle of Antietam Creek, on the 17th inst., was wounded at the head of his corps while leading it forward in action, I most urgently recommend him for the appointment of brigadier-general in the United States Army, to fill the vacancy created by the death of the late Brigadier-General Mansfield. This would be but a fit reward for the service General Hooker rendered his country. I feel sure his appointment would gratify the whole army.

"GEORGE B. McCLELLAN,
"*Major-General.*

"Major-General H. W. HALLECK,
"*General-in-Chief.*"

This suggestion was adopted, and General Hooker was made a brigadier-general in the regular army of the United States, his commission bearing date September 2, 1862.

The result of the victories at South Mountain and Antietam was to drive the enemy from Maryland, to secure Pennsylvania from invasion, and to put Harper's Ferry once more into our possession.

This was much to have been done in a fortnight's time by an army in the shattered and demoralized condition that General McClellan's was in when he took it in hand on the second day of September. How strong a sense of the value of these services was felt by those who were most nearly interested may be learned by an executive order of the Governor of Maryland, as follows:—

"STATE OF MARYLAND, EXECUTIVE DEPARTMENT,
ANNAPOLIS, September 29, 1862.

"The expulsion of the rebel army from the soil of Maryland should not be suffered to pass without a proper acknowledgment, and the cordial thanks of her authorities to those who were chiefly instrumental in compelling that evacuation.

"I would tender, therefore, on behalf of the State of Maryland, to Major-General McClellan, and the gallant officers and men under his command, my earnest and hearty thanks for the distinguished courage, skill, and gallantry with which the achievement was accomplished. It reflects a lustre upon the ability of the commander-in-chief, and the heroism and endurance of his followers, that the country everywhere recognizes, and that even our enemies are constrained to acknowledge.

"A. W. BRADFORD.

"By the Governor:
"WM. B. HILL,
"*Secretary of State.*"

CHAPTER XI.

IT now became a grave question with General McClellan whether or not he should pursue the retreating enemy into Virginia. Our losses had been heavy; the army was greatly exhausted by hard work, fatiguing marches, hunger, and want of sleep. Many of the troops were new levies; and, though they had fought well, they had not the steadiness and discipline that were needed for an expedition so formidable. The means of transportation at our disposal, on the 19th of September, were not enough to furnish a single day's subsistence in advance. Under these circumstances, General McClellan did not deem it wise to cross the river with his army, over a deep and difficult ford, in pursuit of a retreating enemy, and thus place between himself and his base of supplies a stream liable at any time to rise above a fording stage.

This decision was made known to the authorities at Washington, and they were duly informed of the movements of our own troops, and of those of the enemy, as far as the latter could be ascertained. The commander-in-chief, to whom, in general, the communications were addressed, was urged to push forward all the old troops that could be dispensed with around Washington and other places, so that the old skeleton regiments might be filled up at once, and officers appointed to supply the numerous existing vacancies. The work of reorganizing, drilling, and supplying the army was begun at the earliest moment. The different corps were stationed along the river in the best position to cover and guard the fords. Reconnoissances upon the Virginia side of the Potomac, for the purpose of learning the enemy's positions and movements, were frequently made. This was a trying and exhausting service for our cavalry, with which the army was inadequately supplied.

On the first day of October the President of the United States paid a visit to the Army of the Potomac, and remained several days, during which time he passed through the different encampments, reviewed the troops, and went over the battle-fields of South Mountain and Antietam. During this visit, General McClellan explained to him fully, in conversation, the movements of the army since it had left Washington, and gave the reasons why the enemy was not pursued after he had crossed the Potomac.

The twenty-second day of September, 1862, was a memorable day in the history of the war and the history of the country; for on that day the President issued his proclamation in which he announced that on the first day of January, 1863, all persons held as slaves within any State, or any designated part of a State, the people whereof should then be in rebellion against the United States, should be thenceforth and forever free. All discussion of the expediency of this proclamation, or of its legal effect, would be inopportune; but it will be admitted, alike by those who approve and those who disapprove it, that it gave a new character to the war and changed its objects. It is hardly necessary to add that this proclamation became at once, throughout the country, a subject of earnest debate and vehement controversy, which have, indeed, continued to the present time. From the character of the men composing the Army of the Potomac, who were voters and citizens as well as soldiers, accustomed to read the newspapers and talk politics, it was obvious that the same division of opinion upon the President's proclamation would be found among them as was found in the public at large; and there was danger that this conflict of views might impair that unity of action and patriotic zeal which are so essential to the success of all military movements. General McClellan felt himself called upon to remind the officers and soldiers under his command of the relations between the civil authorities and the military forces of the country, and of the duties of the latter in regard to the political questions of the day and the path of civil policy marked out by the Government; and he may have done this with the more promptness and emphasis from the fact that he was known not to belong to that party by whose influence the proclamation had been extorted from a too-yielding President. With these views, the following general order was issued, which may unhesitatingly be pronounced admirable alike in substance and in form, animated by a high-toned patriotism, defining with precision the line where the duty of the citizen ends and the duty of the soldier begins, and giving to every candid mind an assurance that General McClellan himself would serve his country as faithfully and zealously in the future as he had done in the past:—

"HEAD-QUARTERS ARMY OF THE POTOMAC,
CAMP NEAR SHARPSBURG, MARYLAND, October 7, 1862.

General Order No. 163.

"The attention of the officers and soldiers of the Army of the Potomac is called to General Order No. 139, War Department, publishing to the army the President's proclamation of September 22.

"A proclamation of such grave moment to the nation, officially communicated to the army, affords to the general commanding an opportunity of defining specifically to the officers and soldiers under his command, the relation borne by all persons in the military service of the United States towards the civil authorities of the Government.

"The Constitution confides to the civil authorities, legislative, judicial, and executive, the power and duty of making, expounding, and executing the federal laws. Armed forces are raised and supported simply to sustain the civil authorities, and are to be held in strict subordination thereto in all respects.

"This fundamental rule of our political system is essential to the security of our republican institutions, and should be thoroughly understood and observed by every soldier. The principle upon which, and the object for which, armies shall be employed in suppressing rebellion, must be determined and declared by the civil authorities; and the chief executive, who is charged with the administration of the national affairs, is the proper and only source through which the needs and orders of the Government can be made known to the armies of the nation.

"Discussions by officers and soldiers concerning public measures determined upon and declared by the Government, when carried once beyond temperate and respectful expressions of opinion, tend greatly to impair and destroy the discipline and efficiency of troops, by substituting the spirit of political faction for that firm, steady, and earnest support of the authority of the Government, which is the highest duty of the American soldier. The remedy for political errors, if any are committed, is to be found only in the action of the people at the polls.

"In thus calling the attention of this army to the true relation between the soldier and the Government, the general commanding merely adverts to an evil against which it has been thought advisable, during our whole history, to guard the armies of the republic, and in so doing he will not be considered by any right-minded person as casting any reflection upon that loyalty and good conduct which has been so fully illustrated upon so many battle-fields.

"In carrying out all measures of public policy, this army will, of course, be guided by the same rules of mercy and Christianity that have ever controlled their conduct towards the defenceless.

"By order of Major-General McClellan.

JAMES A. HARDEE,

"*Lieut.-Col., Aide-de-Camp, Acting Assistant Adjutant-General.*

"GEORGE B. McCLELLAN,

"*Major-General commanding.*"

The seeming inactivity of the Army of the Potomac after the battle of Antietam was a disappointment to the public, and an annoyance to the Administration. It was expected that Lee's retreating forces would be instantly and vigorously pursued, and a new path to Richmond opened through his broken columns.

The earnest desire of the Administration for a forward movement at length took the form of a positive and peremptory order, which was received on the 7th of October, and is as follows:—

"WASHINGTON, D. C., October 6, 1862.

"I am instructed to telegraph you as follows. The President directs that you cross the Potomac and give battle to the enemy, or drive him south. Your army must move now, while the roads are good. If you cross the river between the enemy and Washington, and cover the latter by your operations, you can be reinforced with thirty thousand men. If you move up the valley of the Shenandoah, not more than twelve thousand or fifteen thousand can be sent to you. The President advises the interior line between Washington and the enemy, but does not order it. He is very desirous that your army move as soon as possible. You will immediately report what line you adopt, and when you intend to cross the river; also to what point the reinforcements are to be sent. It is necessary that the plan of your operations be positively determined on, before orders are given for building bridges and repairing railroads. I am directed to add that the Secretary of War and the General-in-Chief fully concur with the President in these instructions.

"H. W. HALLECK,
"*General-in-Chief.*

"Major-General McCLELLAN."

This order was not immediately carried out, for a forward movement at that moment was an impossibility, and, had it been insisted upon, General McClellan must at once have resigned his command; but, on the other hand, it cannot be said that it was disobeyed, for every possible effort was made to comply with its directions, and the general-in-chief was day by day informed of the progress that was making, and of the reasons why the desired advance was delayed.

These reasons are set forth in full in General McClellan's Report, and are substantiated by the testimony of the chief quartermaster, Colonel Ingalls, and of other officers. The army was wholly deficient in cavalry, and a large part of our troops were in want of shoes, clothing, blankets, knapsacks, and shelter-tents. It should be borne in mind that the presence of the Confederates in Maryland, and the imperative necessity of driving them out, had made excessive demands upon the strength and endurance of the Army of the Potomac. It was one of those cases in which nervous energy is called upon to do the work of muscular strength: for a while the claim is answered, but sooner or later the time of reaction must come. After the battle of Antietam a natural exhaustion followed the unnatural excitement which had been kept up for a fortnight previous. Had the army been furnished with clothing and supplies, a rest of some days would still have been required before a forward movement would have been expedient or even safe; but, in consequence of the deficiencies above mentioned, a yet further delay was compelled.

The order to cross the Potomac was dated on the 6th of October, as has been seen, but the movement did not begin till the 26th; and during the intermediate period the Administration and General McClellan were fairly at issue. The case on behalf of the latter may be found stated in his Report; that on behalf of the Administration, in the report of the Congressional Committee on the Conduct of the War, and in the appendix to the testimony of General Halleck, and is summed up in a letter of his, addressed to the Secretary of War, dated October 28, 1862, which was published in the newspapers of the day at the same time with the order for removing General McClellan. Without going into minute detail, without spreading the whole evidence upon the record, the points of difference were these:—

General McClellan says that the army is deficient in clothing and supplies of all kinds, and especially in horses, that requisitions for the needed articles had been duly made upon the War Department at Washington, but that in point of fact they had not been received, and that until they were received it was not possible for the army to advance.

On the other hand, the Administration, represented by the general-in-chief, says that all General McClellan's requisitions had been promptly referred to the proper functionaries, that all the supplies asked for, horses included, had been procured and forwarded without delay, and that it was not possible that the army could have been in the destitute condition alleged. A long letter from General Meigs, the Quartermaster-General, is given in support of these positions.

It is easy to see that the statements of the Administration are not inconsistent with the statements of General McClellan. The former say, substantially, that certain supplies were put on board freight-trains at Washington to be forwarded to an army stationed at different points in the neighborhood of Harper's Ferry, forty or fifty miles off. General McClellan says that these articles were not received; and if credible and unimpeached witnesses, speaking upon matters within their knowledge, are to be believed, he proves it. It is obvious that proof that articles have been received is not made when it is shown that they have been despatched to their point of destination. General McClellan, be it remembered, is only defending or justifying himself for not advancing, and is not making any complaint against the Administration, or against any officer, civil or military, at Washington. This distinctly appears by the following despatch, which was published in connection with General Halleck's letter to the Secretary of War, before referred to, as a document in justification of General McClellan's removal:—

"HEAD-QUARTERS ARMY OF THE POTOMAC, Oct. 22, 1862.

"Your despatch of this date is received. I have never intended in any letter or despatch to make any accusation against yourself or your department for not furnishing or forwarding clothing as rapidly as it was possible for you to do. I believe that every thing has been done that could be done in this respect. The idea that I have tried to convey was that certain portions of the command were without clothing, and the army could not move until it was supplied.

"G. B. MCCLELLAN.

"TO BRIG.-GEN. MEIGS,
"*Quartermaster-General.*"

That supplies sent from Washington in season were not seasonably received by General McClellan is further shown by the letter of General Meigs before referred to, which is one of the documents in the case on the side of the Administration. At the commencement of this letter he says that "all the articles of clothing called for by requisition from General McClellan's head-quarters were not only ordered, but had been shipped, on the 14th of October,"—a date, it will be observed, eight days later than the day on which the army had been ordered to cross the Potomac; but in subsequent portions of the letter statements and admissions are made which show that further delays may have taken place in the transportation, and that indeed they did. Some of these are transcribed without further comment:—

"This department cannot control the trains upon railroads of which the War Department has not taken the management into its own hands."

"The railroad companies complain that cars are not unloaded at their destinations, and that their sidings are occupied with cars which are needed for forwarding supplies. I presume that the missing articles are in some of these cars, or that they have been unloaded and have not yet reached the particular corps or detachment for which they are intended."

"The fact is that no railroad can provide facilities for unloading cars and transacting the business attending the supply of an army of the size of General McClellan's in a short time or in a contracted space. Sidings, switches, depots, and turn-outs do not exist, and cannot be laid down at once, for such a traffic."

"The railroads are heavily taxed, and transportation has been delayed. A case is reported in which horses remained fifty hours on the cars without food or water."

There is yet another piece of evidence showing that there had been delays in the transportation of supplies to the army of General McClellan. In August, 1862, the superintendence and management of all the railways used by the Government for military purposes were intrusted to Brigadier-General Haupt, a competent and energetic officer. On the 10th of November, five days after the date of the order removing General McClellan, he addressed, from Washington, a circular letter to post-quartermasters, commissaries, officers and agents of military railroads, from which we make a few extracts:—

"GENTLEMEN:—The exceedingly critical condition of affairs compels me to address to you this circular, and to endeavor, with all the earnestness and force of language I can command, to explain some of the difficulties connected with military railroad transportation, and ask your co-operation and assistance in forwarding supplies.

"The army is dependent for its supplies upon a single-track railroad, in bad condition, without sidings of sufficient length, without wood, with a short supply of water, and with insufficient equipments. This road is taxed with an amount of business equal to the ordinary freights of a large city,—an amount four times as large as it has ever before been called on to accommodate, and twice as large as I reported to General McClellan its capacity for transportation.

"There cannot be the most distant prospect of keeping the army supplied without constant, uninterrupted movement of trains day and night. The delicate machinery of the road must not be deranged by any detention or interference. It must be directed by one mind, and one only.

* * * * * * * *

"Again I say that, if the army is to be supplied, the condition which, in its importance, transcends all others, is that no delay—not even a minute—should be allowed to occur in unloading cars, if it can be avoided. Movement, unceasing movement, in the trains, is our only salvation. Without it, the army must either retreat or starve."

The above extracts alone are enough to make out General McClellan's case; for they show that the road upon which the army was exclusively dependent for supplies was taxed beyond its capacity, and that there was a want of system in its management by which unnecessary delays were incurred; and this was all General McClellan ever asked the Administration to believe.

In the opinion of General McClellan, the most important want in the army was the want of horses, —not merely for cavalry and artillery, but for transportation. From the commencement the army had been deficient in cavalry; and after the battle of Antietam constant reconnoissances upon the Virginia side of the river, to learn the enemy's position and movements, had broken down the greater part of the cavalry-horses. A violent disease, attacking the hoof and tongue, soon after broke out among the animals, and at one time put nearly four thousand of them out of condition for service. To such an extent had the cavalry arm become reduced, that when the Confederate general Stuart made his raid into Pennsylvania, on the 11th of October, with two thousand men, penetrating as far as Chambersburg, General McClellan could only mount eight hundred men to follow him. Few civilians have any notion of the number of horses which are required by an army of a hundred thousand men. Indeed, we may go further, and say that few civilians have any distinct notion of what an army of a hundred thousand men is. We repeat the words mechanically, as we repeat the distances of the solar system, without any very definite impressions of numbers and mass in one case, or of space in the other. The following extract from General McClellan's Report will, we presume, be read with some surprise by most of our readers, as well as with interest.

"In a letter dated October 14, 1862, the general-in-chief says,—

"'It is also reported to me that the number of animals with your army in the field is about thirty-one thousand. It is believed that your present proportion of cavalry and of animals is much larger than that of any other of our armies.'

"What number of animals our other armies had," says General McClellan, "I am not prepared to say; but military men in European armies have been of the opinion that an army, to be efficient, while carrying on active operations in the field, should have a cavalry force equal in numbers to from one-sixth to one-fourth of the infantry force. My cavalry did not amount to one-twentieth part of the army, and hence the necessity of giving every one of my cavalry-soldiers a serviceable horse.

"Cavalry may be said to constitute the *antennæ* of an army. It scouts all the roads in front, on the flanks, and in the rear of the advancing columns, and constantly feels the enemy. The amount of labor falling upon this arm during the Maryland campaign was excessive.

"To persons not familiar with the movements of troops, and the amount of transportation required for a large army marching away from water or railroad communications, the number of animals mentioned by the general-in-chief may have appeared unnecessarily large; but to a military man, who takes the trouble to enter into an accurate and detailed computation of the number of pounds of subsistence and forage required for such an army as that of the Potomac, it will be seen that the thirty-one thousand animals were considerably less than was absolutely necessary to an advance.

"As we were required to move through a country which could not be depended upon for any of our supplies, it became necessary to transport every thing in wagons, and to be prepared for all emergencies. I did not consider it safe to leave the river without subsistence and forage for ten days.

"The official returns of that date show the aggregate strength of the army for duty to have been about one hundred and ten thousand men of all arms. This did not include teamsters, citizen-employees, officers' servants, &c., amounting to some twelve thousand men, which gives a total of one hundred and twenty-two thousand men.

"The subsistence alone of this army for ten days required for its transportation eighteen hundred and thirty wagons, at two thousand pounds to the wagon, and ten thousand nine hundred and eighty animals.

"Our cavalry-horses at that time amounted to five thousand and forty-six, and our artillery-horses to six thousand eight hundred and thirty-six.

"To transport full forage for these twenty-two thousand eight hundred and sixty-two animals for ten days required seventeen thousand eight hundred and thirty-two additional animals; and this forage would only supply the entire number (forty thousand six hundred and ninety-four) of animals with a small fraction over half-allowance for the time specified.

"It will be observed that this estimate does not embrace the animals necessary to transport quartermasters' supplies, baggage, camp-equipage, ambulances, reserve ammunition, forage for officers' horses, &c., which would greatly augment the necessary transportation.

"It may very truly be said that we did make the march with the means at our disposal; but it will be remembered that we met with no serious opposition from the enemy, neither did we encounter delays from any other cause. The roads were in excellent condition, and the troops marched with the most commendable order and celerity.

"If we had met with a determined resistance from the enemy, and our progress had been very much retarded thereby, we would have consumed our supplies before they could have been renewed. A proper estimate of my responsibilities as the commander of that army did not justify me in basing my preparations for the expedition upon the supposition that I was to have an uninterrupted march. On the contrary, it was my duty to be prepared for all emergencies; and not the least important of my responsibilities was the duty of making ample provision for supplying my men and animals with rations and forage."

In regard to the supply of horses, and the conflicting views of General McClellan and the Administration thereupon, one or two points are worthy of notice. General Meigs, in a letter written on the 14th of October and addressed to the general-in-chief, states, "There have been issued, therefore, to the Army of the Potomac, since the battles in front of Washington, to replace losses, (9254) nine thousand two hundred and fifty-four horses." From this statement a reader would naturally infer that this number had been sent to the army under General McClellan; but it appears from a report of Colonel Myers, the chief quartermaster with that army, that only (3813) three thousand eight hundred and thirteen came to the forces with which General McClellan was ordered to follow and attack the enemy, and that these were not enough to supply the places of the animals disabled by sickness and overwork; and General McClellan distinctly states that on the 21st of October, after deducting the force engaged in picketing the river, he had but about a thousand serviceable cavalry-horses.

General Halleck, in a letter to General McClellan dated October 14, 1862, in reply to a despatch of the 12th, says,—

> "In regard to horses, you say that the present rate of supply is only one hundred and fifty per week for the entire army here and in front of Washington. I find from the records that the issues for the last six weeks have been eight thousand seven hundred and fifty-four, making an average per week of one thousand four hundred and fifty-nine."

The same charge is repeated in his letter to the Secretary of War of October 28, and is also found in General Meigs's letter of October 14. In the original despatch to which General Halleck's letter is a reply, one thousand and fifty (1050), and not one hundred and fifty, is the number stated; and, as it was written out in letters in full, it is difficult to see how the telegraphic operator could have made a mistake in transmitting the message. The gross injustice done to General McClellan in thus holding him up to the public as guilty either of deliberate untruth or of enormous carelessness, need not be commented upon.

The question between the authorities at Washington and General McClellan was a question of fact. Neither the President nor the general-in-chief nor the Secretary of War would have insisted upon the army's advancing without shoes, clothing, and horses; but it was charged, or at least intimated, that the army, in point of fact, was sufficiently supplied with them all, and that the alleged want of them was a mere pretext put forward by the general in command to excuse his slowness, indolence, or lack of zeal in the cause. Upon this issue we may repeat, what was said before as to the charge of needless delay in forwarding the troops from Harrison's Bar, that General McClellan stands upon the ground of knowledge and the Administration upon the ground of inference. The testimony of one credible witness swearing affirmatively to what he knows outweighs that of twenty who can only contradict him by a process of deductive reasoning. The case cannot be put more simply or more forcibly than has been done by General McClellan himself in his Report:—

"The general-in-chief, in a letter to the Secretary of War on the 28th of October, says, 'In my opinion, there has been no such want of supplies in the army under General McClellan as to prevent his compliance with the orders to advance against the enemy.'

"Notwithstanding this opinion expressed by such high authority, I am compelled to say again that the delay in the reception of necessary supplies up to that date had left the army in a condition totally unfit to advance against the enemy; that an advance under the existing circumstances would, in my judgment, have been attended with the highest degree of peril, with great suffering and sickness among the men, and with imminent danger of being cut off from our supplies by the superior cavalry force of the enemy, and with no reasonable prospect of gaining any advantage over him.

"I dismiss this subject with the remark that I have found it impossible to resist the force of my own convictions, that the commander of an army, who from the time of its organization has for eighteen months been in constant communication with its officers and men, the greater part of the time engaged in active service in the field, and who has exercised this command in many battles, must certainly be considered competent to determine whether his army is in proper condition to advance on the enemy or not; and he must necessarily possess greater facilities for forming a correct judgment in regard to the wants of his men and the condition of his supplies than the general-in-chief in his office at Washington City."

In justice to General McClellan, and that it may be understood that he was not at all open to the charge of disobedience of orders, it should be stated that the President's peremptory instructions of October 6, to cross the Potomac and give battle to the enemy or drive him south, were never distinctly repeated. From the moment of receiving them, General McClellan set himself diligently at work to get his army in condition to obey them; and from day to day, almost from hour to hour, he sent to Washington reports of his condition and progress. His telegraphic despatches between September 6 and November 7, mostly addressed to the general-in-chief, were one hundred and fifty-eight in number; and no stronger proof can be adduced of his attention to his duties, and of his earnest desire that the Government should be fully informed alike of the state of his own army, and of the movements of the enemy as far as he could learn them. As the orders to cross the river were not renewed, General McClellan had a right to suppose that the Administration were satisfied that he was straining every nerve to get the army in order for a forward movement, and on that account forbore to repeat the command. But the evidence on this point is not merely negative, but positive, as appears from the following extract from his Report:—

"Knowing the solicitude of the President for an early movement, and sharing with him fully his anxiety for prompt action, on the 21st of October I telegraphed to the general-in-chief as follows:—

"'HEAD-QUARTERS ARMY OF THE POTOMAC,
October 21, 1862.

"'Since the receipt of the President's order to move on the enemy, I have been making every exertion to get this army supplied with clothing absolutely necessary for marching.

"'This, I am happy to say, is now nearly accomplished. I have also, during the same time, repeatedly urged upon you the importance of supplying cavalry and artillery horses to replace those broken down by hard service; and steps have been taken to insure a prompt delivery.

"'Our cavalry, even when well supplied with horses, is much inferior in numbers to that of the enemy, but in efficiency has proved itself superior. So forcibly has this been impressed upon our old regiments by repeated successes, that the men are fully persuaded that they are equal to twice their number of rebel cavalry.

"'Exclusive of the cavalry force now engaged in picketing the river, I have not at present over about one thousand (1000) horses for service. Officers have been sent in various directions to purchase horses, and I expect them soon. Without more cavalry-horses, our communications, from the moment we march, would be at the mercy of the large cavalry forces of the enemy, and it would not be possible for us to cover our flanks properly, or to obtain the necessary information of the position and movements of the enemy, in such a way as to insure success. My experience has shown the necessity of a large and efficient cavalry force.

"'Under the foregoing circumstances, I beg leave to ask whether the President desires me to march on the enemy at once, or to await the reception of the new horses, every possible step having been taken to insure their prompt arrival. GEORGE B. MCCLELLAN,

"'*Major-General commanding.*

"'Major-General H. W. HALLECK,

"'*General-in-Chief, Washington.*'

"On the same day General Halleck replied as follows:—

"'WASHINGTON, October 21, 1862, 3 P. M.

"'Your telegram of 12 M. has been submitted to the

President. He directs me to say that he has no change to make in his order of the 6th instant.

"'If you have not been, and are not now, in condition to obey it, you will be able to show such want of ability. The President does not expect impossibilities; but he is very anxious that all this good weather should not be wasted in inactivity. Telegraph when you will move, and on what lines you propose to march.

"'H. W. HALLECK, *General-in-Chief.*

"Major-General GEORGE B. McCLELLAN.'"

General Halleck's reply is ambiguous, wary, cold; but General McClellan had a right to draw from it the inference which he says he did, as follows:—

"From the tenor of this despatch I conceived that it was left for my judgment to decide whether or not it was possible to move with safety to the army at that time; and this responsibility I exercised with the more confidence in view of the strong assurances of his trust in me, as commander of that army, with which the President had seen fit to honor me during his last visit.

"The cavalry requirements, without which an advance would have been in the highest degree injudicious and unsafe, were still wanting.

"The country before us was an enemy's country, where the inhabitants furnished to the enemy every possible assistance; providing food for men and forage for animals, giving all information concerning our movements, and rendering every aid in their power to the enemy's cause.

"It was manifest that we should find it, as we subsequently did, a hostile district, where we could derive no aid from the inhabitants that would justify dispensing with the active co-operation of an efficient cavalry force. Accordingly, I fixed upon the 1st of November as the earliest date at which the forward movement could well be commenced."

The above inference is strengthened by a subsequent despatch from General Halleck, dated October 26, in which he says,—

"Since you left Washington, I have advised and suggested in relation to your movements; but I have given you no orders. I do not give you any now. The Government has intrusted you with defeating and driving back the rebel army in your front. I shall not attempt to control you in the measures you may adopt for that purpose. You are informed of my views; but the President has left you at liberty to adopt them or not, as you may deem best."

On the 26th of October the army began to cross the Potomac, and by the 2d of November all the corps were on the right bank, marching to the South, on a line east of the Blue Ridge, which had been selected by General McClellan partly because it would secure him the largest accession of force and partly because the President had always been in favor of it. His purpose was to march his army to a point where it could derive its supplies from the Manassas Gap Railway, and where it could be held in hand ready for action or movement in any direction.

On the 7th of November the several corps of the army were at or near Warrenton, and, as General McClellan says, "in admirable condition and spirits. I doubt whether during the whole period that I had the honor to command the Army of the Potomac, it was in such excellent condition to fight a great battle." Of the Confederate army, Longstreet's corps was in front at Culpepper, and the remaining portion was west of the Blue Ridge, near Chester's and Thornton's Gaps. General McClellan's plan was to separate the two wings of the enemy's forces, and either beat Longstreet separately, or force him to fall back at least upon Gordonsville so as to effect his junction with the rest of the army. In the event of a battle he felt confident of a brilliant victory. Late on the evening of the 7th, the following orders were delivered to him by General Buckingham:—

"HEAD-QUARTERS OF THE ARMY,
WASHINGTON, D. C., November 5, 1862.

"GENERAL:—On the receipt of the order of the President sent herewith, you will immediately turn over your command to Major-General Burnside, and repair to Trenton, N. J., reporting on your arrival at that place by telegraph for further orders.

"Very respectfully, your obedient servant,

"H. W. HALLECK, *General-in-Chief.*

"Major-General McCLELLAN."

"WAR DEPARTMENT, ADJUTANT-GENERAL'S OFFICE,
WASHINGTON, November 5, 1862.

"*General Orders No.* 182.

"By direction of the President of the United States, it is ordered that Major-General McClellan be relieved from the command of the Army of the Potomac, and that Major-General Burnside take the command of that army.

"By order of the Secretary of War:

"E. D. TOWNSEND, *Adjutant-General.*"

CHAPTER XII.

THE reasons for this summary and abrupt dismissal of General McClellan, strange to say, have never been distinctly and officially given to the people of the United States. The President, in his annual message to Congress, only twenty-six days later than the date of his order of removal, says nothing upon the subject.

The general-in-chief, in his Report, addressed to the Secretary of War, says, "From the 17th of September till the 26th of October, McClellan's main army remained on the north bank of the Potomac, in the vicinity of Sharpsburg and Harper's Ferry. The long inactivity of so large an army in the face of a defeated foe and during the most favorable season for rapid movements and a vigorous campaign, was a matter of great disappointment and regret. Your letter of the 27th and my reply on the 28th of October, in regard to the alleged causes of this unhappy delay, I herewith submit, marked Exhibit No. 5. In reply to the telegraphic order of the 6th of October, quoted in my letter of the 28th, above referred to, General McClellan disapproved of the plan of crossing the Potomac south of the Blue Ridge, and said that he would cross at Harper's Ferry and advance upon Winchester. He, however, did not begin to cross till the 26th of October, and then at Berlin.

"The passage occupied several days, and was

completed about the 3d of November. What caused him to change his views, or what his plan of campaign was, I am ignorant; for about this time he ceased to communicate with me in regard to his operations, sending his reports directly to the President.* On the 5th instant I received

---

* This is a curious sentence, and deserves a little examination. The date of the document on which it appears is December 2, 1862, and the general-in-chief says that on that day he was ignorant of General McClellan's plans because the latter, from a date about a month previous, had ceased to communicate with him personally and had sent his reports directly to the President. Are we to understand that the relations between the President and the general-in-chief were such during the whole month of November, 1862, that the latter never saw, never was informed of, the communications addressed to the former by the general commanding the largest army in the field? But, if the statement does not mean this, it is a mere gratuitous effusion of spite against General McClellan. If it means this, will any body believe it?

Again, "about this time" General McClellan ceased to communicate with the general-in-chief. About what time? Two dates had just before been mentioned,—October 26 and November 3; and there is nothing to indicate which of the two was meant. If it were the latter, General McClellan could not have had time to send many communications to anybody after that day, as he was deprived of his command on the 7th: if it were the former, then the statement is not true; for in the appendix to General Halleck's testimony, as published by the Congressional Committee on the Conduct of the War, there appear no less than six despatches addressed to him by General McClellan after October 26.

General McClellan's communications to the President were generally in reply to inquiries or suggestions from the latter, whose restless and meddlesome spirit was constantly moving

the written order of the President relieving General McClellan and placing General Burnside in command of the Army of the Potomac. This order was transmitted by a special messenger, who delivered it to General McClellan at Rectortown on the 7th."

Here it will be seen that no reason is assigned for what the general-in-chief chooses to call "relieving" General McClellan; but, from the whole evidence before him, the reader is left to infer that he was removed because he had disobeyed the orders of the President without cause or excuse. The orders in question, to cross the river and attack the enemy, were given on the 6th of October, the forward movement began on the 26th of the same month, and the removal of General McClellan was made on the 5th of November, when the army were thirty or forty miles on their march, in splendid condition and high spirits.

---

him to ask questions, obtrude advice, and make comments upon military matters, which were as much out of his sphere as they were beyond his comprehension.

It is true that General McClellan did not communicate his plans of the campaign either to the President or the general-in-chief; but surely he is to be commended for this. The success of a military movement often depends upon its being kept an entire secret from the enemy. General McClellan had learned by experience the danger of revealing, even in official conversation, his future operations; and it would have been an increased risk if he had made the telegraph-wire a confidant.

The whole passage is characteristic of the inventive ingenuity which has been shown, from first to last, in devising pretexts to find fault with General McClellan.

In other words, an officer is removed for disobeying orders not only one month after they were given, but eleven days after he had begun to obey them! The Administration must have great confidence in the credulity of the public if they suppose this will be received as the real cause why General McClellan was deprived of his command. Had this been done immediately after the 6th of October, or at least soon after, the pretext would have had some show of seeming.

The real reasons for which General McClellan was removed were political, and not military. They are to be found in the wide difference of views between his letter of July 7, 1862, written at Harrison's Landing, on the policy and conduct of the war, and the President's Proclamation of September 22. That letter incurred for General McClellan the unrelenting hostility of the political party which constrained the President to issue the Proclamation; and the same influences, or "pressure," which procured the document in question, compelled the removal of General McClellan. And that a strong "pressure" was brought to bear upon the President is unquestionable; for on the 13th of September, in an interview with a deputation from Chicago, when urged to issue a proclamation of emancipation, he distinctly declined it, saying, among other things, "What good would a proclamation of emancipation from me do, especially as we are now situated? I do not want to issue a document that the whole world will see must necessarily be inoperative, like the Pope's bull against the comet. Would my word free the slaves, when I cannot even enforce the Constitution in the rebel States? Is there a single court or individual that would be influenced by it there? And what reason is there to think it would have any greater effect upon the slaves than the late law of Congress which I approved, and which offers protection and freedom to the slaves of rebel masters who come within our lines? Yet I cannot learn that the law has caused a single slave to come over to us." It is hardly possible to suppose that in the short space of eleven days the mind of the President had undergone a process of natural conversion upon a point of such vital moment.

But General McClellan's political opinions, and his manly avowal of them, afford no justification for his removal from the command of the army. He had shown by word and deed that he would do his duty as a soldier, within his sphere, whatever political policy the Administration might adopt or whatever political aspects the war might assume. This was all the Administration had a right to ask. That he had the confidence and affection of his army is beyond question. His removal was due to a fact stated affirmatively—though put in the form of a question to General McDowell—by a member of the Congressional Committee on the Conduct of the War, December 26, 1861,—that "there is a political element connected with this war which must not be overlooked." There has indeed been such an "element" from the beginning in the conduct of this war; it never has been "overlooked," but has always been prominent, and set in the front of the battle, and has been the fruitful source of mistakes and disasters to our cause. In the present instance it led to the dangerous experiment of changing commanders in front of an enemy; and the bitter experience of Fredericksburg was the direct result.

The first act of General McClellan on receiving the order relieving him of command was to draw up a farewell address to the army, as follows,—which was read to them at dress-parade on the 10th:—

"HEAD-QUARTERS ARMY OF THE POTOMAC,
CAMP NEAR RECTORTOWN, November 7, 1862.

"OFFICERS AND SOLDIERS OF THE ARMY OF THE POTOMAC:—

"An order of the President devolves upon Major-General Burnside the command of this army. In parting from you, I cannot express the love and gratitude I bear you. As an army you have grown up under my care. In you I have never found doubt or coldness. The battles you have fought under my command will proudly live in our nation's history. The glory you have achieved, our mutual perils and fatigues, the graves of our comrades fallen in battle and by disease, the broken forms of those whom wounds and sickness have disabled,—the strongest associations which can exist among men,—unite us still by an indissoluble tie. We shall ever be comrades in supporting the Constitution of our country and the nationality of its people.

"GEORGE B. McCLELLAN,
"*Major-General, U. S. A.*"

On Saturday, November 8, General McClellan was busily occupied in making the arrangements necessary for transferring his command to General Burnside. The two generals, between whom the personal relations were entirely friendly, were in consultation for several hours.

At nine o'clock on the evening of Sunday, the 9th, General McClellan took leave of his staff officers by appointment. It was a touching and impressive scene. A large fire of logs was blazing within the enclosure formed by the tents of the head-quarters. General McClellan stood just inside of his marquee, the curtains of which were parted and drawn up. As the officers of his staff approached, he grasped each warmly by the hand, and, with a few words of friendly greeting, ushered him inside. The tent was soon filled, and many were compelled to remain outside. Filling a glass of wine, General McClellan raised it, and said, "To the Army of the Potomac," to which an officer present added, "and to its old commander." An hour or two of social converse passed, and the officers took leave of their beloved commander,—sadly, sorrowfully.

Monday, the 10th, was occupied in visiting the various camps and bidding farewell to his troops. A person present at this scene has thus described it:—"As General McClellan, mounted upon a fine horse, attended by a retinue of fine-looking military men, riding rapidly through the ranks, gracefully recognized and bade a farewell to the army, the cries and demonstrations of the men were beyond bounds,—wild, impassioned, and unrestrained. Disregarding all military forms, they rushed from their ranks, and thronged around him with the bitterest complaints against those who had removed from command their beloved leader."

As he rode up to the head-quarters of General Fitz-John Porter, he was met by a large delegation of officers in that command, and addressed by General Butterfield, who, in a few well-chosen words, alluded to the affection existing between General McClellan and his officers, and stated that those on behalf of whom he spoke were there to bid him a personal farewell. In reply, General McClellan said, "I hardly know what to say to you, my friends, officers associated with me so long in the Army of the Potomac. I can only bid you farewell. History will do justice to the deeds of the Army of the Potomac, if the present generation does not. I feel as if I had been intimately connected with each and all of you. Nothing is more binding than the friendship of companions in arms. May you all in future preserve the high reputation of our army, and serve all as well and faithfully as you have served me. I will say farewell now, if I must say it. Good-bye: God bless you."

On the 11th, General McClellan left Warrenton. On reaching Warrenton Junction, a salute was fired. The troops, who had been drawn up in line, afterwards broke their ranks; the soldiers crowded around him, and many eagerly called for a few parting words. He said, in response, while standing on the platform of the railroad-station, "I wish you to stand by General Burnside as you have stood by me, and all will be well."

He reached Washington, but, without stopping, went to the station of the Philadelphia Railroad, and proceeded to the latter city in the train which started at five P.M. He arrived at Philadelphia about midnight, and was there greeted with music and cheers from a crowd assembled to welcome him. He appeared upon the platform, and said,—

"Fellow-citizens of Philadelphia, I thank you for your kindness. I have parted with your brothers and sons in the Army of the Potomac too recently to make a speech. Our parting was sad. I can say nothing more to you; and I do not think you ought to expect a speech from me."

He arrived at Trenton, his point of destination, at four o'clock on the morning of the 12th.

On the evening of the 13th, an address of welcome was made to General McClellan, on behalf of the citizens of Trenton, by Andrew Dutcher, Esq. A large number of interested and sympathizing spectators were present. In reply, he said,—

"My friends,—for I feel that you are all my friends,—I stand before you not as a maker of speeches, not as a politician, but as a soldier. I came among you to seek quiet and repose, and from the moment I came among you I have received nothing but kindness; and, although I came among you a stranger, I am well acquainted with your history. From the time I took command, your gallant sons were with me, from the siege of Yorktown to the battle of Antietam. I was with them, and witnessed their bravery, and that of the ever-faithful and ever-true Taylor and the intrepid and dashing Kearney. One word more. While the army is fighting, you, as citizens, should see that the war is prosecuted for the preservation of the Union and the Constitution, for your nationality and rights as citizens."

Since the time of his removal from the command of the Army of the Potomac, General McClellan has not had any military duties assigned to him, but has been living, unemployed, the life of a private citizen. At this moment of writing (July, 1864), he resides at Orange, in the State of New Jersey, where his home has been for some months past.

In the winter of 1863, General McClellan, accompanied by his wife and two or three officers of his staff, paid a visit to Boston, arriving there on the 29th of January and remaining till the 8th of February. He came upon the invitation of several gentlemen, not all of one political party, but all uniting in their desire to testify to him in person their gratitude for his services and the esteem in which they held him as an officer and a citizen. Though the visit was thus strictly private, the general and earnest desire of the people to see him gave to it something of the nature of a public reception. His movements were followed and his steps watched by earnest and interested crowds, who greeted him, whenever he was seen, with hearty enthusiasm. His time was busily employed in visiting the points of attraction in Boston and its neighborhood, and in receiving those social attentions which were tendered to him with a most liberal hand. His visit must have been highly gratifying to him; and it is certain that he left a most agreeable impression upon all who met him, from his quiet and simple manners, and his careful abstinence from self-reference and complaints of others. It was easy to see that he had qualified himself to command others by first learning to command himself.

During his stay in Boston a very handsome sword was presented to him; and the value of the testimonial was enhanced by the fact that the cost, amounting to several hundred dollars, was defrayed by a subscription limited to one dollar from each person. Among the subscribers—to their honor be it said—were not a few members of the Republican party, who, while they supported the Administration, were willing to acknowledge its mistakes. The inscription which the sword bore, "Pro rege sæpe, pro patriâ semper," excited an amount of discussion and comment in the newspaper press in which future observers will recognize an amusing instance of the importance which trifles may assume when viewed through a properly magnifying medium.

While in Boston, he was invited to visit Concord, New Hampshire, Portland and Augusta, in Maine, and other places; but he was not able to accept any of these gratifying invitations.

In October, 1863, the State election in Pennsylvania took place. Governor Curtin was the Republican candidate for Governor, and Judge Woodward the Democratic. The election was contested with great ardor, and all over the country much interest was felt in the result. It was thought that the vote of the soldiers, who were coming into the State in great numbers, was of much importance, and would, perhaps, decide the contest. They were all devoted to General McClellan; but an impression was spread among them that he was in favor of Governor Curtin. A correspondent of "The Press," a leading political journal, had so stated. Under these circumstances, it was deemed by the friends of Judge Woodward highly important that this erroneous impression should be removed by a distinct contradiction under General McClellan's own hand. Accordingly, one of Judge Woodward's friends left Philadelphia on Sunday evening, October 11,—the day of the election being Tuesday, October 13,—and went to Orange, New Jersey, and laid the whole matter before General McClellan. The result was the following letter:—

"ORANGE, NEW JERSEY, October 12, 1863.

"Hon. CHARLES J. INGERSOLL, Philadelphia.

"DEAR SIR:—My attention has been called to an article in the Philadelphia 'Press,' asserting that I had written to the managers of a Democratic meeting at Allentown, disapproving the objects of the meeting, and that, if I voted or spoke, it would be in favor of Governor Curtin. I am informed that similar assertions have been made throughout the State. It has been my earnest endeavor heretofore to avoid participating in party politics, and I am determined to adhere to this course.

"But it is obvious that I cannot longer maintain silence under such misrepresentations.

"I therefore request you to deny that I have written any such letter or entertained any such views as those attributed to me in the Philadelphia 'Press,' and I desire to state, clearly and distinctly, that, having some few days ago had a full conversation with Judge Woodward, I find that our views agree, and I regard his election as Governor of Pennsylvania called for by the interests of the nation.

"I understand Judge Woodward to be in favor of the prosecution of the war, with all the means at the command of the loyal States, until the military power of the rebellion is destroyed. I understand him to be of the opinion that, while the war is waged with all possible decision and energy, the policy directing it should be in consonance with the principles of humanity and civilization, working no injury to private rights and property not demanded by military law among civilized nations; and, finally, I understand him to agree with me in the opinion that the sole great objects of this war are the restoration of the unity of the nation, the preservation of the Constitution, and the supremacy of the laws of the country.

"Believing that our opinions entirely agree on these points, I would, were it in my power, give to Judge Woodward my voice and my vote.

"I am, very respectfully, yours,

"GEORGE B. McCLELLAN."

The above letter was immediately telegraphed to Philadelphia, but it was not published till late in the afternoon of Monday, the 12th, and then it was freely denounced as a forgery; and thus it failed to exert the influence upon the election which it might have done had it appeared earlier.

General McClellan must have been flattered by the amount and character of the discussion which this letter called forth, since it proved how much weight was attached to his name and opinion. There are occasions in the life of every public man in which he will be blamed whether he does a certain act or declines to do it; and this was one of those occasions. Those who were loudest in denouncing him for writing and publishing the letter would have been entitled to a better hearing had they uttered a word of censure upon the shameful fraud which drew it forth from a man always disinclined to embrace opportunities for public display, and who now only exercised the undoubted right of every freeman.

On the 18th of February, 1864, an incident occurred in the city of New York, which showed how much the soldiers of the Army of the Potomac were attached to their old commander. On that day, an official reception was given by the municipal authorities to the veterans of the First New York Cavalry, at which General McClellan, under whom they had served, was present. When the approach of their old commander was announced, the soldiers rushed to the door to meet him; and as he entered the room they crowded round him so that he could hardly walk. After an interchange of greetings between him and the officers, Colonel McReynolds, who commanded the regiment, spoke as follows:—

"SOLDIERS:—But a short time ago the chairman of this occasion did us the honor to refer to the fact that the First New York Cavalry were the last on the Chickahominy and the first to reach the James River. It was a proud announcement, gentlemen, and it was true. I now have the honor, and the great pleasure, to announce to you that the noble chieftain who led the Army of the

Potomac on that occasion, that matchless chieftain, General George B. McClellan—[cheers lasting several minutes], —I do not blame you for your enthusiasm,—General George B. McClellan, has honored you with his presence. If you will keep still for a moment, I have no doubt he will speak to you."

General McClellan replied, as follows:—

"MY FRIENDS AND COMRADES:—I came here not to make a speech to you, but to welcome you home, and express to you the pride I have always felt in watching your career, not only when you were with me, but since I left the Army of the Potomac, while you have been fighting battles under others, and your old commander. I can tell you now, conscientiously and truly, I am proud of you in every respect. There is not one page of your record—not a line of it—of which you, your State, and your country may not be proud. I congratulate you on the patriotism that so many of you have evinced in your desire to re-enter the service. I hope, I pray, and I know that your future career will be as glorious as your past. I have one other hope; and that is that we may yet serve together some day again."

Loud cheers followed the conclusion of this speech, and officers and men cried out, "We'll follow you anywhere, general!"

After a speech from Major Harkins, General McClellan took leave with a few words of farewell, the soldiers cheering and crowding round him as he went out of the room.

General McClellan has recently appeared before the public, with much honor to himself, in a literary capacity. In the autumn of 1863, the officers of the army stationed at West Point formed an association for erecting at that post a monument in commemoration of such officers of the regular army as shall have fallen in the service during the present war. The permission of the Secretary of War to erect the proposed monument at West Point was obtained, and letters were addressed to commanding generals and others, describing the project and soliciting co-operation. Many favorable replies were received; and in January, 1864, a general circular was sent to the officers of the army, setting forth the plan and asking subscriptions. The response to this appeal was so universal, prompt, and earnest that the committee who had the enterprise in charge felt authorized to make choice of a site for the proposed monument and have it consecrated by appropriate religious ceremonies. Trophy Point, on the northern brow of the plain on which West Point stands, was accordingly selected, and the 15th of June, 1864, was named as the day for its dedication. General McClellan was requested to deliver the oration.

On the appointed day the site for the proposed monument was consecrated by appropriate religious services. The oration by General McClellan was heard with great interest and deep attention by a very large audience, and, after its delivery, was immediately published in many of the Democratic newspapers of the country. It was much commended by all who had the opportunity to read it and were unprejudiced enough to avail themselves of such opportunity, for its high-toned patriotism, its judicious choice of topics, its natural eloquence, and manly energy of style.*

In the course of a brief excursion which followed the delivery of the address above alluded to, General McClellan received many gratifying proofs of the affectionate attachment felt for him by the people of the country generally, and of the lively interest with which they follow his movements. On the evening of the 18th of June, at Fort William Henry, on the banks of Lake George, he was serenaded; and, at the close of the music, having been introduced by Judge Brown to the numerous party which had assembled to pay their respects to him, he addressed them, as follows:—

"I thank you, my friends, for this welcome and pleasing evidence of your regard. It is a most happy termination of the delightful week I have passed in the midst of this beautiful region, among such warm and friendly hearts. When men come, as you have done, some many miles from the mountains and valleys, it means something more than empty compliment or idle courtesy. At all events, I so regard it, and understand this sudden gathering of men who are in truth the strength of the nation as intended to show your love and gratitude to the gallant men who have so long fought under my command,

---

* On account of the striking merits both of substance and form of this discourse,—and it is of no more than moderate length,—it is inserted in the Appendix in full, in the belief that General McClellan's friends will be glad to possess, in a shape less fleeting than that of a newspaper or pamphlet, a production so strongly stamped with the characteristics of his mind and character.

and as an evidence to any who may dare to doubt, whether abroad, at home, or in the rebellious States, that the people of this portion of the country intend to support to the last the Union of our great nation, the sacredness of its Constitution and laws, against whoever may attack them. I do not flatter myself that this kind demonstration is a mark of personal regard to me, but that it means far more than that. You add to the cogent arguments afforded by the deeds of your sons and brothers in the field the sanction and weight of your opinion in favor of the justice and vital importance of the real cause for which we are fighting, and the cause which should never be perverted or lost sight of.

"It has been my good fortune to have had near me in very trying times many of your near relations. In truth, there must be among you now men who went with me through the memorable seven days of battle that commenced just two years ago to-day. It is only just that I should thank you now for the valor and patriotism of your sons and brothers who were with me in the Army of the Potomac, from Yorktown to Antietam. Yet how could they be other than brave and patriotic? for they first saw the light amid scenes classical in our earliest history, and sprang from ancestors who won and held their mountains in hundreds of combats against the Indians, the French, and the English. After a gallant defence of the now ruined ramparts of William Henry, the blood of many of your grandsires moistened the very ground on which you now stand, in a butchery permitted by the cruel apathy of Montcalm, who, two years afterwards, suffered for his crimes in the great battle under the walls of Quebec, where others of your ancestors bore a most honorable part. Ticonderoga, Crown Point, Saratoga, are all names made sacred to you by the bravery of your fathers, who there made illustrious the name of American troops.

"In this latter and more dreadful war you and yours have proved worthy of the reputation of your predecessors. And, whatever sacrifice may yet be necessary, I am confident that you will never consent willingly to be citizens of a divided and degraded nation, but that you will so support the actions of your fellow-countrymen in the field that we shall be victorious, and again have peace and a reunited country, when the hearts of the North and South shall again beat in unison, as they did in the good old times of the Revolution, when our Union and Constitution shall be as firm as the mountains which encircle this lovely lake, and the future of the Republic shall be as serene as the waters of Horicon when no breeze ripples its surface."

CHAPTER XIII.

THE final chapter of the biography of General McClellan can find no more appropriate opening than the concluding pages of his Report, in which he gives a brief abstract of the history and fortunes of the Army of the Potomac, comprising what they did, what they failed to do, and the reasons for both.

"In this Report I have confined myself to a plain narrative of such facts as are necessary for the purposes of history.

"Where it was possible, I have preferred to give these facts in the language of despatches, written at the time of their occurrence, rather than to attempt a new relation.

"The reports of the subordinate commanders, hereto

annexed, recite what time and space would fail me to mention here,—those individual instances of conspicuous bravery and skill by which every battle was marked. To them I must especially refer; for without them this narrative would be incomplete, and justice fail to be done. But I cannot omit to tender to my corps commanders, and to the general officers under them, such ample recognition of their cordial co-operation and their devoted services as those reports abundantly avouch.

"I have not sought to defend the army which I had the honor to command, nor myself, against the hostile criticisms once so rife.

"It has seemed to me that nothing more was required than such a plain and truthful narrative to enable those whose right it is to form a correct judgment on the important matters involved.

"This Report is, in fact, a history of the Army of the Potomac.

"During the period occupied in the organization of that army, it served as a barrier against the advance of a lately victorious enemy while the fortification of the capital was in progress; and, under the discipline which it then received, it acquired strength, education, and some of that experience which is necessary to success in active operations, and which enabled it afterwards to sustain itself under circumstances trying to the most heroic men. Frequent skirmishes occurred along the lines, conducted with great gallantry, which inured our troops to the realities of war.

"The army grew into shape but slowly; and the delays which attended on the obtaining of arms, continuing late into the winter of 1861–62, were no less trying to the soldiers than to the people of the country. Even at the time of the organization of the Peninsular campaign, some of the finest regiments were without rifles; nor were the utmost exertions on the part of the military authorities adequate to overcome the obstacles to active service.

"When, at length, the army was in condition to take the field, the Peninsular campaign was planned and entered upon with enthusiasm by officers and men. Had this campaign been followed up as it was designed, I cannot doubt that it would have resulted in a glorious triumph to our arms and the permanent restoration of the power of the Government in Virginia and North Carolina, if not throughout the revolting States. It was, however, otherwise ordered; and, instead of reporting a victorious campaign, it has been my duty to relate the heroism of a reduced army, sent upon an expedition into an enemy's country, there to abandon one and originate another and new plan of campaign, which might and would have been successful if supported with appreciation of its necessities, but which failed because of the repeated failure of promised support at the most critical and, as it proved, the most fatal moments. That heroism surpasses ordinary description. Its illustration must be left for the pen of the historian in times of calm reflection, when the nation shall be looking back to the past from the midst of peaceful days.

"For me, now, it is sufficient to say that my comrades were victors on every field save one; and there the endurance of a single corps accomplished the object of its fighting, and, by securing to the army its transit to the James, left to the enemy a ruinous and barren victory.

"The Army of the Potomac was first reduced by the withdrawal from my command of the division of General Blenker, which was ordered to the Mountain Department, under General Frémont. We had scarcely landed on the Peninsula when it was further reduced by a despatch revoking a previous order giving me command of Fortress Monroe, and under which I had expected to take ten thousand men from that point to aid in our operations. Then, when under fire before the defences of Yorktown, we received the news of the withdrawal of General McDowell's corps of about thirty-five thousand men. This completed the overthrow of the original plan of the campaign.

"About one-third of my entire army (five divisions out of fourteen; one of the nine remaining being but little larger than a brigade) was thus taken from me. Instead of a rapid advance which I had planned, aided by a flank movement up the York River, it was only left to besiege Yorktown. That siege was successfully conducted by the army; and when these strong works at length yielded to our approaches, the troops rushed forward to the sanguinary but successful battle of Williamsburg, and thus opened an almost unresisted advance to the banks of the Chickahominy. Richmond lay before them, surrounded with fortifications, and guarded by an army larger than our own; but the prospect did not shake the courage of the brave men who composed my command. Relying still on the support which the vastness of our undertaking and the grand results depending on our success seemed to insure us, we pressed forward. The weather was stormy beyond precedent. The deep soil of the Peninsula was at times one vast morass. The Chickahominy rose to a higher stage than had been known for years before. Pursuing the advance, the crossings were seized, and the right wing extended to effect a junction with reinforcements now promised and earnestly desired, and upon the arrival of which the complete success of the campaign seemed clear.

"The brilliant battle of Hanover Court-House was fought, which opened the way for the First Corps,—with the aid of which, had it come, we should then have gone into the enemy's capital. It never came. The bravest army could not do more, under such overwhelming disappointment, than the Army of the Potomac then did. Fair Oaks attests their courage and endurance when they hurled back, again and again, the vastly superior masses of the enemy. But mortal men could not accomplish the miracles that seemed to have been expected of them. But one course was left,—a flank march, in the face of a powerful enemy, to another and better base,—one of the most hazardous movements in war. The Army of the Potomac, holding its own safety, and almost the safety of our cause, in its hands, was equal to the occasion. The seven days are classical in American history,—those days in which the noble soldiers of the Union and Constitution fought an overwhelming enemy by day, and retreated from successive victories by night, through a week of battle, closing the terrible scenes of conflicts with the ever-memorable victory at Malvern, where they drove back, beaten and shattered, the entire Eastern army of the Confederacy, and thus secured for themselves a place of rest and a point for a new advance upon the capital from the banks of the James. Richmond was still within our grasp, had the Army of the Potomac been reinforced and permitted to advance. But counsels which I cannot but think subsequent events proved unwise prevailed in Washington, and we were ordered to abandon the campaign. Never did soldiers better deserve the thanks of a nation than the Army of the Potomac for the deeds of the Peninsular campaign; and, although that meed was withheld from them by the authorities, I am persuaded they have received the applause of the American people.

"The Army of the Potomac was recalled from within sight of Richmond, and incorporated with the Army of Virginia. The disappointments of the campaign on the Peninsula had not damped their ardor nor diminished their patriotism. They fought well, faithfully, gallantly, under General Pope, yet were compelled to fall back on Washington, defeated and almost demoralized.

"The enemy, no longer occupied in guarding his own capital, poured his troops northward, entered Maryland, threatened Pennsylvania, and even Washington itself. Elated by his recent victories, and assured that our troops were disorganized and dispirited, he was confident that the seat of war was now permanently transferred to the loyal States, and that his own exhausted soil was to be relieved from the burden of supporting two hostile armies. But he did not understand the spirit which animated the soldiers of the Union. I shall not, nor can I, living, forget that, when I was ordered to the command of the troops for the defence of the capital, the soldiers with whom I had shared so much of the anxiety and pain and suffering of the war had not lost their confidence in me as their commander. They sprang to my call with all their ancient vigor, discipline, and courage. I led them into Maryland. Fifteen days after they had fallen back, defeated, before Washington, they vanquished the enemy on the rugged heights of South Mountain, pursued him to the hard-fought field of Antietam, and drove him, broken and disappointed, across the Potomac into Virginia.

"The army had need of rest. After the terrible experiences of battles and marches, with scarcely an interval of repose, which they had gone through from the time of leaving for the Peninsula, the return to Washington, the defeat in Virginia, the victory at South Mountain, and again at Antietam, it was not surprising that they were in a large degree destitute of the absolute necessaries to effective duty. Shoes were worn out; blankets were lost; clothing was in rags: in short, the army was unfit for active service, and an interval for rest and equipment was necessary. When the slowly-forwarded supplies came to us, I led the army across the river, renovated and refreshed, in good order and discipline, and followed the retreating foe to a position where I was confident of decisive victory,—when, in the midst of the movement, while my advance-guard was actually in contact with the enemy, I was removed from the command.

"I am devoutly grateful to God that my last campaign with this brave army was crowned with a victory which saved the nation from the greatest peril it had then undergone. I have not accomplished my purpose if by this Report the Army of the Potomac is not placed high on the roll of the historic armies of the world. Its deeds ennoble the nation to which it belongs. Always ready for battle, always firm, steadfast, and trustworthy, I never called on it in vain; nor will the nation ever have cause to attribute its want of success under myself, or under other commanders, to any failure of patriotism or bravery in that noble body of American soldiers.

"No man can justly charge upon any portion of that army, from the commanding general to the private, any lack of devotion to the service of the United States Government and to the cause of the Constitution and the Union. They have proved their fealty in much sorrow, suffering, danger, and through the very shadow of death. Their comrades, dead on all the fields where we fought, have scarcely more claim to the honor of a nation's reverence than the survivors to the justice of a nation's gratitude."

To this mournful, eloquent, and modest summing up of the case there is not much to be added. At the close of the biography of a distinguished military commander, the reader naturally looks for an analysis and exposition of his military genius, and, if not a comparison with the great generals of other countries and other times, at least some statement of his merits, some enumeration of his claims. But there is an obvious embarrassment in thus dealing with one who is still living, and may chance to read the pages in which his military character is delineated. What is just praise when spoken of the dead may sound like flattery when spoken of the living. In the interview between Solon and Crœsus, so beautifully narrated by Herodotus, the king was told by his wise guest that no man could be called happy until a fortunate life had been closed by a peaceful death; for that so long as a man was alive he was the sport and prey of fortune, and no one could tell what the future had in store for him. In like manner, no accurate estimate can be made of the worth and services of a soldier or statesman until the seal of death is set upon his rounded life and there is no more for him any earthly future. Far distant, we trust, is the day when it will be seasonable to take the gauge and dimensions of General McClellan's powers and accomplishments and assign to him his due place on the roll of departed worth.

And there are other reasons why we must be content to wait for a calm and dispassionate estimate of General McClellan's services and merits. A civil war was raging when he was dismissed from the command of the Army of the Potomac, and it is raging still; and the end seems neither near nor certain. A nation engaged in so fierce a struggle as ours is in no condition to weigh, to examine, to compare, and to decide,—as a lake lashed into fury by the tempest can return no true image of the sky that bends over it. The passions which civil war fosters and creates forbid the exercise of a judicial understanding. A court of justice must needs adjourn if a battle be going on under its windows. All our energies, all our faculties, are absorbed in action, and all questions that require deliberation must be postponed to a more quiet season. We cannot afford to listen. The only pause we can brook is such brief interval of repose as exhausted nature demands. Before justice can be done him, General McClellan must wait for more peaceful times and minds less agitated and absorbed. To-day we adjourn the hearing, as Neptune, in the Æneid, adjourned the punishment of his rebellious winds, because of the instant need of stilling the tempest they had raised:—

> "Quos ego—sed motos præstat componere fluctus."

Besides, at this moment a considerable portion of his countrymen have their minds barred against all arguments and considerations in defence of General McClellan, by political prejudice. To deny him all military capacity is part of the creed of a great political party. Most supporters of the present Administration hold it to be a point of duty to disparage and decry him. This is no strange phenomenon. Parallel cases may be found in the history of every country in which public opinion is allowed free expression. There was a time—and the period lasted for years—in which every whig statesman in England felt bound to call in question the military genius of the Duke of Wellington,*

* Lord Brougham says that some very eminent statesmen constantly and greatly misjudged the Duke of Wellington till

and just so the Bourbons and their followers constantly denied the military greatness of Bonaparte.

But General McClellan has been so unjustly treated and so unscrupulously slandered that something more is required, simply as a matter of truth and fair dealing, in vindication and defence of him. After what has passed, silence might seem like acquiescence in charges which are as false as they are injurious. It is no fault of General McClellan that events have taken such a turn that it is impossible to write a life of him without taking a somewhat controversial attitude. A few remarks are, consequently, submitted, which are in the nature of a comment upon some points of the evidence presented in the preceding pages.

First of all: there are some persons who deny to General McClellan all merit whatever as a commander, maintaining that he has neither the capacity to plan a campaign nor to fight a battle, and that every thing successfully done by him was either the work of others or the result of pure accident. With such persons it is useless to reason, as to do so would be simply a waste of time. No arguments or considerations would have any power to shake an impression like this. Men who hold this opinion of the conqueror of Malvern Hill and Antietam are, in the intellectual line, legitimate

---

the publication of his Despatches, when they at once, and in the strongest terms, declared how grievously they had erred. —*Statesmen of the Time of George III.*, ii. p. 355.

descendants of those subjects of George the Third who used to maintain that Napoleon Bonaparte was deficient in the quality of personal courage. A prejudice of this kind is as much proof against reason as the diseased fancy of a hypochondriac who believes that his legs are made of glass, or that he is followed everywhere by a blue dog. "You must have observed," said Mr. Grenville, in a letter to Mr. Pitt, "that of all impressions the most difficult to be removed are those which have no reason to support them; because against them no reason can be applied."

But there are other persons, more reasonable, more discriminating, who, while they allow General McClellan to be an accomplished and meritorious officer, capable of doing excellent service in a subordinate sphere, hold also the opinion that when at the head of an army his good qualities are neutralized by his slowness, his over-cautiousness, his want of dash, his inability to take advantage of the sudden opportunities which the fortune of war presents. The force of this objection is in some measure neutralized by the fact that it is so common in military history. The popular mind is always eager for results in war, and ignorant of the conditions essential to success. Without citing any further examples, Washington and Wellington,*

* "This spirit of faction, however, was not confined to one side. There was a ministerial person at this time, who, in his dread of the opposition, wrote to Lord Wellington complaining of his inaction, and calling upon him to do something that would excite a public sensation; any thing, provided blood

while their campaigns were going on, were constantly censured for their slowness. It is a charge easily made, and not easily answered; for the defence must often rest upon a variety of considerations which the critic is too impatient to listen to. General McClellan is, by nature and temperament, wisely cautious, prudent, and deliberate,—the reverse of rash and impulsive; and these traits are, of course, shown in his military career. He never incurs great risks or plays a desperate game. He is, besides, a humane man, very careful of the lives of his soldiers, and not needlessly shedding human blood. And, lastly, he is a man of moral firmness and just self-reliance, who will never be induced by popular clamor to take a step which he deems unwise, or forego a precaution which he deems necessary. A man like this at the head of an army will often incur the charge of slowness and inertness, and the charge will be made most positively by those who are the least qualified to form a correct judgment in the premises. Public opinion—that is, contemporaneous public opinion—is not of any great value on a question like this. Ignorance and prejudice are both obstacles in the way to a correct understanding of military measures and military men. A battle won is a fact which all can understand; but comparatively few are competent to determine how much merit is due,

---

was spilt. A calm but severe rebuke, and the cessation of all friendly intercourse with the writer, discovered the general's abhorrence of this detestable policy."—NAPIER.

or rather how little blame should be attached, to the general who has had the misfortune to lose a battle. Upon a charge of slowness and over-cautiousness General McClellan has a right to be tried by his peers,—that is, by the officers of the regular army, and especially by those who have served under him. To their judgment he can confidently appeal, and by their verdict he is ready to stand or fall.

Indecision and unreadiness are, no doubt, defects of mind or infirmities of temperament, arising from not having any plans of conduct, or from not carrying them out with promptness. In either case, they are traits which taint the whole being, and lay their paralyzing touch upon all the currents of life. A sluggish, dawdling, and dilatory man may have spasms of activity, but he never acts continuously and consecutively with energetic quickness. When in a commanding general we see a campaign, or a military enterprise, marked by rapidity of movement, by plans promptly formed and vigorously executed, and when in the same man we see at another time pauses, delays, which bring upon him the reproach of slowness, it is fair to infer that his conduct in the latter case is the result of a cautious and far-seeing wisdom, which comprehends all the difficulties of the position, and knows that the more haste the less speed, so far as the matter in hand is concerned. The evidence as to general character is important in an issue like this.

Let us apply these principles to General McClellan's military career.

In the first place, no one has ever pretended, no one can pretend, that he is a military commander who acts without previously-formed plans, without having determined beforehand what he shall do and how he shall do it. On the contrary, he is peculiarly and singularly thoughtful of the future, carefully meditating every step of his progress, and vigilant in providing against all possible contingencies. Upon this point the evidence is irresistible and overwhelming.

But, say General McClellan's assailants and detractors, though his plans are judicious and carefully formed, he lacks quickness and vigor in carrying them out; he is slow in the saddle; he does not take time by the forelock; he lets opportunities slip by which never come a second time. But what is the evidence to support these charges? Look at his campaign in Western Virginia in 1861, —a part of his military career conveniently ignored by his enemies. Here he had a separate command, a defined field of action, and was not hampered and trammelled by interference from Washington; and do we see any signs of indecision and want of promptness here? On the contrary, we observe the happiest combination of judgment in design and vigor in execution: one skilful and powerful blow was instantly followed by another, and the result was absolute and permanent military success.

Then look at the brilliant and crowded period between the second and seventeenth days of September, 1862. On the former of these dates, the forces in and around Washington were little better than a tumultuary and disorganized mob; and within forty-eight hours, as if at the touch of a magician's wand, they were converted into an effective and disciplined army. Within a fortnight from the time of their leaving Washington, they had marched fifty miles, fought two battles, gained two victories, driven out of Maryland a foe flushed with recent success, given a sense of security to Washington, and raised the spirits of every patriot in the land. Was there any time lost here? Is there any evidence here of want of decision, want of energy, want of promptness? Surely not, but all the reverse.

But all this is neutralized and made of no effect because, after the battle of Antietam, he did not cross the Potomac, pursue Lee's retreating army, and utterly destroy it! Nothing but ignorance or prejudice, one or both, could make this delay a ground for disparaging General McClellan's military reputation. Are we to suppose that the man who for fifteen days had been acting with the most extraordinary energy and vigor was suddenly so paralyzed, so smitten with procrastination, that he folded up his hands, went to sleep, and from mere indolence forbore to gather the new laurels which were within reach of his hand if he had only stretched it out? Such sudden change is inconsistent with the laws of human nature. Men are not one week brimful of fiery energy and the next eaten up by the rust of inaction. The pause made after the battle of Antietam must be interpreted by the fortnight of crowded and intense action which preceded it; and to an unprejudiced and instructed mind it is vindicated by the soundest military reasoning.

But he failed to take Richmond, it is said. This is true; but it is equally true that this failure was no fault of his. To what causes it was due is set forth in the preceding pages, and especially in the concluding portion of General McClellan's Report, copied into this chapter. He never would have undertaken to capture Richmond with a force so small as that to which he was finally reduced by the interference of the Administration with his plans, and their broken faith. It is no disparagement to a general that, having only ninety thousand men, he did not succeed in an enterprise which he had undertaken upon the assurance that he should have a hundred and forty thousand. Besides, he was forbidden to go on with it, and his army sent to General Pope; with what result need not be repeated. The Peninsular campaign of 1862, as planned, was General McClellan's; as executed, it was that of the President and the Secretary of War: and upon them the responsibility of failure must rest. Had they kept their faith, had they sent to General McClellan the reinforcements which again and again had been promised him, and which he again and again demanded, there is very little question that Richmond would have been taken. The military chances were greatly in favor of such a result.

Of course, as Richmond in point of fact was not captured, the enemies of General McClellan may say that it would not have been, even if he had had all the forces he asked for or desired. An assertion like this cannot be denied point-blank. To bandy opinions about the past is only one whit less unprofitable than to bandy predictions about the future. All that can be affirmed is that General McClellan's plans were such that, in all human probability, success would have followed had he been permitted to carry them out.

So much may be said by way of defence of General McClellan against the charges most commonly brought against him, and in rebuttal of the evidence put in on the other side; but there are some considerations which are in the nature of distinct and positive testimony in his behalf, on which it is but just to him to say a few words.

In the first place, with the single exception of the battle of Gaines's Mill, in which some thirty-five thousand men retired, without disorder or demoralization, before twice their number, no army led by General McClellan, or that was under his control, has ever been defeated. This is a significant and important fact, and all the more so from the comparisons which are forced upon every unbiassed mind by the unjust treatment which General McClellan has received at the hands of the Administration. In August, 1862, the Army of the Potomac was taken from him and intrusted to General Pope; and the consequence was the disaster at Bull Run on the 30th of the same month, the second misfortune to our arms on that ill-omened field. In November of the same year he was "relieved" of the command of the same army, and General Burnside was put in his place; and then came the mournful defeat at Fredericksburg on the 13th of December. Here is Malvern Hill against Bull Run; here are South Mountain and Antietam against Fredericksburg. But General McClellan was practically dismissed from the army, with every mark of ignominy and disgrace, and General Burnside and General Pope are now, and always have been, in honorable and responsible military commands. We have nothing to do with these two last-named officers, nor do we care to discuss the policy of the Administration towards them; but it is unjust and unreasonable that the tenderness and consideration which have been so liberally extended to them should be so utterly withheld from General McClellan, and that he should be disgraced for his victories while they are rewarded, or at least forgiven, for their defeats. He asks no favors; but he has a right to demand consistency and justice.

In the next place, General McClellan has always had the love and trust of the soldiers he has commanded, and, with a few exceptions, has enjoyed the respect, confidence, and affection of the officers who have served under him. At this moment his name is a tower of strength with the Army of the Potomac. This is an important fact, a weighty piece of evidence in his behalf. Upon the merits of a general in command, the opinion of the army which serves under him is of far more value than the opinion of the public. The former cannot be deceived or imposed upon by a reputation made to order by politicians, editors, and army-correspondents. The judgment of the army is like the judgment of experts in a patent-case, or of nautical men in an insurance-case. The consequences of incapacity are too serious to permit any delusion or mystification on the subject. And the value of this favorable judgment is enhanced by the high standard of intelligence in our army, by the fact that the rank and file, in general, is made up of men who read, write, think, and discuss their civil and military leaders. They know, by personal experience, his skill, judgment, and wisdom.

It is beyond question that General McClellan is an accomplished officer, well read in his profession, and master of such knowledge of the art of war as can be learned from books. And many of those who deny to him the praise of rapid and brilliant execution in the field admit his merit in that department of the art of war which is called strategy, as distinguished from tactics. "Strategy," says Jomini, "is the art of properly directing masses upon the theatre of war, whether for the invasion of a country or for the defence of one's own." It includes the choice of a fixed base of operations, of zones and lines of operations, of strategic lines, and of vital geographical points to occupy offensively or to cover defensively; or, in popular language, it is the planning and laying out beforehand of a campaign. It supposes an intimate knowledge of the physical features of the country comprised within the zone of operations, and a prophetic sagacity in determining and selecting those decisive strategic points the possession of which insures the control of a region important to hold. It selects the spots where magazines of supplies should be formed, as well as where permanent fortifications should be constructed. The strategist is to the tactician what the architect is to the builder. Blücher and Ney, among others, were instances of men of the most brilliant conduct on the field of battle who had no power of strategy, no capacity of organizing a campaign or of directing the movements of detached bodies of troops so as to bring them to bear upon a given point at the same time. On the other hand, the Archduke Charles, who as a strategist had no rival but Napoleon himself, is thought to have sometimes shown a want of quickness and decision on the field of battle. That General McClellan is capable of planning and organizing a campaign, of designating movements to be executed by others, can be doubted by no man of candid mind who will read his memorandum on the conduct of the war, addressed to the President, and to be found in the fifth chapter of the present work, and his letters of instruction to Generals Halleck, Buell, Sherman, and Butler, contained in his Report. Strategy is the most important department of the art of war, and strategical skill is the highest and rarest function of military genius. To handle troops well on the field of battle, to retain self-possession amid "all the currents of a heady fight," to take advantage of any mistake made by the enemy, to repair the mischances and disasters in his own ranks, requires a man of no common capacity; but yet higher powers are demanded of him who at the head of a great army executes a series of movements, extending over several weeks perhaps, which finally compel an adversary to give battle at a point and under conditions which insure his defeat. The superiority of the Archduke Charles in this the most intellectual part of his profession has given him the second place on the roll of honor of the great generals in the wars of the French Revolution.

But General McClellan has shown great moral qualities in his career of public service, which are elements of what may be called character, in distinction from pure intellectual force. The spotless purity of his private life has never been called in question. The rancor of partisan or personal malignity has never accused him of pecuniary corruption, of rapacity, of turning his official opportunities to his own gain or the gain of others. No swarm of unworthy favorites or needy dependants has ever buzzed around him. His record is without a blot; his hands are without a stain. His name has never been mixed up with disreputable or doubtful transactions. The charges against him are aimed at him solely in his military capacity. And this is not merely negative praise. The life of a soldier is a life of moral danger and exposures, as well as physical; and only the noblest and purest natures entirely escape reproach.* There are no eyes so sharp as the eyes of hatred; and now, for two long years, has General McClellan been watched and scanned by these, in hope to find some speck or flaw in his record; but vain has been the quest, fruitless the search. As a shield of steel dazzles and blinds the eye, so does the spotless purity of his character repel the envious and sinister glance. No slanderer, however base, no courtier, however fawning, has ever dared to accuse him of intemperance, licentiousness, rapacity, or profanity: nay, more, he has never been even suspected of them. No unscrupulous partisan sheet has ever insinuated or hinted at any such charges; no reckless platform-orator has ever suggested any thing of the kind; it has never been whispered round a camp-fire, or a dinner-table, or in a committee-room, a base Congressional mess, or a baser legislative lobby. The moral instincts of the American people are sound and good; and they have an instinctive and well-founded perception of General McClellan's moral worth which is proof against all the insinuations of malice, all the devices of calumny. The hold he has upon their hearts is due to their strong sense of his integrity, his sincerity, his disinterestedness, his loyalty to duty, his moral purity, his unspotted life; and it is a hold which cannot be lost or shaken.

---

* "I never knew a Warryer yet, but thee,
From wine, tobacco, debts, dice, oaths, so free."
Thomas Carlton to Captain John Smith.

But this is not all. The training and education of a soldier tend to make a man keenly sensitive on the point of honor, and to feel a stain on his professional reputation like a wound. Observe the way in which the Administration has dealt with him. First, he was made general-in-chief of all the armies of the United States, then reduced to the command of the Army of the Potomac, then degraded to the post of a quartermaster at Alexandria, then suddenly and in fright made commander of the Army of the Potomac once more, then dismissed from that command as unceremoniously and abruptly as one flings a torn envelope into a waste-paper basket; and all within a single year. Such capricious changes are more like the shifting scenes of a novel or drama than like real life. But, wounding as such treatment must have been, we hear no complaint from General McClellan. He makes no appeal to the public, no protest against injustice, no demand for sympathy. If any expressions of impatience are wrung from him, it is because of his army, and not because of any thing done to, or suffered by, himself. He submits in silence to the will of the Administration; he discharges faithfully the duties of every position devolved upon him; he asks only for the privilege of serving his country. During the long period of his enforced idleness, not one word of complaint has been heard from him: he has made no proclamation of his wrongs, no denunciation of those who have wronged him. Yet this is not an age of self-renunciation and self-sacrifice :—

"Now our life is only drest
For show,—mean handiwork of craftsman, cook,
Or groom! We must run glittering like a brook
In the open sunshine, or we are unblest."

Our times are times of self-assertion and self-vindication: men push their own claims, vaunt their own services, sound their own trumpets. The virtues of manly silence, of dignified self-command, of magnanimous fortitude, which General McClellan has shown, are to be the more valued because of their rarity.

And yet the future historian of the crowded period in which we live will have to record the fact that the services of this accomplished officer, patriotic citizen, and good man were denied to his country during a civil war unparalleled in history alike for the magnitude of its movements and the intensity of the passions by which it was sustained, in which all the energies of the people were taxed to the utmost limit of endurance, and not only their wealth, but their best blood, was poured out on behalf of the Union and the Constitution with a noble devotion which caused every patriot heart to swell with pride and admiration. And he will also record the further fact that, during the long period in which this man was languishing in inaction, civilian generals, grossly and notoriously incompetent, were allowed to play at the game of war, for political stakes, with the lives of our bravest and best for their counters. Such historian will find in the events which he relates fresh illustration of the bitterness of political hatred, the ferocity of partisan zeal, and the rank growth of low passions in high places; for a sullen and smouldering hate, which never goes out and never bursts forth into a generous blaze, is a low passion, which debases and degrades the breast which it haunts. And he will draw from them the further moral that there is a harmony and consistency in the works of Nature. The venom that chills and curdles the warm current of life in man is secreted only in creeping and cold-blooded creatures; and the inveterate malignity that never forgets or forgives is found only in base and ignoble natures, whose aims are selfish, whose means are indirect, cowardly, and treacherous. Anger is a fierce and sudden flame, which may be kindled in the noblest breasts; but in these the slow droppings of an unforgiving temper never take the shape and consistency of enduring hatred. The natural instincts of a generous heart shrink from an inveterate hater as the child shrinks from the snake in his path. The enemies of General McClellan, in the persistency and malignity of their attacks, furnish a key to unlock their own characters. As for him, "he will remember," to borrow what Burke said of Fox, "that obloquy is a necessary ingredient in the composition of all true glory; he will remember that it was not only in the Roman customs, but it is in the nature and constitution of things, that calumny and abuse are essential parts of triumph. These thoughts will support a mind which exists only for honor, under the burden of temporary reproach." And if detraction has been the meed of patriotic faith, if persecution has been the reward of arduous service, if calumny has followed desert, General McClellan must find comfort in the reflection that his is no new experience, but that every generation has had similar examples of the power of the weak over the strong, and the triumph, sometimes transient and sometimes enduring, of the low and base over the high and noble. How soon the future is to right the wrongs of the past, cannot be predicted; but he is sure what the verdict of time will be, and thus he may wait patiently till it shall be rendered.

APPENDIX.

ORATION DELIVERED BY GENERAL McCLELLAN AT WEST POINT, JUNE 15, 1864, AT THE DEDICATION OF THE SITE OF A MONUMENT PROPOSED TO BE ERECTED IN MEMORY OF THE OFFICERS OF THE REGULAR ARMY WHO SHALL HAVE FALLEN IN BATTLE DURING THE PRESENT WAR.

All nations have days sacred to the remembrance of joy and of grief. They have thanksgivings for success, fasting and prayers in the hour of humiliation and defeat, triumphs and pæans to greet the living and laurel-crowned victor. They have obsequies and eulogies for the warrior slain on the field of battle. Such is the duty we are to perform to-day. The poetry, the histories, the orations of antiquity, all resound with the clang of arms; they dwell rather upon rough deeds of war than the gentle arts of peace. They have preserved to us the names of heroes, and the memory of their deeds, even to this distant day. Our own Old Testament teems with the narrations of the brave actions and heroic deaths of Jewish patriots, while the New Testament of our meek and suffering Saviour often selects the soldier and his weapons to typify and illustrate religious heroism and duty. These stories of the actions of the dead have frequently survived, in the lapse of ages, the names of those whose fall was thus commemorated centuries ago. But, although we know not now the names of all the brave men who fought and fell upon the plain of Marathon, in the pass of Thermopylæ, and on the hills of Palestine, we have not lost the memory of their examples. As long as the warm blood courses the veins of man, as long as the human heart beats high and quick at the recital of brave deeds and patriotic sacrifices, so long will the lesson still incite generous men to emulate the heroism of the past.

Among the Greeks, it was the custom that the fathers of the most valiant of the slain should pronounce the eulogies of the dead. Sometimes it devolved upon their great statesmen and orators to perform this mournful duty. Would that a new Demosthenes or a second Pericles could arise and take my place to-day! for he would find a theme worthy of his most brilliant powers, of his most touching eloquence. I stand here now, not as an orator, but as a whilom commander, and in the place of the fathers, of the most valiant dead,—as their comrade, too, on many a hard-fought field against domestic and foreign foe,—in early youth and mature manhood,—moved by all the love that David felt when he poured forth his lamentations for the mighty father and son who fell on Mount Gilboa. God knows that David's love for Jonathan was no more deep than mine for the tried friends of many long and eventful years, whose names are to be recorded upon the structure that is to rise upon this spot. Would that his more than mortal eloquence could grace my lips and do justice to the theme!

We have met to-day, my comrades, to do honor to our own dead; brothers united to us by the closest and dearest ties, who have freely given their lives for their country in this war,—so just and righteous, so long as its purpose is to crush rebellion and to save our nation from the infinite evils of dismemberment. Such an occasion as this should call forth the deepest and noblest emotions of our nature,—pride, sorrow, and prayer: pride that our country has possessed such sons; sorrow that she has lost them; prayer that she may have others like them,—that we and our successors may adorn her annals as they have done, and that when our parting hour arrives, whenever and however it may be, our souls may be prepared for the great change.

We have assembled to consecrate a cenotaph, which shall remind our children's children, in the distant future, of their fathers' struggles in the days of the great rebellion. This monument is to perpetuate the memory of a portion only of those who have fallen for the nation in this unhappy war: it is dedicated to the officers and soldiers of the regular army. Yet this is done in no class or exclusive spirit, and in the act we remember with reverence and love our comrades of the volunteers, who have so gloriously fought and fallen by our sides. Each State will, no doubt, commemorate in some fitting way the services of its sons who abandoned the avocations of peace and shed their blood in the ranks of the volunteers. How richly they have earned a nation's love, a nation's gratitude, with what heroism they have confronted death, have wrested victory from a stubborn foe, and have illustrated defeat, it well becomes me to say; for it has been my lot to command them on many a sanguinary field. I know that I but echo the feeling of the regulars, when I award the high credit they deserve to their brave brethren of the volunteers.

But we of the regular army have no States to look to for the honors due our dead. We belong to the whole country, and can neither expect nor desire the General Government to make a perhaps invidious distinction in our favor. We are few in number, a small band of comrades, united by peculiar and very binding ties; for with many of us our friendships were commenced in boyhood, when we rested here in the shadow of the granite hills which look down upon us where we stand; with others the ties of brotherhood were formed in more mature years, while fighting among the rugged mountains and the fertile valleys of Mexico, within hearing of the eternal waves of the Pacific, or in the lonely grandeur of the great plains of the far West. With all, our love and confidence have been cemented by common dangers and sufferings, on the toilsome march, in the dreary bivouac, amid the clash of arms, and in the presence of death on scores of battle-fields. West Point, with her large heart, adopts us all,—graduates and those appointed from civil life, officers and privates. In her eyes we are all her children, jealous of her fame and eager to sustain her world-wide reputation. Generals and private soldiers, men who have cheerfully offered our all for our dear country, we stand here before this shrine, ever hereafter sacred to our dead, equals and brothers in the presence of the common death which awaits us all, perhaps on the same field and at the same hour. Such are the ties which unite us,—the most endearing which exist among men; such the relations which bind us together,—the closest of the sacred brotherhood of arms.

It has therefore seemed, and it is, fitting that we should erect upon this spot, so sacred to us all, an enduring monument to our dear brothers who have preceded us on the path of peril and of honor which it is the destiny of many of us to tread.

What is this regular army to which we belong?

Who were the men whose death merits such honors from the living?

What is the cause for which they have laid down their lives?

Our regular or permanent army is the nucleus which, in time of peace, preserves the military traditions of the nation, as well as the organization, science, and instruction indispensable to modern armies. It may be regarded as coeval with the nation. It derives its origin from the old continental and State lines of the Revolution, whence, with some interruptions and many changes, it has attained its present condition. In fact, we may with propriety go even beyond the Revolution to seek the roots of our genealogical tree in the old French wars; for the cis-Atlantic campaigns of the seven years' war were not confined to the "red men scalping each other by the great lakes of North America," and it was in them that our ancestors first participated as Americans in the large operations of civilized armies. American regiments then fought on the banks of the St. Lawrence and the Ohio, on the shores of Ontario and Lake George, on the islands of the Caribbean and in South America. Louisburgh, Quebec, Duquesne, the Moro, and Porto Bello, attest the valor of the provincial troops; and in that school were educated such soldiers as WASHINGTON, PUTNAM, LEE, MONTGOMERY, and GATES. These, and men like GREENE, KNOX, WAYNE, and STEUBEN, were the fathers of our permanent army; and under them our troops acquired that discipline and steadiness which enabled them to meet upon equal terms, and often to defeat, the tried veterans of England. The study of the history of the Revolution, and a perusal of the despatches of WASHINGTON, will convince the most skeptical of the value of the permanent army in achieving our independence and establishing the civil edifice which we are now fighting to preserve.

The War of 1812 found the army on a footing far from adequate to the emergency; but it was rapidly increased, and of the new generation of soldiers many proved equal to the requirements of the occasion. Lundy's Lane, Chippewa, Queenstown, Plattsburgh, New Orleans,—all bear witness to the gallantry of the regulars.

Then came an interval of more than thirty years of external peace, marked by many changes in the organization and strength of the regular army, and broken at times by tedious and bloody Indian wars. Of these the most remarkable were the Black Hawk War, in which our troops met unflinchingly a foe as relentless and far more destructive than the Indians,—that terrible scourge, the cholera; and the tedious Florida War, where for so many years the Seminoles eluded in the pestilential swamps our utmost efforts, and in which were displayed such traits of heroism as that commemorated by yonder monument to DADE and his command,—"when all fell, save three, without an attempt to retreat." At last came the Mexican War, to replace Indian combats and the monotony of the frontier service; and for the first time in many years the mass of the regular army was concentrated, and took the principal part in the battles of that remarkable and romantic war. Palo Alto, Resaca, and Fort Brown were the achievements of the regulars unaided; and as to the battles of Monterey, Buena Vista, Vera Cruz, Cerro Gordo, and the final triumphs in the valley, none can truly say that they could have been won without the regulars. When peace crowned our victories in the capital of the Montezumas, the army was at once dispersed over the long frontier and engaged in harassing and dangerous wars with the Indians of the plains. Thus thirteen long years were spent, until the present war broke out, and the mass of the army was drawn in, to be employed against a domestic foe.

I cannot proceed to the events of the recent past and the present without adverting to the gallant men who were so long of our number, but who have now gone to their last home; for no small portion of the glory of which we boast was reflected from such men as TAYLOR, WORTH, BRADY, BROOKS, TOTTEN, and DUNCAN.

There is a sad story of Venetian history that has moved many a heart, and often employed the poet's pen and the painter's pencil. It is of an old man whose long life was gloriously spent in the service of the state as a warrior and a statesman, and who, when his hair was white and his feeble limbs could scarce carry his bent form towards the grave, attained the highest honors that a Venetian citizen could reach. He was Doge of Venice. Convicted of treason against the state, he not only lost his life, but suffered besides a penalty which will endure as long as the name of Venice is remembered. The spot where his portrait should have hung in the great hall of the doge's palace was veiled with black, and there still remains the frame, with its black mass of canvas; and this vacant frame is the most conspicuous in the long line of effigies of illustrious doges!

Oh that such a pall as that which replaces the portrait of MARINO FALIERO could conceal from history the names of those, once our comrades, who are now in arms against the flag under which we fought side by side in years gone by! But no veil can cover the anguish that fills our hearts when we look back upon the sad memory of the past and recall the affection and respect we entertained towards men against whom it is our duty to act in mortal combat. Would that the courage, ability, and steadfastness they have displayed had been employed in the defence of the "Stars and Stripes" against a foreign foe, rather than in this gratuitous and unjustifiable rebellion, which could not be so long maintained but for the skill and energy of those our former comrades!

But we have reason to rejoice that upon this day, so sacred and so eventful for us, one grand old mortal monument of the past still lifts high his head amongst us, and graces by his presence the consecration of this tomb of his children. We may well be proud that we have been commanded by the hero who purchased victory with his blood near the great waters of Niagara, who repeated and eclipsed the achievements of CORTEZ,—who, although a consummate and confident commander, ever preferred, when duty and honor would permit, the olive-branch of peace to the blood-stained laurels of war, and who stands, at the close of a long, glorious, and eventful life, a living column of granite against which have beaten in vain alike the blandishments and the storms of treason. His name will ever be one of our proudest boasts and most moving inspirations. In long-distant ages, when this incipient monument has become venerable, moss-clad, and perhaps ruinous, when the names inscribed upon it shall seem, to those who pause to read them, indistinct mementos of an almost mythical past, the name of WINFIELD SCOTT will still be clear-cut upon the memory of them all, like the still fresh carving upon the monuments of long-forgotten Pharaohs.

But it is time to approach the present.

In the war which now shakes the land to its foundation, the regular army has borne a most honorable part. Too few in numbers to act by themselves, regular regiments have participated in every great battle in the East and in most of those west of the Alleghanies. Their terrible losses and diminished numbers prove that they have been in the thickest of the fights, and the testimony of their comrades and commanders shows with what undaunted heroism they have upheld their ancient renown. Their vigorous charges have often won the day; and in defeat they have more than once saved the army from destruction or terrible losses by the obstinacy with which they resisted overpowering numbers. They can refer with pride to the part they played upon the glorious fields of Mexico, and exult at the recollection of what they did at Manassas, Gaines's Mill, Malvern, Antietam, Shiloh, Stone River, Gettysburg, and the great battles just fought from the Rapidan to the Chickahominy. They can also point to the officers who have risen among them and achieved great deeds for their country in this war,—to the living warriors whose names are on the nation's tongue and heart, too numerous to be repeated here, yet not one of whom I would willingly omit.

But perhaps the proudest episode in the history of the regular army is that touching instance of fidelity on the part of the non-commissioned officers and privates, who, treacherously made prisoners in Texas, resisted every temptation to violate their oath and desert their flag. Offered commissions in the rebel service, money and land freely tendered them, they all scorned the inducements held out to them, submitted to every hardship, and, when at last exchanged, avenged themselves on the field of battle for the unavailing insult offered their integrity. History affords no brighter example of honor than that of these brave men, tempted, as I blush to say they were, by some of their former officers, who, having themselves proved false to their flag, endeavored to seduce the men who had often followed them in combat and who had naturally regarded them with respect and love.

Such is the regular army,—such its history and antecedents,—such its officers and men. It needs no herald to trumpet forth its praises; it can proudly appeal to the numerous fields, from the tropics to the frozen banks of the St. Lawrence, from the Atlantic to the Pacific, fertilized by the blood and whitened by the bones of its members. But I will not pause to eulogize it. Let its deeds speak for it: they are more eloquent than tongue of mine.

Why are we here to-day?

This is not the funeral of one brave warrior, nor even of the harvest of death on a single battle-field, but these are the obsequies of the best and bravest of the children of the land, who have fallen in actions almost numberless, many of them among the most sanguinary and desperate of which history bears record. The men whose names and deeds we now seek to perpetuate, rendering them the highest honor in our power, have fallen wherever armed rebellion showed its front,—in far-distant New Mexico, in the broad valley of the Mississippi, on the bloody hunting-grounds of Kentucky, in the mountains of Tennessee, amid the swamps of Carolina, on the fertile fields of Maryland, and in the blood-stained thickets of Virginia. They were of all the grades,—from the general officer to the private; of all ages,—from the gray-haired veteran of fifty years' service, to the beardless youth; of all degrees of cultivation,—from the man of science to the uneducated boy. It is not necessary, nor is it possible, to repeat the mournful yet illustrious roll of dead heroes whom we have met to honor. Nor shall I attempt to name all of those who most merit praise,—simply a few who will exemplify the classes to which they belong.

Among the last slain, but among the first in honor and reputation, was that hero of twenty battles,—JOHN SEDGWICK,—gentle and kind as a woman, brave as a brave man can be, honest, sincere, and able: he was a model that all may strive to imitate, but whom few can equal. In the terrible battles which just preceded his death, he had occasion to display the highest qualities of a commander and a soldier; yet, after escaping the stroke of death when men fell around him by thousands, he at last met his fate, at a moment of comparative quiet, by the ball of a single rifleman. He died as a soldier would choose to die,—with truth in his heart, and a sweet, tranquil smile upon his face. Alas! our great nation possesses few such sons as true JOHN SEDGWICK.

Like him fell, too, at the very head of their corps, the white-haired MANSFIELD, after a long career of usefulness, illustrated by his skill and cool courage at Fort Brown, Monterey, and Buena Vista, JOHN F. REYNOLDS, and RENO, both in the full vigor of manhood and intellect,—men who have proved their ability and chivalry on many a field in Mexico and in this civil war,—gallant gentlemen, of whom their country had much to hope, had it pleased God to spare their lives. LYON fell in the prime of life, leading his little army against superior numbers, his brief career affording a brilliant example of patriotism and ability. The impetuous KEARNEY, and such brave generals as RICHARDSON, WILLIAMS, TERRILL, STEVENS, WEED, STRONG, SAUNDERS, and HAYES, lost their lives while in the midst of a career of usefulness. Young BAYARD, so like the most renowned of his name, that "knight above fear and above reproach," was cut off too early for his country, and that excellent staff-officer, Colonel GARESCHÉ, fell while gallantly doing his duty.

No regiments can spare such gallant, devoted, and able commanders as ROSSELL, DAVIS, GOVE, SIMMONS, BAILEY, PUTNAM, and KINGSBURY,—all of whom fell in the thickest of the combat,—some of them veterans, and others young in service, all good men and well-beloved.

Our batteries have partially paid their terrible debt to fate in the loss of such commanders as GREBLE, the first to fall in this war, BENSON, HAZZARD, SMEAD, DE HART, HAZLITT, and those gallant boys, KIRBY, WOODRUFF, DIMMICK, and CUSHING; while the engineers lament the promising and gallant WAGNER and CROSS.

Beneath remote battle-fields rest the corpses of the heroic McREA, REED, BASCOM, STONE, SWEET, and many other company officers.

Besides these were hosts of veteran sergeants, corporals, and privates, who had fought under SCOTT in Mexico, or contended in many combats with the savages of the far West and Florida, and, mingled with them, young soldiers who, courageous, steady, and true, met death unflinchingly, without the hope of personal glory. These men, in their more humble sphere, served their country with as much faith and honor as the most illustrious generals, and all of them with perfect singleness of heart. Although their names may not live in history, their actions, loyalty, and courage will live. Their memories will long be preserved in their regiments; for there were many of them who merited as proud a distinction as that accorded to the "first grenadier of France," or to that Russian soldier who gave his life for his comrades.

But there is another class of men who have gone from us since this war commenced, whose fate it was not to die in battle, but who are none the less entitled to be mentioned here. There was SUMNER, a brave, honest, chivalrous veteran, of more than half a century's service, who had confronted death unflinchingly on scores of battlefields, had shown his gray head serene and cheerful where death most revelled, who more than once told me that he believed and hoped that his long career would end amid the din of battle: he died at home from the effects of the hardships of his campaigns.

That most excellent soldier, the elegant C. F. SMITH, whom many of us remember to have seen so often on this plain, with his superb bearing, escaped the bullet to fall a victim to the disease which has deprived the army of so many of its best soldiers.

JOHN BUFORD, cool and intrepid; MITCHEL, eminent in science; PLUMMER, PALMER, and many other officers and men, lost their lives by sickness contracted in the field.

But I cannot close this long list of glorious martyrs without paying a sacred debt of official duty and personal friendship. There was one dead soldier who possessed peculiar claims upon my love and gratitude. He was an ardent patriot, an unselfish man, a true soldier, the beau ideal of a staff officer: he was my aide-de-camp, Colonel COLBURN.

There is a lesson to be drawn from the death and services of these glorious men which we should read for the present and future benefit of the nation. War in these modern days is a science, and it should now be clear to the most prejudiced that for the organization and command of armies, and the high combinations of strategy, perfect familiarity with the theoretical science of war is requisite. To count upon success when the plans or execution of campaigns are intrusted to men who have no knowledge of war, is as idle as to expect the legal wisdom of a STORY or a KENT from a skilful physician.

But what is the honorable and holy cause for which

these men laid down their lives, and for which the nation still demands the sacrifice of the precious blood of so many of her children?

Soon after the close of the Revolutionary War, it was found that the confederacy, which had grown up during that memorable contest, was fast falling to pieces from its own weight. The central power was too weak; it could only recommend to the different States such measures as seemed best; and it possessed no real power to legislate, because it lacked the executive force to compel obedience to its laws. The national credit and self-respect had disappeared, and it was feared by the friends of human liberty throughout the world that ours was but another added to the long list of fruitless attempts at self-government. The nation was evidently upon the brink of ruin and dissolution, when, some eighty years ago, many of the wisest and most patriotic of the land met to seek a remedy for the great evils which threatened to destroy the great work of the Revolution. Their sessions were long, and often stormy: for a time the most sanguine doubted the possibility of a successful termination to their labors. But from amidst the conflict of sectional interests, of party prejudices, and of personal selfishness, the spirit of wisdom and conciliation at length evoked the Constitution, under which we have lived so long.

It was not formed in a day, but was the result of patient labor, of lofty wisdom, and of the purest patriotism. It was at last adopted by the people of all the States,—although by some reluctantly,—not as being exactly what all desired, but as being the best possible under the circumstances. It was accepted as giving us a form of government under which the nation might live happily and prosper, so long as the people should continue to be influenced by the same sentiments which actuated those who formed it, and which would not be liable to destruction from internal causes, so long as the people preserved the recollection of the miseries and calamities which led to its adoption.

Under this beneficent Constitution the progress of the nation was unexampled in history. The rights and liberties of its citizens were secure at home and abroad; vast territories were rescued from the control of the savage and the wild beast and added to the domain of civilization and the Union. The arts, the sciences, and commerce, grew apace: our flag floated upon every sea, and we took our place among the great nations of the earth.

But under the smooth surface of prosperity upon which we glided swiftly, with all sails set before the summer breeze, dangerous reefs were hidden, which now and then caused ripples upon the surface and made anxious the more cautious pilots. Elated by success, the ship swept on, the crew not heeding the warnings they received, forgetful of the dangers they escaped in the beginning of the voyage, and blind to the hideous maelstrom which gaped to receive and destroy them. The same elements of discordant sectional prejudices, interests, and institutions which had rendered the formation of the Constitution so difficult, threatened more than once to destroy it. But for a long time the nation was so fortunate as to possess a series of political leaders who to the highest abilities united the same spirit of conciliation which animated the founders of the Republic; and thus for many years the threatened evils were averted. Time and long-continued good fortune obliterated the recollection of the calamities and wretchedness of the years preceding the adoption of the Constitution. Men forgot that conciliation, common interest, and mutual charity had been the foundation and must be the support of our government, —as is, indeed, the case with all governments and all the relations of life. At length men appeared with whom sectional and personal prejudices and interests outweighed all considerations for the general good. Extremists of one section furnished the occasion, eagerly seized as a pretext by equally extreme men in the other, for abandoning the pacific remedies and protection afforded by the Constitution and seeking redress for possible future evils in war and the destruction of the Union.

Stripped of all sophistry and side issues, the direct cause of the war, as it presented itself to the honest and patriotic citizens of the North, was simply this. Certain States, or rather a portion of the inhabitants of certain States, feared, or professed to fear, that injury would result to their rights and property from the elevation of a particular party to power. Although the Constitution and the actual condition of the government provided them with a peaceable and sure protection against the apprehended evil, they preferred to seek security in the destruction of the government which could protect them, and in the use of force against the national troops holding a national fortress.

To efface the insult offered our flag, to save ourselves from the fate of the divided republics of Italy and South America, to preserve our government from destruction, to enforce its just power and laws, to maintain our very existence as a nation,—these were the causes that compelled us to draw the sword.

Rebellion against a government like ours, which contains the means of self-adjustment and a pacific remedy for evils, should never be confounded with a revolution against despotic power, which refuses redress of wrongs. Such a rebellion cannot be justified upon ethical grounds; and the only alternative for our choice is its suppression, or the destruction of our nationality. At such a time as this, and in such a struggle, political partisanship should be merged in a true and brave patriotism, which thinks only of the good of the whole country.

It was in this cause and with these motives that so

many of our comrades gave their lives; and to this we are all personally pledged in all honor and fidelity. Shall such a devotion as that of our dead comrades be of no avail? Shall it be said in after-ages that we lacked the vigor to complete the work thus begun?—that, after all these noble lives freely given, we hesitated, and failed to keep straight on until our land was saved? Forbid it, Heaven, and give us firmer, truer hearts than that!

O spirits of the valiant dead, souls of our slain heroes, lend us your own indomitable will, and, if it be permitted you to commune with those still chained by the trammels of mortality, hover around us in the midst of danger and tribulation, cheer the firm, strengthen the weak, that none may doubt the salvation of the Republic and the triumph of our grand old flag!

In the midst of the storms which toss our ship of state, there is one great beacon-light to which we can ever turn with confidence and hope. It cannot be that this great nation has played its part in history; it cannot be that our sun, which arose with such bright promises for the future, has already set forever. It must be the intention of the overruling Deity that this land, so long the asylum of the oppressed, the refuge of civil and religious liberty, shall again stand forth in bright relief, united, purified, and chastened by our trials, as an example and encouragement for those who desire the progress of the human race. It is not given to our weak intellects to understand the steps of Providence as they occur: we comprehend them only as we look back upon them in the far-distant past.

So is it now.

We cannot unravel the seemingly tangled skein of the purposes of the Creator: they are too high and far-reaching for our limited minds. But all history and his own revealed word teach us that his ways, although inscrutable, are ever righteous. Let us, then, honestly and manfully play our part, seek to understand and perform our whole duty, and trust unwaveringly in the beneficence of the God who led our ancestors across the sea, and sustained them afterward amid dangers more appalling even than those encountered by his own chosen people in their great exodus. He did not bring us here in vain, nor has he supported us thus far for naught. If we do our duty and trust in him, he will not desert us in our need.

Firm in our faith that God will save our country, we now dedicate this site to the memory of brave men, to loyalty, patriotism, and honor.

INDEX.

www.ingramcontent.com/pod-product-compliance
Lightning Source LLC
LaVergne TN
LVHW020113110826
845151LV00001B/142

9781425543457